Burnout Immunity

Burnout Immunity

How Emotional Intelligence
Can Help You Build Resilience and
Heal Your Relationship with Work

Kandi Wiens, EdD

HARPER
BUSINESS

An Imprint of HarperCollins*Publishers*

 For information, address HarperCollins Publishers, 195 Broadway, New York, NY 10007.

HarperCollins books may be purchased for educational, business, or sales promotional use. For information, please email the Special Markets Department at SPsales@harpercollins.com.

FIRST EDITION

Fig 1.1: From "Emotional Intelligence Has 12 Elements. Which Do You Need to Work On?" by Daniel Goleman and Richard E. Boyatzis, Harvard Business Review, *February 6, 2017. Reprinted with the permission of More than Sound / Key Step Media.*

Fig 5.1: From "The Secret to Building Resilience" by Rob Cross, Karen Dillon, and Danna Greenberg, Harvard Business Review, *September 17, 2021. Reprinted with the permission of Harvard Business Publishing.*

Fig 7.1: From "Empathy and Compassion" by Tano Singer and Olga M. Klimecki, Current Biology, *September 22, 2014. Copyright © 2014 Elsevier Ltd. All rights reserved. Reprinted by permission.*

Library of Congress Cataloging-in-Publication Data has been applied for.

ISBN 978-0-06-332366-7

24 25 26 27 28 LBC 5 4 3 2 1

For Spencer, Colsen, and Sawyer.

You have my whole heart for my whole life.

Contents

Burnout Immunity

1

Breaking Free of Burnout

The nurse checked my blood pressure twice, a third time, then a fourth. She quietly exited the exam room, and I grabbed my BlackBerry to check on work. This was supposed to be a routine physical. The kind where I popped in for half an hour, got my A, and went back to work.

Minutes later the doctor came in. "What's going on, Kandi?" she asked. "How are you feeling?"

"I'm fine," I said.

And I really did feel fine. The problem was, what had come to feel normal to me was a life-threatening blood pressure reading of 200/110. As I would soon learn, a reading that high is considered a "hypertensive emergency." If it's not treated, it can lead to any number of terrifying outcomes: organ failure, vision loss, a stroke, heart attack. Death.

My doctor shook her head. "You are not fine. We need to get this under control ASAP." She immediately gave me medication to lower my blood pressure and a strong dose of Xanax. She then personally called my husband to pick me up, and, once I was stable, ordered me to go straight home and remain on bed rest for three days. If I experienced so much as a slight headache, I was to go to the ER.

My first thought? *I can't call in sick—I have a leadership development program to run next week!*

My second thought, which even then I recognized as unhealthy: *Thank God. I finally have a legitimate excuse to sleep.*

My third: *She's absolutely right. I am not fine.*

*   *   *

That day in the doctor's office happened in 2011. In a way, I'd been heading there my entire life.

I grew up on an Indian reservation in eastern Montana. Picture big blue skies, golden wheat fields, and the rich beauty of Native American culture—alongside abject poverty, little opportunity for education, and, on my mom's side of the family, a long history of mental illness and alcoholism. My parents divorced after the tragic death of my two-year-old middle sister, leaving my mom to care for a newborn and me.

Needless to say, we struggled. A lot. My mom was traumatized and grieving in ways I couldn't begin to understand, and we lived in government-subsidized housing and relied on food stamps and Indian health care for basics. I was constantly bullied at school for being too skinny. *Not my fault,* I would think to myself, *I've barely eaten in the last five days!*

So began my struggle with adversity-induced stress and insecurity-driven anxiety.

*   *   *

I blame 1970s sitcoms *The Love Boat* and *Fantasy Island* for awakening the inner overachiever in me. Before we got our first TV in 1978, I had no idea there was a life outside of poverty. Those two shows introduced me to characters who had important jobs, fancy clothes, and enough money to travel. Seeing another way to live gave me a vision of what life could be like one day, if I worked really, really hard. I pictured myself traveling for work, carrying a shiny briefcase, and doing some kind of job where I was an expert (in what, it didn't matter) and people came to me for guidance.

When I was twelve years old the Montana judicial system allowed me to decide where to live, and I moved to my dad's house. Life changed overnight. Dad, who came from a long line of hardy, German Mennonite homesteaders, was disciplined and industrious. He had a "real" job—as a loan officer at a small bank—so suddenly I was in a stable home environment. He made sure I did my homework and never missed school. I found that I loved learning, and for the first time, I experienced the exhilaration of accomplishing goals. Within six months I went from almost straight F's to almost straight A's, and my taciturn dad nearly burst with pride.

And so began my addiction to external validation and an overactive need to achieve.

As did a strong fear of disappointing my dad, especially after he'd rescued me from a life of hardship.

*   *   *

With this mix of motivations, I excelled in high school, and college started to look like a realistic possibility. Though we were no longer poor there was no money for extras, so I knew I'd have to figure out tuition on my own. I got a job as a dishwasher at the Busy Bee Truck Stop in Roundup, Montana, and saved every penny I could. I won three small academic scholarships and took out student loans to cover the rest, and just like that I was off to college, the first in my family to do so.

I supported myself by working three jobs—bookkeeper at a law firm, cocktail waitress at a dive bar, and selling software in the mall. When I ran out of money, I'd take a semester off and work more until I could save up enough to cover my living expenses.

I kept that up throughout college, always with one if not two jobs while carrying a full load of courses. Some days I didn't know whether I was coming or going, and I felt frequently overwhelmed. But I was terrified of running out of money. And even more terrified of not finishing.

Thus began my habit of playing through the pain.

*   *   *

It was my junior year in college when I had my first run-in with major stress and burnout. I was doing a full course load of upper-level classes I'd really been looking forward to, but my boss at the law firm loved my work and wanted me to add hours. The approval was like a drug, and I couldn't say no. Plus, who was I to turn down extra money?

At the same time, the classes were everything I'd hoped for. I threw myself into studying, and, I'm not gonna lie, the thrill of succeeding, whether it was acing an exam or coming up with another tuition payment, was downright addictive. I worked even harder, got by on a few hours' sleep a night, and subsisted on turkey sausage and sauerkraut (straight out of the frugal German Mennonite handbook). My sole form of stress relief was to party like it was 1999.

By midterms I was exhausted, both physically and mentally. I'd developed an ulcer and could barely eat, which left me even more fatigued. Still I didn't slow down. I didn't know how and, truthfully, didn't want to. I was desperately afraid of failing and being thrust back into my former life.

A concerned friend suggested I try counseling. It helped, insofar as I was willing and able to let it. I gained some awareness of how deeply stressed I was, and of how my bad coping routines (drinking, overwork, perfectionism) were exacerbating my stress. But I wasn't ready to give them up, or put in the deep work that was needed to examine where my unhealthy coping mechanisms came from.

Honestly, I don't blame myself. No one is ready for that sort of work until they're ready, and for me it would be many more years. And of course, I'm telling you this story with the benefit of hindsight. Back then, I just knew that I was full of doubt and fear. Remaining very, very busy helped me stay two steps ahead of it.

*　　*　　*

Then, a silver lining appeared.

After graduation I enrolled in an MBA program, and I absolutely loved it. I was so taken with the experience—the coursework, the brilliant professors and students, the possibilities opening up exponentially—that it was as if there were no extra room for all my old self-doubts and fears. For the first time, I re-experienced the joy of learning just for the sake of learning. It was there that I learned about the concept of *eustress*, or good stress. This is the kind of stress that leaves you feeling motivated and challenged, instead of overwhelmed and ineffective.

In this state, my overachieving habits seemed to deliver excellent results but without the high price that bad stress exacts. I sailed through the program in a sort of flow state and graduated at the top of my class.

I applied for six jobs and received offers from all of them. I accepted a job at a consulting firm whose mission was to make health care more affordable and accessible for low-income families. I was made for this! I gleefully deposited my signing bonus in my checking account and bought a shiny leather briefcase to celebrate. This was it. Finally—I was about to step into the life I'd dreamed of since childhood.

*　　*　　*

My "baptism by fire," which is literally what the company called it, began on Day 1. It meant that every new hire was simply thrown into the deep end, no onboarding other than to fill out some HR forms and be shown to a cubicle. Mine, by the way, just happened to be in the back dark corner of a windowless janitor's closet. (I wish I were joking!)

I smile now at my naïveté, but I wasn't worried about the lack of training. I was fresh out of grad school and full of optimism, confident I could overachieve my way through the nearly vertical learning curve. I was also a true believer in the firm's mission, and I believed I was joining a team of equally committed colleagues. By the end of the first quarter I thought I'd be skipping off hand in hand into the sunset with my very happy clients.

Then came my first assignment.

I was to be the acting supervisor for a client group of nine financial counselors at four hospitals. My job was to improve the financial performance of the team by 200 percent in one year by implementing productivity and quality standards, changing numerous processes, and implementing a new technology. Lo and behold, two of the financial counselors hated the changes, and therefore hated me. One regularly screamed at me, and one got so mad she threw a three-ring binder at me when I walked into her office. So much for happy client sunset scenes.

Then about three months in, a guy on my team I'll call Ben pulled me aside to say he'd overheard our project leaders talking about me. They thought I was a hiring mistake and were trying to figure out what to do with me.

I was stunned. How could I already be failing? There were three other young women who'd been hired right around the time I was, and none of them appeared to be struggling. What was I doing wrong?

My worst nightmare was coming to life. I'd been found out—I didn't deserve to be there and everyone knew it.

There was only one thing for an insecure overachiever to do: double down and try harder. Asking for help was not an option. This was a culture where seeking support was seen as a sign of weakness or incompetence, where we were explicitly told to "embrace the suck." You either proved you could "handle the grind" or you got benched. I was also so young and inexperienced that I simply assumed this was just the way the corporate world *was*, and I had no idea how to question that or advocate for myself.

So it never once occurred to me to ask for feedback on my job performance or speak with leadership to see if there was any truth to Ben's words. (I would learn many months later that he was an inveterate gaslighter.)

Caught in a vicious cycle of perfectionism and overwork, my weekly work hours crept up to fifty-five, sixty, then sixty-five. All I did was work, travel for work (while working on the plane), and grab a few hours' sleep at night, when often my dreams were of work.

Before long I was miserable, exhausted, and painfully disillusioned. This was not how things were supposed to go. Every Sunday evening I was filled with dread and anxiety, and I'd calculate how much of my signing bonus I would have to repay if I quit. But I knew I never would. That would be confirmation of my failure, I still had $37,000 in student loans to repay, and I desperately wanted to prove that I wasn't a hiring mistake.

True to form, I "embraced the suck" and kept going.

*   *   *

Things did improve over the next several years as I became proficient at my job, and it helped that I really loved my client work. The churn never let up, though, and my firm, like many, was only too happy to have an ambitious, insecure overachiever like me around. I had a new project, a new client, a new team, a new city, and a new set of responsibilities every ten to twelve months. Often, just when I felt I'd adapted, I was told I was needed on another project in another city the next week. I had to quickly wrap things up, say goodbye to clients and teammates I'd bonded with, and move on.

Still, I excelled, garnering multiple promotions and big bonuses and raises. Meanwhile on the personal front, things were wonderful. I got married in 2001. We had our first child in 2003 and our second in 2004.

On the outside, I was the emblem of success. I seemed to have it all—cool job, impressive title, smart, talented colleagues, great family, beautiful home, more money than the skinny little girl on the rez could have dreamed of.

But behind the scenes I still carried a ton of self-doubt and a deep need to prove that I was good enough. Despite bringing in millions in revenue for my company and getting steadily promoted, I felt as though on any day, someone up the chain of command would realize that I was "a hiring mistake." And now in addition to routinely working ten- and twelve-hour days, I worried constantly that I was failing at home. Was I spending enough time with my husband? My two babies? How badly were my long absences screwing them up?

Sunday evenings started to feel dreadful again. It was becoming harder and harder to motivate myself, and, on some days, even to get out of bed. I chalked this up to exhaustion—what new mom wouldn't be tired?—and told myself that once I hit the next big deliverable, I could ease off a little. Or if I could just hang on until summer, I could take a vacation and recharge and spend quality time with my family, which would allay some of my constant guilt.

I told myself that the kind of success I was after required this kind of sacrifice.

*   *   *

I hit the wall in 2005. My mom passed away in June, when my sons were two years old and six months. The grief and the postpartum baby blues walloped me. For the first time in my life, I couldn't work at all. Not that I didn't try. I'd drag myself to my computer, only to collapse in tears. Or I'd start in on a project, and I just couldn't make my brain work. I felt bone-tired, and my job didn't make sense anymore. Was there any point to it? Were all my efforts even making a difference?

I decided to take a leave of absence to stay home with the boys and recover. I felt guilty about it (and enormously grateful that I had the option), but some gut instinct in me knew that if I ever wanted to be effective and fulfilled at work again—if I ever wanted to *work* again—I needed to heal.

Despite two very young children and our third son's arrival in 2006, I remember that two-year period as a positive—and, get this, *leisurely*—time compared to the pace of work. Yep, even with a newborn and two toddlers, my life felt easier and calmer, and I actually slept *more* than when I was in the consulting grind. It was serious renewal time for me.

But after a while, I started to feel like not working was not working for me. As delightful as it may sound to spend all day with the three-and-under set, there was a serious lack of intellectual stimulation. I went back to work in 2007, determined to do things differently. I protected my time, didn't work on weekends, and built really positive relationships with my team members. I loved my new role leading our new-hire and leadership-development programs, and I began to love work again.

Ironically, leadership was so pleased with my performance that I was promoted yet again—which meant more work, more responsibility, more travel. My hours started to creep right back up, as did my stress levels. But I didn't want to let anyone down—especially after they'd put so much faith in me.

Slowly but steadily, I was back to the grind. I would've kept going if my body hadn't issued an SOS in 2011.

At home on bed rest, I remember lying on the couch, feeling pretty chill from the Xanax, when the realization suddenly hit me. *Holy shit*, I thought. *I nearly killed myself! Something has to change. I need to change.*

During those days at home, I finally started to take a hard look at my stress, my unhealthy relationship with work and success, and my self-destructive coping patterns. My entire career, I'd been too busy to stop and consider why I was so driven and so willing to sacrifice all the things outside of work—time with family and friends, sleep, exercise, vacations, leisure activities—that made life meaningful. Finally forced to come to a full stop, I realized how burned-out I felt, even though I loved my client work and still believed in the firm's mission.

And I realized something else: The gathering dread I'd tried so mightily to ignore wasn't about the workload or even the exhaustion I was feeling. It came from constantly chasing other people's goals rather than my own.

I dissolved into tears when I finally admitted to myself that I felt deeply disconnected from my true purpose—and worse yet, that I had been so busy overachieving and pushing myself and people-pleasing that I wasn't even sure what that was.

Right there on the couch, I resolved to make some serious changes. What was the worth of any of this success if I was going to stroke out in my early forties?

As soon as I got the okay from my doctor I started a fitness routine, and I began practicing mindfulness—something I knew nothing about until reading *Search Inside Yourself*. Chade-Meng Tan's permission to be a "lazy meditator" ("beditating" is my fave) was a game changer. I began taking vacations. Real ones, where I left work at work and gave myself a digital detox. I started identifying my boundaries and began to practice enforcing them. No more work on weekends. No more road warrior travel schedule. No more saying yes to every request out of fear of disappointing someone.

*   *   *

Then at work, serendipity struck. Part of my job was to train our new hires, and, around this time, research in emotional intelligence (EI) was garnering lots of attention in the corporate world. There are a few different models and schools of thought on EI, but the one that rose to the fore in popular culture and deeply influenced thinking on management and leadership came from Dr. Daniel Goleman, a psychologist and science journalist. Goleman defined EI as "the capacity for recognizing our own feelings and those of others, for motivating ourselves, and for managing emotions well in ourselves and in our relationships." According to Goleman, EI was the one absolutely essential skill for leadership, and the single largest predictor of success in the workplace. I was floored to learn that literally thousands of studies concluded that EI was the key difference between average leaders and exceptional leaders. I incorporated an overview of EI and a few EI-building exercises into our onboarding curriculum, and the new hires loved it.

I did, too. Goleman's original five domains of emotional intelligence—self-awareness, self-regulation, self-motivation, empathy, and social skills—got me thinking seriously about my own leadership style and how a lack of self-awareness and poor self-regulation skills had contributed to the stress I experienced at work. I'd been operating on autopilot, ignoring all the signals that my stress was out of control, until I wound up ill and with what I now recognized to be full-blown burnout. Before, I'd pictured burnout to be an experience of profound exhaustion, or of being so stressed-out and fed up that you wanted to give up. But burnout actually covers a wide range of physical, mental, and emotional symptoms, and can look very different from person to person. I hadn't recognized mine in part because of my lack of awareness and in part because my experience of burnout didn't fit the very narrow portrait I had in my head. Burnout, as I soon discovered, was a distinct and well-studied workplace phenomenon, with its own body of research and subject-matter experts. According to the World Health Organization, burnout is characterized by three things:

1. feelings of exhaustion and depleted energy,
2. feelings of cynicism or negativism toward one's job, and
3. reduced professional efficacy (feeling that you're ineffective or not performing at your best).

My experience checked every box. Now, I wondered, if I could somehow strengthen my emotional intelligence, could I apply those skills to stress management? And if I'd had more self-awareness and better stress management skills back then, could I have avoided burnout entirely?

WHAT IS EI ANYWAY?

Since Daniel Goleman popularized the concept of emotional intelligence in 1995, he and his colleagues Dr. Richard Boyatzis and Dr. Annie McKee evolved the model to include four domains—self-awareness, self-management, social awareness, and relationship management—along with twelve corresponding EI competencies, which are a group of learned capabilities that enable outstanding performance. (See Figure 1.1.)

In its most practical sense, EI is a set of competencies that help us understand how our emotions affect our thoughts and behaviors, as well as understand our social environment and how to work effectively within it. Essentially, EI is about:

- Understanding yourself
- Managing yourself
- Understanding others
- Managing relationships

The two most fascinating things about EI are this:

- EI competencies are learnable. Our life and work experiences form our early EI foundation, and we can continue to hone, adapt, and evolve these skills with deliberate practices.
- EI competencies improve the more you use them.

Throughout the book, you'll find exercises, assessments, and reflection questions that will help you practice how to develop and apply your EI to manage stress and protect yourself from burnout.

Self-Awareness	Self-Management	Social Awareness	Relationship Management
Emotional self-awareness	Emotional self-control	Empathy	Influence
	Adaptability		Coach and mentor
	Achievement orientation		Conflict management
	Positive outlook	Organizational awareness	Teamwork
			Inspirational leadership

Figure 1.1: Emotional Intelligence Domains and Competencies

I began devouring literature on EI, positive psychology, and burnout, and, pretty quickly, I realized I wanted to study these topics for real—to "science the shit out of it," as they say in academia.

So finally, I decided to follow my own passions instead of someone else's. In 2013 I enrolled in a doctoral program at the University of Pennsylvania. It was the perfect place to explore my nerdy interests and study with EI expert Annie McKee, and I immersed myself in all the literature on emotional intelligence, resilience, stress, and burnout. So much began to make sense: how the lack of stability and security in my early life prompted an excessive need for just that; how I carried stress like a badge of honor; how I fell into the traps of overwork and perfectionism in response to imposter syndrome; how I engaged in comfort activities to alleviate stress (bingeing on Netflix and junk food) rather than renewal activities (spending time with family, hiking, traveling, getting adequate rest).

Then, in the midst of what felt like a huge intellectual and personal awakening, the time arrived for me to shift from student to researcher. I began designing and conducting my own studies on emotional intelligence, stress, and burnout, and expected to find fairly predictable results that I could easily parlay into a strong dissertation.

Instead, I stumbled upon something that was to change the course of my research, and, ultimately, my life.

*   *   *

In a study on burnout and occupational stress I conducted with chief medical officers at thirty-five large hospitals, an overwhelming number—69 percent—reported that their stress levels were severe, very severe, or the worst possible. With that level of workplace stress, I expected to see high rates of burnout. But not only were most of these highly stressed leaders *not* burned out, *they showed no signs of heading toward burnout.*

This was super exciting, but the results of one small study don't exactly represent a scientific breakthrough. So my team and I conducted more studies, zeroing in on leaders in high-stress roles. In each study, we saw the same pattern. Though some of the participants met the diagnostic criteria for burnout, there was always a group of people who, despite experiencing dangerous levels of stress, were not burned-out and showed no signs of impending burnout.

What was going on with these people? Had they hit some sort of genetic lottery that gifted them with stress-busting superpowers? Or did it have more to do with nurture—had they been raised by unusually coolheaded parents? Was it an acquired skill? Were they Jedi-level meditators capable of remaining unflappable even in chronically stressful environments?

Whatever they had, where could I get some?

*   *   *

Though most of the media coverage on burnout centers on its sky-rocketing rates around the world—which is indeed a story worth covering—I became intensely curious about this virtually unknown group of leaders who seemed to be immune to burnout. If I could identify what made them different from others—and what they shared in common—it might just hold the key for the rest of us to learn how to avoid burning out.

So that's what I set out to do. I conducted hundreds of in-depth interviews with leaders who were under dangerous levels of stress at work—we're talking a 7 or above on a 10-point scale—but somehow managed to avoid burnout. Just what was this X factor that prevented them from burning out?

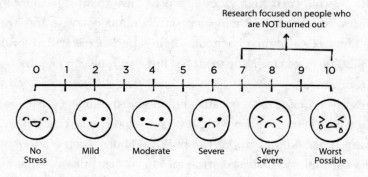

Figure 1.2: The Stress Assessment Tool

Once all the data was in, it turned out there *was* something different about these people, and there *was* something they had in common. The X factor had been staring me in the face all along. It was emotional intelligence.

No matter what role or industry they were in, no matter their level of seniority, no matter how they'd been raised or by whom, the one thing those with burnout immunity shared was a high degree of emotional intelligence.

It wasn't that they were preternaturally calm or that they were aloof, uninvolved leaders. Plenty were what you'd call high-strung or even anxious, and they were all deeply engaged in their work. But they all had the ability to accurately perceive their own emotions as well as their employees' and colleagues', and to handle all those emotions in the midst of the fray, without succumbing to unproductive protective patterns or unhealthy behaviors.

Put another way, they all relied on their EI to regulate their emotions *and* respond effectively to others' emotions in the midst of high-stress situations. Situations like having the weight of an entire community's safety in their hands; or the loss of a key client; or the need to make a momentous decision *right now*; or spearheading the launch of a high-stakes initiative or new venture . . . or just the daily grind of having too much to do and not enough time and support to do it. Overall, their highly developed EI gave them superior coping abilities, which helped them successfully manage stress and immunize themselves against burnout. Their experience clarified for me a key fact: no one is immune to stress, but everyone can acquire burnout immunity.

Yes, everyone. That's because emotional intelligence isn't something a lucky few are born with. It's a skill that can be developed, just like any other skill. *Everyone* can build and boost their emotional intelligence and use EI-based strategies to successfully manage workplace stress and immunize themselves against burnout.

And that's exactly what I'm going to teach you how to do.

*   *   *

One of the first, and most important, steps to immunize yourself against burnout is to determine your risk level. What's your current degree of workplace stress? Are you stressed-out, in danger of burning out, at high risk for burnout, or already burned-out? To see where you are on the burnout risk spectrum, complete the Burnout Risk Assessment on page 252. You'll have the option of filling it out right here in the book, or you can use your smartphone to scan the QR code and complete the survey online, where you can access additional tools and resources to lower your risk of burning out or mitigate the effects of burnout that's already present.

Wherever your experience happens to fall on the spectrum, if you've picked up this book, I'm going to assume that you're stressed at work and you're worried about burning out—or maybe, like millions of others and myself back in 2011, you're already burned-out. To get you the help you need, I distilled the results of my research into a set of EI-based skills, principles, and strategies that came up again and again in my research on folks with burnout immunity. That's exactly what I'll be sharing with you in this book. Each chapter will walk you through one of the following skills, and I'll show you how to develop it and incorporate it into your particular work context:

1. Awareness
2. Regulation
3. Meaningful connections
4. Mindset
5. Recover, Reconnect, and Reimagine

Awareness of our emotional makeup and how our emotions drive our thoughts and behaviors is the foundation upon which all the other burnout immunity skills are built. Greater awareness enables us to know what triggers us and why, what makes us more sensitive to stress, what puts us over the tipping point from good stress that gives us energy and focus to bad stress that depletes and overwhelms us, our protective patterns under stress, the impact we have on colleagues and culture when we're stressed, and what we can control and what we can't.

Regulation is about the ability to skillfully manage our emotions, thoughts, and behaviors. Especially when we're stressed-out and overwhelmed, our emotions can gain the upper hand, and our thoughts can spiral out of control. And we all know what happens when we're in an agitated state—we often act in ways that aren't productive or are even downright harmful, which ends up stressing us (and our colleagues) out even more. Learning self-regulation helps prevent us from succumbing to negative thoughts, unproductive emotions, and impulsive, unexamined behaviors that put us at risk of burnout and that distract us from our vision of our ideal self.

Meaningful connections help us reduce stress and prevent overwork, and they offer us healthy forms of renewal. Research shows that people who have meaningful connections of any type—with their personal or community relationships, their jobs or sense of mission, their goals, or their hobbies and passion projects—enjoy greater well-being, less stress, and are more physically and emotionally healthy. We'll look at how meaningful connections with our work, our relationships, and our values lower stress and protect against burnout.

Mindset has to do with our general beliefs and attitude about work, life, and everything in between. Do we come from a hopeful, optimistic orientation, or a more negative and pessimistic one? Do we believe that the world is a place that is delightful, beautiful, safe, abundant, full of meaning, and capable of getting better? Or are we convinced that everything is going to hell in a handbasket? Research attests that people who have a positive, hopeful outlook and who believe they can effect positive change even if their outer circumstances are very negative are more resilient, less stressed, and have better personal and professional relationships. In my own research, I've observed that the people with the strongest natural burnout immunity are those with the most positive outlooks, those who believe that stress can be enhancing, those who have a servant leadership mindset, and those who practice regular self-compassion. We'll look at proven ways even the most negative among us can cultivate hope and positivity, even in times of acute stress.

Recover, Reconnect, and Reimagine—what I call 3Rx, the three-R prescription—is a burnout immunity strategy unto itself. Workers who engage in regular times to recover from work stress lower their risk of burning out. And certainly, adequate recovery is needed once we're in a state of burnout. Those who periodically take time to reconnect with their values and vision, especially when they're grappling with major stressors at work such as a new role, a change in company culture, or a setback, are better equipped to avoid burnout. And finally, workers who can reimagine a new way forward, whether that's after burnout has struck or, hopefully, when they first notice stress escalating, are empowered to move beyond the stress they're currently feeling and tame the flames of burnout.

As you make your way through the book, I'll give you the latest research on stress management, resilience, and burnout prevention and recovery; real-life stories from people with natural burnout immunity *and* those like me who acquired it later in life; and a variety of exercises and self-assessments so you can start building your personalized plan for burnout immunity right away.

Before we dive in, I want to offer a couple of caveats. In the best-case scenario, we can prevent burnout well before it occurs. If you're already in a state of burnout, however, *and* you want to remain in your job, I'll show you how to use EI and burnout immunity skills to open up a path to recovery, and to having a healthier relationship with work.

But if you're in a toxic or abusive work environment, or your job is so demanding that it's compromising your mental or physical health, you need to start planning your exit. There's no need to tough it out under unbearable working conditions. I had to learn that the hard way, and, in retrospect, I'm grateful for the health crisis that made me reexamine my relationship with work and that set me on a career path that's more aligned with my values and my vision of my ideal self. But I really hope you don't get to that point. If you're in that kind of situation, it's my hope that you'll reach out for help this very day, and, that a little later, this book will help in giving you the fortitude to leave and pursue a new, healthier career path much sooner than I did.

Though I'm encouraged by the new emphasis on mental health and well-being in the workplace that has come about in the wake of the Covid-19 pandemic, there are still too many indications that burnout is a systemic problem, deeply embedded in many organizational cultures. My former student Dr. Carmen Allison, now chief human resources manager at Stanford's Hoover Institution, studied the effects of extreme stress and intrapersonal pressure on executives. While stress and high-stakes situations will always be a part of work, she observes, business culture lauds and even insists on high-pressure assignments as "an expected rite of passage." Employees feel they have no choice but to endure this "trial by fire," which is seen as a badge of honor.

Sadly, that's no different from when I was a consultant. Even though we know this path is not sustainable, the same patterns persist. Eleven percent of Allison's participants ranked their work pressure as *higher* than 10 on a 10-point scale, and many experienced severe mental anguish. "Intense pressure experiences were detrimental to the health and well-being, cognition, and focus of these executives and disruptive to the organization," she wrote, "causing irreversible harm to some of our most valuable human resources." In the end, Allison came to a chilling conclusion: "Given the lack of care placed on selecting leaders for difficult assignments and providing them with support led me to conclude that executive leaders are seen as disposable."

Disposable? Something is deeply wrong here.

Meanwhile, I'm currently mentoring Alexa, a local high school student who's doing her senior project on the rates and severity of burnout among high school seniors. The same day she told me that 55 percent of her classmates agree or strongly agree that they're feeling overwhelmed and burned-out, a friend forwarded a report with alarming statistics. While global levels of burnout improved slightly in 2022—falling from 71 percent to 63 percent—a staggering 84 percent of Gen Z workers reported burnout in the previous year. These are horrifying numbers. But the stat that really got me was that 40 percent of the respondents believe burnout is *an inevitable part of success.*

From seasoned professionals to those just entering the workforce to *teenagers*, we're burned-out and exhausted and demoralized, and close to half of us think burnout is necessary to succeed. Something is indeed deeply wrong here.

I can't claim to know all the answers on how to make the kind of systemic and cultural changes needed to render burnout nonexistent. But I do know that we need a collective effort, led by workers who are aware, energized, and ready to change the culture of work from what Carmen Allison calls "sink or swim" to "support and succeed," so that everyone has the work conditions they need to flourish. Burnout robs individuals of the chance to be effective and impactful, and to feel fulfilled and happy at work. It costs organizations more than $190 billion a year in absenteeism, lost productivity, and turnover. And it robs the world of the contributions and solutions that our health care workers, teachers, innovators, executives, entrepreneurs, public safety officers, child care providers, and policy-makers could offer if they didn't feel exhausted, overwhelmed, unsupported, and unproductive.

So let's not allow that to happen. Whether you're in a high-stress role that you love and want to keep, or you're starting to feel the worrying signs of chronic stress and encroaching burnout, life is too short to spend it feeling exhausted, sick, stuck in an unfulfilling job, and burned-out. I've taught burnout immunity principles to thousands of people around the world, and I continue to be amazed by their stories of how much better life is, at work and elsewhere, when they learn to boost their EI skills and find more productive ways to deal with workplace stress. I'm thrilled to share their stories here, along with an abundance of practical tools and strategies you can use to protect yourself against burnout.

This book is written with deep gratitude to all the amazing people who helped me understand why some people don't get burned-out and what we can learn from them. And it's dedicated to all the wonderful readers who want to take control of their own well-being and enjoy a happier and healthier relationship with work.

2

Case Study: YOU

What Makes You Vulnerable to Burnout?

I hope you had a chance to take the Burnout Risk Assessment. If not, take a few moments to flip to the back of the book and complete it. Becoming aware of your degree of burnout risk is the first step in awareness and helps to chart a path forward, according to your unique experience and needs.

I'm sure some of you already knew you were burned-out and hardly needed a quiz to confirm it. Or maybe, like many who've completed the assessment, you were surprised by your results and are now concerned to see that you're at moderate or high risk for burnout. What do your results reveal?

After discovering she was at high risk, one of my coaching clients said something I'll never forget: "I exist in two modes. When I'm at work, I'm a machine—nothing but the grind exists. At home, I'm completely checked out and numb. Sometimes I don't even remember falling asleep."

I'll just come right out and say it: this is no way to live. While it's possible to keep up the grind for short bursts of time, the kind of pace and intensity this leader was enduring are not sustainable.

What I really want you to notice about her story, however, is that she was actually checked out and numb in *both* modes. Day and night, she functioned in a numbed-out, autopilot state—and is there really any wonder? It was how she was getting through a life with too much work and far too few of the things that could recharge and support her, like time with friends, exercise, or a hobby. It was only when the Burnout Risk Assessment yielded results that surprised her that she paused to pay attention to herself and became aware of the effects of her workplace stress.

She's hardly the only one who's functioning on autopilot. I hear it from my research participants, graduate students, and workshop participants daily. (And I still find myself there once in a while.) After one of my corporate workshops, a participant came up to talk to me, and he had tears in his eyes. Earlier that day he'd won a sales award, and the room of three hundred leaders had erupted in applause as he strode to the stage. Now he stood by me on the same stage, apologizing for being emotional.

"Not at all," I said, and invited him to sit down and talk.

"I just want to tell you," he said, "that I took your assessment and it scared the crap out of me. That award I got today? I've won it four out of the last five years. Everybody thinks I'm at the top of my game—and a couple hours ago I would've said the same thing. But this assessment says I'm at high risk for burnout."

"Does that feel true to you?" I asked him.

"This is exactly why it's hitting me so hard!" he said. "I think I've known for a while I was reaching a breaking point, but I didn't want to admit it."

He went on to tell me a story of how he had been working so hard and had sacrificed so much to support his family. "They're the most important thing to me, but if I'm burning myself out to support them, what good does that do?" he said. "And all this work I'm doing means I'm not even with them. What's the point?"

I nodded in recognition. Like this young man, I hear all too often from people who tell me they sensed something was off but weren't pausing to become aware of what was going on at a deeper level. There are endless reasons we avoid bringing focused attention to ourselves, but here are some of the top reasons I've heard and observed:

- We're afraid that if we slow down or take a break, we'll get passed over for opportunities.
- We're afraid that we'll need to ask for help, which feels like failure or weakness.
- We feel that focusing on ourselves is indulgent or somehow shameful.
- We're fearful that we'll discover that we need to make changes that require considerable effort.
- We simply feel we don't have the time to do anything other than work.

Whatever our reasons, many of us would rather stay busy, all the while unwittingly escalating our risk of burnout, rather than pause to pay attention to our own experience. "My firm isn't paying me to look under the hood," a workshop participant once told me. "They're paying me to deliver."

I get where this person is coming from. Honestly, I've *been* that person. But what I would say to him (and to my younger self) is that first of all, this is a severely limited notion of awareness. Awareness, as we'll see, isn't just about introspection, and it isn't navel-gazing—it isn't even solely about yourself. And second, anyone who wants to become the happiest and most effective version of themselves *and* serve and succeed for the long term must develop their awareness skills. You actually can't afford not to.

Research bears this out. Numerous studies have shown that people who are self-aware are more confident and creative, make better decisions, build stronger relationships, communicate more effectively, earn more promotions, and even create more-profitable companies. At the same time, awareness of *others* (social awareness) is essential for good leadership, teamwork, and overall effectiveness. Those who practice empathy, or the ability to understand and share the feelings of another, are better at coaching, engaging others, and decision-making, and they communicate and collaborate more effectively.

On the flip side, when we lack awareness, our personal growth and the growth of the organization can suffer. Employees who lack self-awareness aren't able to accurately assess their own strengths and weaknesses, have greater trouble regulating their emotions, and are less likely to consider the perspectives of others. It's no fun to work for this type of person, either. Research has shown that working with unaware people can translate to increased stress, decreased motivation, a higher chance of quitting, and even negative impacts to performance, as collaborating with unaware colleagues cuts a team's chance of success by *half.*

Awareness is necessary to know who we really are (not who others want us to be or who we think we should be), what type of work environment best suits our temperament and our skills, the impact we want to have, and the values that underpin the choices we make and the actions we take. Awareness is essential to becoming more resilient, and to immunizing ourselves against burnout.

At its simplest level, *self-awareness* is the ability to accurately recognize and understand our own emotions, thoughts, and behaviors, and the underlying reasons for each. When we're self-aware, we have a clear, objective view of what we're feeling, thinking, and doing, and we also have an accurate assessment of how others see and experience us. Self-awareness is critical to psychological health.

Social awareness is the ability to accurately recognize and understand the impact of our emotions, thoughts, and behaviors on others. This includes empathy, which requires us to understand how other people feel so that we can accurately anticipate and understand how our emotions and behaviors will affect the people around us. Social awareness is critical to organizational health.

Notice that for both self-awareness and social awareness, accuracy is key—which turns out to be a lot harder than you'd think. After a five-year study involving nearly 5,000 participants, organizational psychologist Tasha Eurich concluded that although 95 percent of people believe they're self-aware, only 10–15 percent actually are. Eurich's findings are consistent with the emotional intelligence assessments I've conducted with my coaching clients. After completing a self-assessment of their EI competencies, clients are asked to have several colleagues (their boss, peers, direct reports, and often teammates as well as external customers and clients) complete the same assessment of them. My most recent comprehensive analysis of these assessments found that just 19 percent had an accurate assessment of their EI competencies.

That's really an extraordinary disparity between perceived self-awareness and the self-awareness we actually possess, but if you consider the many ways we can lose awareness, even temporarily, the gulf begins to make more sense. Have you ever been in a bad mood for no reason you can identify? Have you ever "come to" after being mindlessly involved in some activity—doom-scrolling or snacking or daydreaming, for example—and wonder where on earth the time has gone? Ever been taken aback by your reaction to an event at work or blurted out a regretful comment and have no idea where it came from? Or how about this: Have you ever worked with (or for) someone whose skills or performance don't come close to the inflated image they have of themselves? How about a top performer who consistently underrates themselves or undervalues their contributions? Have you ever been blindsided by a performance review—either because it's a lot worse or a lot better than you expected? Ever angered or hurt someone because something you said or did was taken in a way you did not expect at all?

These are all ways that a lack of awareness can show up. Some are more serious than others, of course, but in all cases, a lack of awareness means we're missing vital information about who we are, our true strengths and shortcomings, and how we're coming across.

It can mean we're out of touch with our own experience, oblivious to the effects that our emotions, thoughts, and behaviors are having on ourselves and on others. And when it comes to burnout, chronic un-awareness can cause us to miss the clues that our work-related stress is creeping into burnout territory.

Now that the Burnout Risk Assessment has given you a baseline awareness of your personal burnout risk, we'll spend the rest of this chapter deepening that awareness—of your internal makeup as well as the external factors that may be elevating your risk of burning out. The first order of business is simply to gather some data. Together we'll discover how work-related stress is affecting you, the early influences that taught you how to handle stress, and the unique, innate traits that make you who you are and that may increase your sensitivity to certain stressors. It's there, at the inter-section of nature (your innate traits) and nurture (your environ-mental influences), that we'll uncover the particular set of factors that increase *your* vulnerability to burnout, as well as your ability to handle stress, build resilience, and, ultimately, avoid burning out.

There is no more powerful way to immunize yourself against burnout than to know exactly what makes YOU vulnerable to burn-ing out—not your boss, not your competitor, not your seemingly in-defatigable coworker—and then taking measures that will protect YOU from the career killer that's been called "an equal-opportunity international crisis."

BURNOUT KEYWORDS

According to the WHO, burnout is characterized by feelings of **exhaus-tion** and **depleted energy**, **cynicism** or **negative attitude** toward one's job, and **reduced professional efficacy**. People describe their expe-riences of burnout in many different ways, however, and the words we choose offer a window into our experience. Take a moment to reflect on your language. Do any of these keywords and phrases come up when you talk about work? They could be a signal that you are in a state of burnout or in danger of developing it.

Angry	I'll never get through this
Anxious	Impossible
Bitter	Indifferent
Breaking point	Ineffective
Can't do this anymore	Irritated
Cynical	Listless
Defeated	Low energy
Deflated	Numb
Demoralized	Overloaded
Disconnected	Overwhelmed
Discouraged	Pessimistic
Disengaged	Pointless
Distant	Resentful
Emotionally drained/depleted	Resigned
Exhausted	Spiraling
Fatigued	Stuck
Fed up	Suffering
Frustrated	Unfulfilled
Helpless	Unproductive
Hopeless	Trapped
I want to quit/give up	Withdrawn

Is Burnout Calling?

We tend to think of burnout in its extreme form: the deeply unhappy worker who's at a breaking point, utterly spent and maybe even on the verge of collapse. And while that is an accurate portrayal of many people's experience, one of the more insidious qualities of burnout is that it can sneak up on us, slowly taking hold in micro steps. Think of the old boiling-frog metaphor: a frog in a pot of cold water won't notice that the water is becoming dangerously hot if the heat rises gradually. Likewise, our workplace stress can increase so incrementally that we don't notice we're heading toward burnout until something happens to jolt us into awareness.

Sometimes, like my coaching client, our frantic scrambling to keep on top of the day-to-day takes up our full awareness, and we just don't have the bandwidth to pay attention to what's happening internally. Sometimes, as we saw earlier, we avoid self-awareness, which can happen consciously or subconsciously (yes, you can be unaware that you are unaware!). And don't forget that burnout can happen to people who really love their jobs and who enthusiastically go above and beyond at work.

I saw this recently with a group of K–12 school superintendents I worked with at the University of Pennsylvania. When the pandemic turned their routines and educational lives upside down, they became ultra-absorbed in problem-solving and figuring out how to navigate massive changes while keeping teachers, staff, and families happy—all while prioritizing students' well-being and upholding rigorous learning standards. So much so that they didn't have time to think about themselves, and many of them ended up compartmentalizing their emotions in order to keep up with the drastic change in workload and an entirely new set of demands.

Now that schools are open and educational practices are returning to normal, they're able to attend to their own experience and reflect on the sacrifices they made, and many of them are, in effect, "waking up" to realize that they're burned-out. It's as if they're noticing a shift from subconscious burnout to conscious burnout.

The point is, if we're not aware of the toll that our work-related stress is taking—and it *is* taking a toll, whether we're miserable at work or pursuing our dream job—we're left vulnerable to burning out. When we tune in and become self-aware, however, we can start to notice the signs—even the very subtle ones—that our workplace stress is escalating and that burnout is calling.

Research tells us that problematic workplace stress predominantly shows up in five main areas of our lives. For each one, let's look at the telltale signs that stress is entering the danger zone. As you read through, see if you recognize any of these "distress signals" in your own life, especially if these experiences or behaviors are new for you, or if they're escalating in terms of severity or frequency.

HOW STRESS AFFECTS US

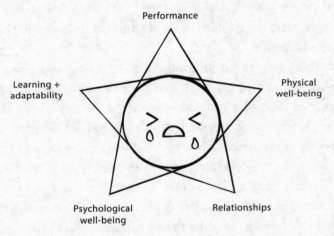

Figure 2.1: The Five Areas in Which Stress Affects Us

Physical Well-Being: You begin experiencing headaches, digestive issues (indigestion, nausea, upset stomach), muscle tension, tightness in the chest or feeling short of breath, insomnia, fatigue, changes in eating habits (eating too much or too little), hair loss, elevated blood pressure, elevated heart rate, excessive sweating, teeth grinding, loss of libido, frequent colds and infections.

Psychological Well-Being: You feel excessively worried, pessimistic, cynical, a lack of interest in things that once engaged you, low self-esteem, a lack of control, overwhelmed, anxious, sad, discouraged or demoralized; you experience stress dreams; you begin relying on unhealthy coping mechanisms (avoidance, substance abuse, excessive spending, excessive use of social media, etc.) to lower stress or "numb out."

Relationships: You find yourself more irritable with colleagues and loved ones; you're experiencing more conflict; you're less tolerant of others' mistakes, shortcomings, or learning curves; you're more argumentative, less willing to engage in teamwork, less willing to listen to others' input; you avoid people; you're simply not enjoying time with other people like you once did.

Learning and Adaptability: You find that you can't focus or concentrate like you used to; you're less comfortable stepping out of your comfort zone; you're more forgetful; you're slower to learn new skills or technologies; you're more resistant to change, more defensive; you're more reluctant to take on new initiatives and projects; you insist on your routine or processes.

Performance: You miss deadlines, become disorganized, make poor decisions, avoid responsibilities, call in sick more often, make mistakes that aren't characteristic of you; you feel unmotivated or disengaged; you work harder but your results don't show it; you're less productive; you require more oversight than you used to; you fantasize about, or even plan for, leaving your job.

Now, the first thing I want to say about this laundry list of negative effects of stress is that *the stress you're feeling at work is not your fault*. I'm living proof that learning healthy coping mechanisms and ways to increase resilience makes an enormous difference, but chronic workplace stress, the kind that steadily grinds you down, is a sign that something is amiss in your work environment. To really address work-related stress and prevent burnout, we need to address the underlying workplace factors that are creating it.

It's Not You, It's Your Job

Among burnout experts, there is universal agreement that burnout is primarily caused by psychologically hazardous factors occurring at your workplace.

In other words, it's not you, it's your job. (I've long wanted to have that printed on a T-shirt and finally did so while writing this book.)

"Burnout in individual workers," write burnout experts Dr. Christina Maslach and Dr. Michael Leiter, "says more about the conditions of their job than it does about them. Contrary to popular opinion, it's not the individual but the organization that needs to change." Elsewhere, Maslach likens burnout to the proverbial canary in the coal mine. If the canary emerges from the mine having trouble breathing and functioning, we don't blame the canary for its lack of resilience or the inability to withstand toxic fumes—we figure out what's wrong with the mine.

When it comes to burnout, it's the *persistence* of psychologically hazardous workplace conditions that makes them toxic. The people who have the greatest vulnerability to burnout are those who experience a high degree of "distress zone" (7 or more on a 10-point scale) stress at work for a prolonged period of time. I had one person tell me recently, "When I'm feeling really burned-out, it's not because something bad happened that day. It's when things build up and intensify, and I'm not stopping to do something about it." Maslach would agree. "Burnout," she says, "is a prolonged response to chronic situational stressors on the job."

Bottom line? When you're trying to determine what makes you more vulnerable to burnout, the first place to look is your organization.

WHAT'S OUT OF ALIGNMENT?

Maslach and Leiter posit that burnout happens when there are "chronic mismatches" between people and their organizations in one or more of these areas: 1) workload, 2) control, 3) reward, 4) values,

5) fairness, and 6) community. What creates a mismatch? Simple. When your personal needs and expectations conflict with the conditions of the organization.

Let's take a more detailed look at each of these six key areas, and how chronic mismatches in each could play out at work. I'll then lead you through an exercise that will help you become more aware of what's going on in your work environment that may be increasing your vulnerability to burnout.

> **Workload**: While increasing workload *is* correlated with burnout (greater demand leads to greater stress and exhaustion), this one isn't a simple matter of having too much work to do. The problem arises when there is a mismatch between the individual employee's capacity and the demands of their work. We each have different capacities for engagement and different thresholds of exhaustion, and we each have different needs for rest and recovery. This is why it's so important to be aware of what we require to thrive and where our physical, emotional, and mental limits are.

I'll never forget the time that I was conducting a weekend retreat for finance leaders from a pharmaceutical company with offices in multiple states. Thirty leaders flew in from around the country, and they'd each completed a personal inventory prior to their arrival so I could get an idea of their roles and their major areas of concern. As always, I received a wide variety of responses, but two immediately stood out for the extremes in their experience. The first basically said, "This is the best job I've ever had. Every day I wake up and feel energized by our company's mission and the work we're doing," while the other was a serious cry for help: "My workload is extremely overwhelming. If something doesn't change, I can't do this anymore."

I had a chance to sit down with both of these individuals, and was shocked to discover that not only did they work in the same office but they were in the same department, reported to the same senior leader, and shared nearly identical workloads. This is a vivid illustration of how people in the same work environment with the same responsibilities can have vastly different subjective experiences of their workload, and thus a vastly different vulnerability to burnout.

> **Control**: Do you have the autonomy to fulfill your job duties in a way that's consistent with your values, your personal needs, and with your desire for when and how to get things done? It will be no surprise that a mismatch between the amount of control you need to perform at your best and the amount of control you're actually afforded at work creates more stress and increases your risk of burnout.

Back in college when I worked at a kiosk in the mall, I became friendly with a number of mall employees. Besides rude customers, their number one complaint was a lack of control over scheduling. Many retail and service industry workers don't know their schedule until days before they're expected at work, and schedules can change unpredictably. Research shows a clear link between a lack of control and burnout in any profession, but burnout rates for retail and other frontline workers are climbing. According to the latest Global State of Frontline Work Experience Study, 58 percent of frontline workers are planning to resign because of burnout, and 68 percent of retail workers reported burnout as being a more motivating factor for resigning than compensation (50 percent).

This study also asked workers what, if anything, could keep them at their jobs. The most popular answer? Flexible scheduling.

> **Reward**: The bottom line here is simple: "Insufficient reward, whether financial, institutional or social, increases staff members' vulnerability to burnout." Feeling that you're not being compensated in a way that matches your effort and time, or feeling

that you're not being recognized or appreciated for your efforts, exacts a high emotional toll that can easily lead to cynicism, feelings of inefficacy, and emotional exhaustion—all three aspects of burnout.

Recently, the Office of the U.S. Surgeon General released the Framework for Workplace Mental Health and Well-Being. It identifies five essentials that workers need to thrive at work, to feel physically and mentally healthy, and to contribute positively to their workplace. (These five essentials share much affinity with Maslach and Leiter's six key areas.) I'd like to highlight three aspects of what it says about Reward, which the Framework treats under an essential called "Mattering at Work."

First, whatever our profession, we want to know that we matter and that our work makes a difference. Knowing that you matter and are valued has a stress-lowering effect, while feeling that you don't matter or are not valued raises your risk of depression, and contributes to feelings of cynicism and withdrawal. Second, there is a direct correlation between well-being and income. According to a recent PricewaterhouseCoopers survey, 49 percent of workers who were financially stressed said that worries about money had a severe or major impact on their mental health in the past year. Third, feeling "seen, respected, needed, and valued" has an outsize positive effect on well-being. According to recent research, "Regardless of their position, when people feel appreciated, recognized, and engaged by their supervisors and coworkers, their sense of value and meaning increases, as well as their capacity to manage stress."

Clearly, insufficient reward in any of its guises has a direct negative impact on mental health and well-being, and is a key factor that increases our vulnerability to burnout. Sufficient reward, on the other hand, has exactly the opposite effect—even to the point that feeling valued lowers stress and builds our capacity to handle additional stress.

Values: When your individual values are incompatible with your organization's demonstrated values, you're in a situation that leaves you vulnerable to burnout. "The strain associated with an enduring mismatch of values," write Maslach and Leiter, "depletes personal energy, reduces involvement, and undermines professional efficacy or accomplishment."

But it's not just a matter of your values versus your organization's. Sometimes the discrepancy comes between an organization's *stated* values and the values that are actually reflected in their behavior or that are encouraged in the culture. Organizations can tout their values all day long, and they do (integrity, respect, inclusion, accountability, innovation, collaboration, and so on), but we often see corporate cultures that do not uphold their own values, or that reward behaviors that are inconsistent with their stated values.

One of the biggest values mismatches I've seen is in health care organizations that say patient safety is their top value. Physicians certainly agree—it's at the top of their list of values as well. Yet, in some organizations, the entire physician compensation structure revolves around physician productivity—which is measured by how many patients they see in a day. This creates a lot of stress for physicians who feel they need more time with their patients in order to achieve the highest levels of patient safety, yet who are also trying to maximize their compensation *and* who are being encouraged by their organization to maximize productivity and revenue. This is both a values and a potential workload mismatch, which leaves health care workers especially vulnerable to burnout.

Another very common example involves collaboration, which is often at the top of many organizations' stated core values. But when incentive structures reward employees for siloed behaviors, it's no wonder that people who highly value collaboration experience a lot of stress. I saw this with one of my clients who recently acquired a smaller tech startup. Prior to their integration, both companies listed collaboration as a core value, and after some cultural integra-tion work, leaders on both sides agreed to keep collaboration on their list of values. But in almost every meeting I attended, I observed si-loed, competitive, turf-protecting behavior. And guess what some of those leaders told me in private conversations? Things like "This is so frustrating. We keep saying we can't get this integration done unless we collaborate, but no one is working together. We're all just trying to protect our territory," and "I'm sorry, but saying that we value collab-oration is bullshit. We can't say we value it and turn around and re-ward people for being a lone wolf. Successful integrations don't work that way."

Ongoing mismatches like these steadily wear you down, mentally and emotionally. Who wouldn't feel frustrated, cynical, ineffective, demoralized, and fed up? Working in an environment like this leaves you ripe for burnout.

> **Fairness**: Are the policies and practices at your organization fairly administered in terms of who gets opportunities, recog-nition, resources, and rewards? Are decisions made in order to meet organizational objectives, rather than give personal advan-tages to privileged individuals? When people aren't treated with equity in any arena, for any reason, they are far more susceptible to burnout. It's demoralizing and demeaning to be treated with disrespect, which, not surprisingly, increases feelings of cynicism and negativity toward one's job. Maslach and Leiter also point out that unfair decisions alienate individuals from their commu-nity and undermine the sense of mutual trust that healthy orga-nizations need.

There is strong evidence that members of marginalized groups, whether due to ethnicity, race, gender, ability, or sexuality, are more likely to experience burnout. While the reasons behind this are com-plex and can differ according to group identity and individual expe-rience, the lack of fairness that marginalized groups can encounter in the workplace plays a primary role. According to a recent Gallup survey of 7,500 full-time employees, the factor that was most highly correlated with burnout was none other than unfair treatment at work. Workers who frequently experienced unfair treatment such as bias, favoritism, or unfair compensation were more than twice as likely to burn out.

> **Community**: This area encompasses all the relationships we have through work: colleagues, supervisors, direct reports, stakeholders. The key insight here is that supportive relationships have a powerful buffering effect against burnout. In fact, Maslach and Leiter tell us that "a lively, attentive and responsive community is incompatible with burnout."

Conversely, a lack of social support and connection makes us feel isolated and makes work feel more demanding, which drains our energy and leaves us more vulnerable to burning out. Sadly, this experience comes in many forms, from feeling disconnected from your coworkers or feeling unappreciated, to working with difficult or toxic colleagues, to outright exclusion or discrimination. Given that human beings are inherently social creatures whose need for connection and interaction is as vital as our need for food, shelter, and security, it's no wonder that a lack of social connection and difficult interpersonal dynamics can be so painful, and can so dramatically undermine our happiness and effectiveness at work.

Ruchika Tulshyan, author of *Inclusion on Purpose*, vividly describes a painful early-career experience in which she had zero community support, and the devastating effect it had on her. In this role she was the only person of color at her organization—which alone is an isolating experience—but she also suffered from exclusion, outright bullying, and unfair promotion and hiring practices. As you read her account—and fair warning, it's not easy—take note of the "burnout keywords" that show up:

My heart would beat faster when the elevator was about to open up to my office's floor. I'd have trouble getting out of bed in the morning, despite being an early riser my whole life. I stopped wanting to socialize with friends, despite being an extrovert. Most of the time, I was just too exhausted to go anywhere. . . .

Having no women of color to turn to, I felt like I was living in an alternative reality. Today, I know there's a word for what I experienced: racial gaslighting. But back then, I questioned myself literally every day. Eventually, the burden became too much to bear. I could see myself turning into a cynical, bitter shell of myself. I saw up close how the rules were different for my white peers—the white men and women who got promoted despite underperforming, the male leaders who only hired attractive white women. I was left out of meetings, social gatherings, and inside jokes, and I never saw anyone who looked like me.

It took a toll—not just the bullying, but the daily acts of exclusion. Eventually, I quit, despite advice from my family and friends that I shouldn't leave such a lucrative opportunity. But I was broken mentally and spiritually.

Tulshyan's painful experience is an accurate portrayal of how profoundly isolating and harmful it is to work in an exclusionary and unwelcoming environment where one is made to feel one doesn't belong, and where there is insufficient social support. Notice, too, how Tulshyan internalized the treatment she received, assuming it was somehow her fault, and even feeling guilt and shame over it. *But remember: It's not you, it's your job.* What was lacking had nothing to do with Tulshyan, and everything to do with the psychologically hazardous conditions at her workplace.

Fortunately, Tulshyan's story has a happy ending. She left her toxic work environment and has gone on to build a successful career as an author, entrepreneur, and inclusion strategist.

EXERCISE: ALIGNMENT CHECK

Read the following statements—do you agree or disagree with each? What do your answers reveal about your current work environment and how it may be making you more vulnerable to burnout?

1. I feel like my boss and colleagues respect my boundaries between work and nonwork time.

2. I have enough support from managers and teammates to perform my job at the level I want.

3. I feel that what I do is meaningful and makes a difference.

4. I feel that I'm fairly compensated for the work that I do.

5. I receive adequate recognition for my accomplishments at work.

6. I'm satisfied with my level of involvement in decisions that impact me.

7. I work with people I can count on for help when I need it.

8. People at my job are given equitable treatment in terms of compensation, recognition, and opportunities for advancement.

9. The culture of my organization celebrates diversity, equity, inclusion, and accessibility.

10. I feel safe at work—physically as well as psychologically.

11. I feel that my contributions are valued.

12. In terms of when and where I get my work done, I am satisfied with the degree of flexibility and autonomy I have.

13. My organization offers adequate opportunities for ongoing education and training.

14. Not only do I have sufficient PTO, but I am encouraged to use it.

15. My organization provides and encourages the use of benefits that support my mental and physical health.

16. For the most part, my colleagues are dependable and easy to get along with.

17. I feel that I can speak up about things that aren't working well, or share my ideas for how to improve the organization.

18. The feedback I receive from my manager(s) is helpful, and delivered in a respectful manner.

Now, reflect further on your answers:
1. Did you notice any tension or angst with a particular question(s)?
2. Did you notice any positive sensations with a particular question(s)?
3. What insights are emerging for you?
4. What surprised you about your answers?
5. What are your instincts telling you about what to do with this information?

If no action steps come to you immediately, that's A-OK! Step one is to increase awareness and deepen your understanding about the degree of alignment between what you need from your organization and what you're getting in return, and you've just done exactly that.

Hell (Can Be) Other People

Speaking of aspects of work that sometimes feel like hell, how about we spend a little time focusing on something that can make or break a good work experience—other people!

If you've ever had the misfortune of working with a toxic colleague or working for a toxic boss, you know how high the personal and professional cost can be. *Toxic* is a word that gets thrown around a lot these days, and there are endless guides on how to identify a toxic employee—and even how to categorize different types. (Apparently there's a lot of bad behavior going on at work.) But I think we all know a toxic colleague when we encounter one. These aren't just *difficult* people, but as a seminal Harvard Business School (HBS) study on toxic workers put it, they are people who engage "in behavior that is harmful to an organization, including either its property or people." In their most extreme form, the authors note, toxic workers can cost organizations billions of dollars or even mortally harm current or past employees. But even "relatively modest levels of toxic behavior," they write, "can cause major organizational cost, including customer loss, loss of employee morale, increased turnover, and loss of legitimacy among important external stakeholders."

Not surprisingly, there is a strong connection between toxic workers and burnout. And I'm not talking about the toxic employee burning out! No, the people who are more vulnerable to burnout are the *coworkers* of toxic employees. In an article for the *Harvard Business Review*, one of the authors of the HBS study, Dylan Minor of the UCLA Anderson School of Management, captures why: Not only do toxic workers cause harm, they also spread their harmful behavior to others. Colleagues, teams, and even entire organizations can suffer for it.

The McKinsey Health Institute conducted a study on toxic workplace conditions and burnout, using data from nearly 15,000 employees and 1,000 HR decision-makers in fifteen countries. They found that toxic workplace behavior was the single biggest driver of employee negative outcomes, including burnout and intent to leave. Employees experiencing high levels of toxic behavior at work were eight times more likely to experience burnout symptoms such as exhaustion, reduced ability to regulate emotional and cognitive processes, and lack of engagement, and burned-out employees were six times more likely to quit within three to six months.

Why do toxic workers pose such a threat to their colleagues' well-being and their risk of burnout? On one hand, the answer is simple: they make work life miserable. Who wouldn't dread work or want to quit when a coworker or boss is disrespectful, demeaning, unfair, unethical, bullying, or engages in harassment? The more contact you have with such people, the higher your likelihood of psychological harm and of burning out.

There's another, subtler thing happening as well, however, and a hint is found in Minor's comment: toxic workers *spread their negative emotions and harmful behavior to others*. That's the key difference, Minor says, between workers who are just difficult to deal with and workers who are genuinely toxic—toxic employees' harmful behavior proliferates throughout the work environment, taking down multiple people or potentially even organizations. In fact, Minor and his coauthor found that exposure to toxic workers increases the likelihood of becoming toxic yourself.

This happens in part because people automatically tend to mimic the emotions—and resulting behaviors—of the people in their environment. I'm sure we've all had experiences where we're having a perfectly fine day until a stressed-out and anxious coworker comes in and unloads on us, leaving us feeling stressed-out and anxious, too, or when a disgruntled colleague frequently vents about the latest thing that's gone wrong, leaving us feeling drained and more pessimistic. Fortunately, though, it works both ways: another person's cheerful, upbeat mood is just as "shareable." Whether it's positive or negative, emotion can transfer from person to person, and it has the potential to drastically change your mood, outlook, and behavior.

The term for this phenomenon is *emotional contagion*. Just like the flu, emotions and emotion-based behaviors can spread from person to person, and it all happens in milliseconds, usually without our conscious awareness. A special part of our brain called the limbic system is wired to pick up on the emotional states of others, which are communicated verbally and nonverbally through body language, facial expression, tone of voice, gesture, and their general "vibe."

At work, emotional contagion can play a powerful role in employees' mood, outlook, productivity, sense of belonging, and overall performance. The effect is even more pronounced when it comes to a *leader's* emotions. Studies in social psychology have shown that emotions are especially contagious in relationships where there is an inequality of power, such as between managers and employees. In addition to the regular, unconscious mimicry that happens between people, employees are more likely to actively try to align their reactions, moods, and emotions to those of their manager—and that happens if the manager's mood is positive or negative, helpful or harmful. A recent study out of Denmark found that not only do managers transmit their stress to employees, but the stress contagion effect lasts up to a full year.

Does this effect occur when it comes to burnout? You bet it does! Just as toxic behavior can beget toxic behavior, burnout begets burnout.

Think about it: if you're in a work environment that's "infected" by high stress, cynicism, disengagement, and low morale, you're likely to absorb and act out those same negative emotions, which leaves you very vulnerable to burnout. This is especially so if your disposition naturally leans more toward the negative (for example, if you tend to be more pessimistic than optimistic), or if you don't have healthy coping strategies for dealing with stress. It also happens more frequently in roles that require high contact with people experiencing negative emotions or moods, such as customer service jobs that involve problem-solving and receiving negative feedback, or high contact with ill or depressed people, such as health care providers. Occasional or short-lived exposure to others' negative emotions and moods is unpleasant and challenging while it lasts. But due to emotional contagion, *long-term* exposure to people's negative emotions and moods can lead to burnout.

Researchers have found that the "burnout contagion effect" can occur between a single employee and another, or it can take root more rapidly, through group transmission. A burned-out employee's negativity, diminished productivity, and lower well-being sets a negative example and influences how others feel and think. And, because burned-out employees tend to be low-performing, others may have to pick up the slack for them and end up developing burnout on their own. Group transmission, on the other hand, usually occurs after some sort of big event that affects an entire team or organization. Layoffs, budget cuts, a new manager, or an acquisition that brings a new culture are all examples of big events that can inspire collective fear, confusion, or anger. If difficult feelings like these aren't addressed by the organization, they can fester, and down the line, spark burnout among workers who interact with each other frequently.

Right now, let's take a moment to assess your work environment. What words would you use to describe the emotional state of your workplace? What's the general mood and tone? Do employees look and sound happy to be there? Is the vibe generally upbeat and optimistic, or does it feel tense, low-energy, or overwhelming? When things get tough, do people rally and support each other? Succumb to anxiety? Throw up their hands?

Whatever the emotional climate of your workplace, and whatever the employees' collective emotional response to stress, remember that no one is an island. Emotional contagion is very real, and very powerful. Working with people who are constantly caught in the grip of negative emotion—and/or who do not respond to stress in healthy, productive ways—is a big red flag. Be aware that you're in a high-risk environment and should take steps to protect yourself from the negative effects of emotional contagion well before it can develop into burnout.

Whether it's coworkers' negative moods or full-blown burnout you want to avoid, here are some ways to protect yourself from these highly transmissible occupational ills.

1. **Prioritize self-care**. I'm a firm believer that self-care is nonnegotiable 365 days a year. But *especially* when you're in an environment that's rife with negativity, make sure that your basic needs are met—good sleep, healthy food and hydration, sufficient exercise, adequate downtime—and that you're engaging in the practices that keep you recharged. Whether it's yoga, a hobby, therapy or coaching, spending time with loved ones, travel, or a spiritual practice, this is the time to lean into your restorative practices.

2. **Identify—and uphold—your boundaries**. This is revolutionary practice! Boundaries can be anything that safeguards your time, energy, productivity, or overall well-being. Reduce your

contact with office energy vampires, be up front and let them know that their negative attitude is rubbing off on you and it's making you uncomfortable, reserve "do not disturb" time on your calendar, negotiate to work from home a few days a week . . . whatever makes sense for your unique situation.

3. **Go on the offensive**. Remember that emotional contagion works both ways: Positive emotions are just as "catching" as negative ones, and in fact, some researchers think they're *more* communicable. Telegraph the mood and attitude you want to see in your workplace (optimism, gratitude, openness, conscientiousness, perseverance, and so on), and then count on emotional contagion to make it happen.

4. **Become aware of your mood—and change it if necessary**. If you realize you're in a negative mood that will bring down your coworkers, take one minute to remember a situation in which you felt really positive, really happy. Can't remember one on the spot? Imagine one! To solidify the effect, smile. Research has consistently shown that your mood follows your facial expression.

5. **Use body language to convey positive emotions**. Emotional contagion is all about mimicry. If you're frowning and standing there with your arms crossed, the people around you are likely to interpret that as anger or defensiveness (even if you're just cold). Project positivity, ease, and warmth by smiling, uncrossing your arms, sitting in an upright but relaxed posture, or nodding encouragingly when someone speaks. Look people in the eyes when they are speaking to you.

6. **Work to create a positive culture**. Through your actions, words, gestures, tone, stated values, and culture, build an environment of psychological safety where positive emotions are encouraged and routinely expressed. Make it clear that destructive negative emotions (rage, contempt) and toxic behaviors (bullying, gossiping, rudeness, gaslighting, harassment) will not be tolerated.

What Makes You Tick

How well do you know yourself? It's a big question, I know, but humor me for a sec. How well do you *really* understand what makes you YOU? Do you deeply understand what motivates you and what values drive you to make certain choices and behave in particular ways?

As we saw earlier, our self-awareness often isn't as accurate as we think it is. Fortunately, there are a number of tools available to help us understand ourselves better, and if you have the opportunity to avail yourself of them, I encourage you to do so. I'm a big fan of people taking valid assessments to learn more about themselves. For some of my clients, assessments have been a huge eye-opener into awareness of their tendencies and whether or not those tendencies are working for them. Some of the more well-known assessments are the HIGH5 Test (formerly StrengthsFinder), the DiSC profile, the Enneagram, the Minnesota Multiphasic Personality Inventory (MMPI), and my personal favorites, the Big Five Personality Test and the Myers-Briggs Type Indicator (MBTI), otherwise known as the 16 Personalities Test. Many personality tests, profiling tools, and self-assessments are available online for free, and, increasingly, are used in the HR field for recruitment and training, or are offered as part of ongoing professional development curricula.

To give you a jump-start on increasing your self-awareness, however, let's take a brief look at your temperament and personality—two aspects of self that are often spoken of interchangeably but actually have an important difference. Temperament is a set of traits that you're born with and that remain relatively stable throughout your life. Personality, on the other hand, develops gradually over time and changes in response to life experiences. This will become an important distinction for us as we look at the innate traits *and* the environmental influences that can make you more vulnerable to burnout.

We'll use the traditional nine temperament traits and the "Big Five" personality traits, and rather than defining each trait one by one, let's jump right in and "learn by doing" with a personal inventory on temperament and personality. Let me emphasize that this is not a scientific assessment but rather a tool to get you quickly acquainted with "what makes you tick." The aim is not only to increase your self-awareness but to begin to identify the workplace conditions that you need to thrive, as well as the conditions and events that you, due to your temperament and personality, will automatically find stressful.

EXERCISE: WHAT MAKES YOU TICK?

As you answer these questions—and remember, there is no wrong answer—try to think about how each aspect of your core self intersects with and impacts your current role and work environment. Based on your answers, do you feel you're in alignment with where you are working and what you are doing?

TEMPERAMENT

Activity level: How physically active do you like to be at work? Are you an "on the go" person who likes to be in motion, or do you prefer a job with less physical activity?

Adaptability: How comfortable are you with transitions and changes in your environment? Do you tend to go with the flow, or do you struggle with change or find yourself resisting it?

Approach/withdrawal: What's your comfort level when a new person or a new object enters your environment? Are you drawn to new people (approach), or do you find yourself shying away from them or even avoiding unfamiliar people (withdrawal)?

Distractibility: To what degree do external stimuli interfere with your attention and focus? Are you easily distracted, or do you tend to laser-focus on one thing at a time?

Intensity: Think of this like the volume button on personality. Are your typical reactions to stimuli effusive and over-the-top, or are you more mild-mannered and reticent?

Persistence: When you encounter an obstacle or an annoyance, do you quickly move on to something else, or do you stick with a task until it's done, despite the obstacle?

Regularity: How predictable are your routines and rhythms like sleep, eating, and work hours? Do you prefer to adhere to a schedule, or is your style more loose and unpredictable?

Sensory threshold: Are you easily overstimulated by sensory input like touch, texture, brightness, volume, taste, or smell? Or do you have a high threshold for sensory stimuli?

Mood: Are you primarily positive or negative in your mood? Do you tend to be more pessimistic (glass half-empty), or optimistic (glass half-full)?

PERSONALITY

Extraversion: Do you thrive on social interaction, and need lots of contact with people in order to feel energized and excited? Are you talkative and emotionally expressive? Or are you more socially reserved and need lots of alone time and quiet in order to recharge and be your best self?

Agreeableness: Do you have a keen interest in other people, and look forward to helping others and promoting their well-being? Are you generally cooperative and trusting of others? Or do you find yourself less interested in others and feel that people should take care of their own problems? Are you competitive and less trusting of others?

Openness: Are you curious about the world and other people, eager to encounter new things, and have a broad range of interests? Or do you prefer for things to stay relatively the same?

Conscientiousness: Are you organized, detail-oriented, and prefer having a set schedule? Do you finish tasks right away and plan ahead? Or do you dislike schedules and structure, and find that you tend to procrastinate or miss deadlines?

Neuroticism: Do you feel that your moods can change dramatically and that you tend to worry and feel lots of stress? Do you get upset easily and struggle to bounce back when things don't go your way? Or do you feel emotionally steady, relaxed most of the time, and generally resilient?

No matter where you land on the spectrum for each answer, here's the thread that runs through them all: *When you are in a work environment that does not align with your temperament or personality, you are more vulnerable to burnout.* Your risk of burning out rises in direct proportion to the degree that your work environment is out of alignment with who you are and the conditions you need to thrive and perform at your best. (To use Maslach and Leiter's language, the greater the number of mismatches between your preferences and your environment, the greater the risk of burnout.) Thus, if my job is misaligned with seven out of nine aspects of my temperament, I'm going to experience a lot more stress, and I'll be at a far higher risk of burning out than if only one or two are out of alignment. This is why it's extremely important to be aware of who you are at your core and what sort of work environment you need to be in.

Let me give you an obvious example to illustrate the point. If I'm a person who thrives on quiet, stillness, stability, regularity, and a low-stimulus environment, I'm going to burn out far more quickly working as, say, a server in a high-volume restaurant, a day trader, or an air traffic controller. Likewise, if I need constant novelty, stimulation, and lots of noise and activity and change in my daily routine, I'll be ill-suited to jobs that require long periods of quiet and focused concentration, such as many research, creative, or administrative roles.

Now, of course, most people know themselves well enough to steer clear of mismatches as obvious as these. But sometimes circumstances undermine our best intentions or deepest wishes. I've had a number of extroverts tell me that working from home and feeling isolated during the pandemic was a major source of stress, and that it left them feeling more depleted and burned-out than they ever had. Meanwhile, when many of us returned to the office in 2021, my introverted clients expressed a lot of anxiety about having to go back to the office and work with a lot of people and distractions. Or sometimes a change in management or ownership triggers a shift in culture that creates a mismatch. The truth is, there are all kinds of reasons our preferences don't match up with the reality of our work environment, and in many cases, it's beyond our control. Just know that the further you stray from *you*, the greater your vulnerability to burnout.

The Past Doesn't Have to Be Permanent

Many years ago, well before I had kids, I was having lunch at a restaurant with several friends. Everyone was enjoying themselves until a woman at the next table began yelling. She was there with two young children—a boy who looked to be three or four, and an infant in a car seat. "Oh my god, Michael, no!" she screamed, and lunged over to yank the little boy's chair closer. "Don't touch!"

We looked up to see a perplexed (and clearly startled) busser holding out a crayon to Michael, who was now crying at the top of his lungs. The busser stammered that he was only trying to help—he'd been passing by and saw Michael drop the crayon. The mom blushed and tried to apologize, but her hands were full with Michael, whose crying was still gathering steam, and now the baby, who'd been woken from a nap.

Although both kids eventually settled down, Michael never fully relaxed. He wouldn't touch any of his crayons, and he scanned the room warily as he ate. On her way out of the restaurant, the mom stopped by our table and apologized for interrupting our lunch. "I didn't realize he worked here," she said. "I thought it was some stranger after my kid. You never know these days!"

I remember feeling bad for the busser and for Michael, both of whom had been scared half to death by this woman's overreaction, and feeling pretty judgmental of this mom. If she could freak out over such a small thing, imagine what it would be like to live with her. To be *raised* by her.

Of course, my attitude changed after I had kids and I experienced for the first time the parental instinct to protect your kids at all costs. While I still believed the mom had overreacted, there was, of course, no telling what she'd been through to cause such a reaction. (Not to mention this happened during the heyday of "stranger danger.")

I thought of this scene when I was studying for my doctorate and reading about how we're socialized from a very early age to deal with stress. Study after study indicates that the early conditioning we experience in childhood becomes the blueprint for how we behave as adults. These early, formative experiences, and how we are supported or not supported through them by experienced adults, shape our beliefs, biases, and patterns of behavior, particularly when it comes to stress encounters. They make a world of difference in how we learn to assess situations (Are they stressful or not stressful? Threatening or not threatening? Insurmountably difficult or a challenge to overcome?) and in how we learn to cope with them.

Now, just to be clear, a parent overreacting the one time an unfamiliar person approaches doesn't mean the child will be scarred for life and will never want to engage with unfamiliar people. But, if the scenario of "my mom rescues me every time *she* senses danger" continues and becomes a pattern, that child is likely to have a lower threat tolerance (that is, will more quickly perceive stressful encounters as a threat or a situation involving harm or loss rather than a challenge). And, because the child comes to rely on a parent or other figure to swoop in and rescue them when things become difficult, the child does not learn to work through challenges and stressful encounters on their own.

I'll never know what happened to Michael or his younger sibling, but check out these stories from two adults I worked with.

"I grew up surrounded by strong Black women," one of the participants in a Police Executive Leadership Institute (PELI) workshop told me. "I was raised by my mom and my grandmother, plus two aunts who were always around. They were tough as nails. When anything went wrong, no matter how big or how small, they wouldn't waste time complaining or worrying about it, they just jumped straight to figuring it out. If it was too big for one to handle, they'd lean on each other. I'm grateful every day I was brought up with a strong support system! I use it as a reminder to myself that I don't have to go through things alone. When the stakes are high and my decision is going to affect an entire community, I call in my leadership team and get their input before I make the final call."

Contrast this leader's experience with the experience of a physician I interviewed. "I had to work very, very hard to learn resilience and manage my anxiety," she said. "We moved a lot when I was a kid because of my dad's job, and my mom does not do well with change and was in a constant anxiety spiral. There were days when she literally could not come out of her bedroom. It took years of therapy and a ton of meditation for me to realize that I had absorbed her anxiety and her avoidance. . . . I was smart and capable but I just wouldn't try anything. Eventually I learned a bunch of coping skills I missed out on as a kid. I may have been the oldest student in my graduating class, but I'd always wanted to be a doc and I finally did it!"

According to author and psychotherapist Linda Graham, our brains begin to learn and encode lessons about coping strategies from the very beginning of brain development. This happens through two mechanisms: conditioning and neuroplasticity. Conditioning is the encoding of experiences and responses into lasting neural patterns. Put another way, it's the wiring of our neural circuitry that occurs as we learn from experience. Conditioned responses can be positive and lead to desirable behaviors—let's say you train your brain to associate drinking a glass of water every time you go downstairs—or negative and lead to problematic behaviors. If a parent panics and yells "Stay away!" every time the family encounters a dog during a walk, a child will become conditioned to fear all dogs, even though the vast majority of our four-legged friends don't pose a threat.

That said, our conditioned responses are never permanently locked in, and that's possible thanks to neuroplasticity. Throughout our life spans our brains remain flexible, able to change our original encoding, learn new patterns, grow new neurons, and create new connections between neurons—all in response to new experiences. That's what happened with the physician I spoke with, who learned healthier coping strategies through therapy and meditation. Graham points out that we can even learn to choose *specific* experiences to deliberately rewire our brains for better coping and stronger resilience, which is the capacity to respond to pressures and difficulties quickly, adaptively, and effectively.

Let's say a kid does develop an excessive fear of dogs as a result of early conditioning and carries that fear into adulthood. One way they might choose specific experiences to "rewire" their brain and create new neural connections is, little by little, to deliberately put themselves in the presence of dogs. This is good old-fashioned exposure therapy, and it could start by watching dogs from afar, and gradually move on to being in the same house (but a different room) with a dog, standing near a dog (say, through a neighbor's fence), being in the same room with a dog who remains with their owner, eventually working up to petting a dog, and so on. The point is, this is actual experience that is influencing neural circuitry, and a great example of how behavior can influence thoughts and feelings. "Although the initial wiring of our brains is based on early experience," Graham writes, "later experiences, especially healthy relational ones, can undo or overwrite that early learning to help us to cope differently and more resiliently with anything, anything at all."

That includes trauma, tragedy, and terrible setbacks.

One of the most dramatic examples of how early socialization affects our long-term development and well-being concerns the effect of what are known as adverse child experiences, or ACEs. ACEs are potentially traumatic events that occur before the age of eighteen, such as:

- experiencing violence, abuse, or neglect
- witnessing violence in the home or the community
- having a family member or caregiver attempt or die by suicide

- having a family member or caregiver suffer from substance abuse problems or mental health problems
- experiencing instability at home due to parental absence.

Researchers estimate that around 61 percent of adults have experienced at least one ACE, and nearly 1 in 6 have experienced four or more ACEs. The more ACEs a child experiences, the greater their risk of suffering ill effects later in life. ACEs have been linked to an increased risk of chronic illness (heart disease, cancer, and diabetes, for example), depression, anxiety, suicidality, substance abuse, poorer academic achievement, relationship difficulties, financial struggles, and early death, and their negative outcomes can even extend into future generations.

Why are ACEs' downstream effects so harmful, so broad, and so long-lasting? Researchers believe it's due to the effects of "toxic stress" on the developing child. Also referred to as chronic stress, what we're talking about is the prolonged or excessive activation of the stress response system. When the brain perceives a threat, the amygdala, an area of the brain responsible for processing and regulating emotions, immediately sends a distress signal to the hypothalamus, which activates the sympathetic nervous system, which triggers the "fight-or-flight" response. All of this happens in milliseconds, sometimes before we're even consciously aware of a threat. (This is why you can jump out of the way of the "stick" on the hiking trail before you've even registered it as a snake.) Once launched, the stress response impacts the entire body. Heart and respiratory rates speed up, blood pressure rises, and the endocrine system pumps out adrenaline—but only for a few minutes. This keeps the body and brain on high alert, digestion slows or temporarily ceases, large muscles contract, readying the body for quick action, and the reproductive system temporarily shuts down in an effort to conserve metabolic resources. After the adrenals burn through adrenaline, your body begins to pump out cortisol. If your stress response is triggering frequently throughout the day, it depletes your adrenaline stores and causes chronically elevated levels of cortisol. This is the physiologic condition that defines "chronic stress" and is associated with symptoms like poor sleep, coronary artery disease, weight gain/obesity, fatigue, headaches, frequent illness, insulin resistance, cancer, etc.

It's a marvelous mechanism, and in the face of an imminent threat, the stress response system can save our lives. But it's only meant to last for short periods of time—just enough to allow us to deal with the threat. Now imagine what could happen when the stress response gets stuck in the On position, and we move through the world in a constant state of physical and emotional overdrive. Many, in fact, have compared this to revving the engine of a car for days or weeks at a time. A constantly revved engine inevitably creates wear and tear on the car, and the damage happens much faster and more intensely than during normal use of the car.

Similar damage can occur when our stress response system is extremely sensitive and goes off frequently, delivering a full-body fight-or-flight response every time the brain detects a threat—even when the stick is really just a stick and your life isn't in imminent danger. It makes no difference to the brain. If it registers something as a threat, it will automatically launch the stress response in order to protect you. An "overreactive amygdala" is not uncommon in those who've experienced ACEs, trauma at any point, or who have grown up with role models who habitually overreacted to perceived threats. (In the next chapter, we're going to look at the stress response system in more detail and at several ways to regulate an overactive amygdala or an overly sensitive stress response system.)

With all of this in mind, it's easy to see why chronic stress takes such a toll on our health and has such comprehensive and far-reaching effects—including, as we'll see, on our performance at work and our risk of developing burnout. Now consider what happens when that kind of heightened, prolonged stress is experienced very early in life, when a child's physical, neurological, social, and emotional faculties are still developing, and when they haven't had the chance to develop effective coping skills. Studies have shown that experiencing ACEs can even alter the structure of a child's brain: decreases in brain volume and brain electrical activity have been noted, resulting in cognitive impairment and learning difficulties down the line.

"ACEs," Dr. Peter Loper told me, "are different ways to violate nurture." Loper is a professor, executive coach, and physician, and an expert on healthy human development. He explained that kids who experience ACEs or who grow up with insufficient nurturing are less able to prevent and manage what's sometimes referred to as an "amygdala hijacking." This is a term first coined by EI expert Daniel Goleman, and it refers to an immediate and intense emotional reaction that's out of proportion to the stressor. When our amygdala is hijacked, we're left awash in intense emotion, and we lose the ability to react rationally and effectively to a perceived threat.

Loper explained that when a child grows up without a resilient role model, they don't learn how to seek proximity to others to help them navigate stressful situations. They miss the opportunity to model their behavior on that of a safe, experienced adult. Left with a trial-and-error approach to coping with stress, whatever they're able to figure out on their own is the pattern they carry into adulthood.

Now, if those patterns are unproductive or even harmful—which wouldn't be surprising if one has a history of ACEs and didn't grow up with a healthy, resilient role model—think about what happens when that adult enters the workforce. As you can imagine, ACEs' effects show up there, too, and can have detrimental effects on our professional development, our success, and our relationships at work. Plenty of research has been done to examine their impact on career outcomes—including employability, job performance, employee retention, and, yes, the potential to experience burnout. Here's just a small sample of recent findings:

- In a study of nearly 28,000 adults, compared to participants with no ACEs, those with three or more ACEs were more likely to report high school noncompletion, unemployment, and living in a household below the federal poverty level.

- In a study of ACEs as a potential "vulnerability factor" in physician burnout, those with higher ACE scores were more likely to experience burnout. Physicians with four or more ACEs had more than 2.5 times the risk of burnout.
- A study of nursing students found that those who had experienced ACEs had higher rates of both burnout and depression.
- In a study of mental health counselors, researchers once again found that higher ACE scores were associated with a higher incidence of burnout. But this study also looked at the impact of *positive* childhood experiences (PCEs) on burnout. Sure enough, those with more PCEs were less likely to experience burnout.

This last study brings up a set of extremely important points—and if you could really use some good news right about now, here it is. Having a history of ACEs does *not* guarantee that you will face negative outcomes later in life. In fact, research has also been conducted on successful, well-adjusted people who have experienced one or more ACE. How are people who endured traumatic or highly stressful events in childhood able to overcome early adversity? There are many factors, but perhaps the most powerful one boils down to *social support*. A recent study sums it up well: "The effects of ACEs may be partially or fully moderated by the presence of an adult who makes a child feel safe, by having adequate social support in the form of a loving, stable adult, or by living in a safe, supportive neighborhood." Why is social support, whether it comes from one person or a community, so powerful? Because it *builds resilience, moderates the stress of adverse experiences*, and has been linked to *lifelong positive results*.

Stop and think about how amazing that is. The presence of even one person who makes a child feel safe can have a protective effect that lasts a lifetime. For me, that person was my stepmom, Cathy. When I moved in with my dad and my stepmom when I was twelve, Cathy made sure we did something that I'd never done before—we sat down together as a family for dinner every night. She asked me about school, gave me advice about how to make new friends, and loved to help me with my homework. She made me feel very safe and loved.

What would my life have been like without Cathy's loving support and mentorship? Or my dad's steady and reliable presence? I don't even want to imagine! What I do know is that my life went from feeling unsafe and unstable to safe, supportive, and stable, and in that environment of physical and psychological safety, I could let down my guard and begin to learn a healthier way to live.

And guess what? Thanks to neuroplasticity, *it works in adulthood, too.* Neuroplasticity is really one of our best reasons for hope: it is possible to change even entrenched ways of thinking and behaving, even if it feels like they're hardwired into us.

This is good news for many of us, especially if we didn't grow up with healthy models for how to handle stress and adversity—or if we picked up some unproductive habits and maladaptive coping mechanisms along the way. For instance, many workers are conditioned to "play through the pain" and suppress their needs for adequate sleep, downtime, and healthy workplace boundaries, whether that's being expected to stay late, never say no, or ignore the unacceptable behavior of a coworker. And there are countless examples of workers who develop unhealthy habits in order to cope with their work-related stress. Just ask one of my UPenn professors Dr. Alexandra Michel, whose studies of hundreds of investment bankers found that many of them cope with the high stress and hypercompetitiveness of their industry by taking dubiously sourced and unregulated prescription drugs in an attempt to enhance cognitive performance, stave off fatigue, and prevent various "body breakdowns." You don't need to look to such extreme examples, though; it's incredibly common for people to turn to alcohol and other substances, avoidance, over- or undereating, and other harmful coping mechanisms in order to deal with workplace stress.

Neuroplasticity and our capacity to strengthen our resilience at any point in life mean we never have to settle for patterns of behavior that are not working for us. This means we can, like the physician I interviewed, learn to establish new, healthier patterns that serve us personally and professionally. In the words of Linda Graham, we can learn to bounce back from setbacks and to regroup and adapt when we're thrown off balance by the unknown, by stress, or even by trauma, whether it was experienced early on or later in life.

One of the best ways to learn new patterns is by learning from people who are getting it right. This is where that resilient role model comes in. "Seeking proximity to other adults when we are an adult is a productive way to continue to scaffold our development," Loper said. "Having an 'experienced other' like a mentor, a boss or colleague we look up to, or other role models helps us learn how to navigate stressful situations." Having a mentor at work has been shown to have stress-lowering effects *and* to prevent burnout—and this is especially the case for those who are high in neuroticism, a personality trait that has been strongly associated with ACEs. There are plenty of ways to break the cycle of early adversity and mitigate its effects in adulthood—and they happen to be many of the same ways we can learn to manage stress and lower our vulnerability to burnout.

So can you find your Cathy at work? Can you identify your resilient role models? Who among your coworkers is steady, reliable, and coolheaded, even in the midst of high-stress situations? Who are the people you can turn to for support when things get tough, as they inevitably will from time to time, and you feel an amygdala hijacking coming on? Who are the people who project optimism and openness, or even, dare I say it, an attitude of love?

"Trees grow in soil and sunlight," Loper told me. "Human beings develop in the medium of love." If you missed your chance to grow up in a medium of love, take heart: you can still offer it to yourself. I will always advocate for working with a good therapist or executive coach, but resilient role models come in many forms. Find the people who are getting it right and develop a relationship with them.

Low E

The third dimension of burnout, *reduced professional efficacy*, grows out of a concept called self-efficacy, which is the belief we have in our abilities and competencies, especially as it relates to our confidence that we can cope with stressful challenges or demands. "I can do this. I can figure this out." That's self-efficacy. Professional efficacy, then, is the belief we have in our job-related abilities and competencies— and again, especially as it relates to our confidence that we can take on stressful challenges or demands. "I'm good at my job. I'm capable of growing and getting even better." That's professional efficacy. The two are closely related . . . even to the point that some researchers refer to the latter as professional self-efficacy.

No matter how you slice it, what's fascinating about self-efficacy is this: it can change according to domain. A person who has high levels of self-efficacy in their ability to navigate their hometown, for instance, may have very low self-efficacy when it comes to finding their way around a foreign city. It can also change within the same environment when circumstances change. For example, an elementary school teacher I know responded to her district's shortage of middle school teachers and took a job working with seventh and eighth graders. As an experienced elementary school teacher she had high levels of professional efficacy and low levels of stress, but in her new role, her professional efficacy plummeted and her work-related stress climbed. (Apparently, tweens and teens serve up a special kind of stress, which I for one can attest to.)

When our professional efficacy is low—when we think, *I have no idea what I'm doing* or *I've lost my mojo* or *I'll never get good at this*—our vulnerability for burnout is high, and that has a lot to do with how we view work-related stress and how we handle it. Take the example of learning a new skill. Even if you're supremely motivated to level up your game, there's a certain degree of stress involved. You're in unfamiliar territory (which brings uncertainty), it will take time and effort to get good at something new, and you've got to juggle your other work responsibilities as well—all of which brings stress. But here's the difference: people who generally trust in their own capabilities (who have high self-efficacy, in other words) tend to perceive difficult tasks as a challenge rather than a threat. They're feeling stress, sure, but it's the positive "eustress" that motivates us, rather than "distress" that can lead to overwhelm, avoidance, or, if it persists over time, burnout.

There is a vicious-cycle aspect to reduced professional efficacy, too. If you become convinced that you can't do something or you'll never master a skill, you're much more likely to give up before you put in the effort it requires to complete the task, learn a new skill, or get really, really good at something. Without the outcome you're looking for, you doubt your abilities and competencies even more, which further diminishes your appetite to take on challenges and expand your skills and impact . . . and off you go into a spiral of doubt and underperformance. A classic self-fulfilling prophecy.

People with high levels of professional efficacy, on the other hand, are much better equipped to handle work-related stress, and much less likely to experience burnout. Across multiple research studies I've conducted, one finding is consistent: individuals who rated their stress as 7+ on a 10-point scale but who also had high levels of professional efficacy were significantly less likely to be burned-out. For them, high rates of professional efficacy served as a mediator in the stress appraisal process, which is a fancy way of saying that high professional efficacy gave them a more positive view of the stressors they encountered at work—they saw stressors as a challenge rather than a threat.

Bear with me as I nerd out for a minute to show you how this works. Stress appraisal occurs in two stages. *Primary appraisal* happens automatically (and often unconsciously) when you encounter a stressor. Your brain immediately determines if the stressor is 1) irrelevant, that is, "This doesn't affect me at all"; 2) benign-positive: "This doesn't affect me, or maybe it will affect me in a good way"; or 3) stressful: "Oh no, this isn't going to be good for me." If your brain determines it's number 3, it then decides whether the stressor will cause harm or loss, pose a threat, or present a challenge. Harm or loss is associated with damage that has already occurred—"I just unexpectedly lost my job; now I have nothing." A threat is the possibility of harm or loss in the future—"This is going to take away something I value. I'd better hurry up and try to protect myself." But a challenge can provide you with an opportunity to gain a sense of mastery and competence by confronting and overcoming the stressful event—"This is gonna be tough, but I'll be ten times better once I get through this." When you have high professional efficacy, you're far more likely to appraise stressors as a welcome challenge, and to have lower levels of burnout.

Secondary appraisal also happens automatically and often subconsciously, and can occur simultaneously with the primary appraisal process. It refers to the process by which you figure out how to deal with the stressful event, and it depends on the perceived personal resources you have to cope with the demands at hand—in other words, in your self-efficacy.

High self-efficacy: "I have the skills I need to get through this stressor." Low self-efficacy: "I don't think I can do this."

What could this actually look like at work? Here's a fictional snapshot. Jake has high professional efficacy. He loves to take on and conquer challenges, throws himself into problem-solving, and relishes skills training and professional development opportunities. He's super engaged and energetic, has a positive attitude, and is constantly leveling up. He's pretty much the opposite of a burned-out employee, right? Bill, on the other hand, has low professional efficacy. When faced with stressors, he instinctively feels defensive and stressed. Instead of seeing (appraising) the stressor as a challenge, he feels it as a threat. To protect himself, he keeps a low profile at work and avoids drawing any attention to himself. Bill, in an effort to avoid stress and the discomfort it brings, has disengaged from his job. He has a negative attitude toward work, and his growth has stagnated. If he continues on this path, his chances of burning out are high.

When self-efficacy is high, as it is with Jake, it acts as a buffer against distress experiences and protects us from burnout. Weak self-efficacy, on the other hand, creates vulnerability in distress experiences, as we saw with Bill, which increases our vulnerability to burnout.

All of which leads us to the $64 million question: How do we increase our self-efficacy, which helps to immunize us against burnout? Here are six tips:

1. **Practice (and practice some more) with patience**. Research indicates that the most powerful driver of self-efficacy is what's known as mastery experiences, which are the experiences of success and confidence we gain when we practice and successfully learn a new skill or overcome a new challenge. Mastery experiences give us direct, personal experience of taking on challenges and succeeding. Not only does this boost our confidence but it also provides direct evidence of our success from the past, which bolsters our belief that we can succeed in the future. Word to the wise: Be patient with yourself. No one is a master of anything on their first try. Give yourself ample time and abundant grace to try, fail, fail better, get better, and, ultimately, master a new skill.

2. **Learn from a resilient role model or mentor**. One of the strengths of resilient role models and more experienced mentors is that they are better equipped at seeing stressful events as challenges rather than threats because of their past successful encounters with stress. They've grown, learned, and developed their confidence as a result of those past experiences. Not only can you learn from their example but you can enjoy and benefit from the social support they offer.

3. **Treat yourself to some verbal persuasion**. This is a social cognitive psychology term for encouragement and positive reinforcement from people you trust and respect. Mentors and executive coaches are great for this, but anyone at work who can

help you identify your strengths and gifts can function in this role. Receiving an objective assessment from a trusted source can do wonders for your confidence and your self-efficacy.

4. **Keep an achievements log**. Especially when we're feeling overwhelmed with stress, and certainly when we're burned-out, it can be easy to forget that we *have* accomplished a great deal and that in all likelihood, we have plenty of mastery experiences in our past performance. An achievements log is a permanent record of your professional efficacy.

5. **Set goals that are challenging yet achievable**. A surefire way to boost your confidence is to meet the goals you set—especially if it's a stretch goal. There are numerous guides on goal-setting that you can access, including the popular SMART goal system (Specific, Measurable, Achievable, Relevant, and Time-bound).

6. **Reframe obstacles**. Obstacles, challenges, setbacks, bottlenecks, impediments, roadblocks . . . these are all natural and perfectly normal parts of work. Facing them with an attitude of defeat, overwhelm, panic, or other unproductive mindsets perpetuates low self-efficacy and undermines our ability to deal with them successfully. Even if it feels unnatural to you, "try on" a high professional efficacy mindset, in whatever language works for you: "I've got this." "I'm not nervous; I'm excited!" "There is no one better suited for this than me." In advocating for *yourself*, you are seeing an obstacle in an all-new way.

When the Shit Hits the Fan

Before we move on, I just want to pause and acknowledge that sometimes it doesn't matter how aware or resilient or emotionally intelligent we are—sometimes life just has a way of throwing more at us than we can handle. Illness, the loss of a loved one, the end of a relationship, a big move—or even positive events that cause major disruptions can consume the energy we once used to deal with work-related stress. When this happens we're left vulnerable to burnout.

Natalie was a senior software engineer who'd worked at her firm for eight years. She'd flourished in her role, despite the stress of having to stay on top of constantly evolving technologies, and she adored her colleagues. Then in 2021, everything seemed to happen at once: She got married, bought a house (after a ten-month search in a challenging real estate market), moved, became an aunt for the first time, and, on top of it all, got promoted to staff engineer. Faster than she could believe, her entire attitude about work changed. She found herself overwhelmed, dreading work, and, on most days, just wanted to stay in bed. To make matters worse, she was confused and anxious because she was "supposed to be" happy. These were all positive life events, after all, and she'd wanted that promotion for years.

The truth is, the amount of energy we have to deal with things—events at work, events at home, and how they all intersect—is *not* infinite. All the things going on in Natalie's life, even though they were welcome, positive events, were simply too much to juggle simultaneously, and they made it impossible to handle her normal work-related stress with the same effectiveness she had before.

When life converges all at once, first of all, cut yourself some slack. Your bandwidth is finite; there's only so much you can do. Second, make self-care nonnegotiable. I can't emphasize enough how important this is. What do you need in order to recharge? In Natalie's case, she took two weeks off to settle into her new home, and she arranged to shadow a mentor to make the transition to staff engineer easier. Third, reach out for help. Can your responsibilities be shared with another? Can you negotiate longer deadlines, or at least temporarily, fewer deliverables? Are there people or services who can help with non-work-related items that will make your life easier? Often, people are happy to help but simply don't know how. Don't be afraid to ask for specific forms of help—now is the time to do so, and you can be that person for others later on.

To Be Aware and Care

There's no doubt about how incredibly stressful and psychologically hazardous work can sometimes be. Managing our work-related stress can consume so much of our attention and energy that we forget to notice the impact it's having in all aspects of our life. We can try to ignore it, outrun it, achieve our way out of it, or pretend it doesn't exist, but burnout will always be knocking at the door if you work in a high-stress environment and you're not taking steps to manage it.

Because here's the thing: even if we have extraordinary powers of denial (hello!), sooner or later, burnout will trigger a distress signal that's impossible to ignore. For me, it was sky-high blood pressure that sent me to the emergency room. I'm willing to bet my 401(k), though, that in every single case of burnout, including mine, there were plenty of smaller signals that your body and your mind were issuing all along. We just missed them because we were unaware.

One of the single most impactful steps I took in my burnout recovery journey was to strengthen my awareness—of what was causing my burnout vulnerability, of what was triggering my stress and why, and of what I wanted and needed in order to have a healthy relationship with work. But most importantly, I became more aware of what needed to change—what *I* needed to change—and it all came down to a new practice of care that I'd been too busy to consider until I had to. Namely, I felt an urgent need to *be aware and care*. To care more for and about myself. To care more about the impact my stress was having on others. To care about having a healthy relationship with work in a way that allows me to make meaningful contributions while living out my values and actualizing my vision of my ideal self.

That's my hope for you after reading this chapter. That you have learned some ways to become more aware—and that you are now ready to begin caring for yourself. People who prioritize healthy self-care—who engage in actions that support their emotional, mental, and physical health, and who seek out or create workplace conditions that support their best performance—are rarely at risk of burning out, and they're happier and more productive besides.

3

Put Your Stress to Good Use

Finding Control Within the
Sweet Spot of Stress

Colin came to me for executive coaching just as his organization was coming out of a year-end crunch time, which had been exacerbated by the sudden departure of his manager. "Everyone's stress levels were at an eleven," he told me, "and things got embarrassingly ugly." Meetings turned into displays of flaring tempers, power struggles, and arguments that devolved into name-calling and public character assassinations. Upper management didn't intervene, choosing to put off "personnel issues" until after everyone hit their year-end goals. So in addition to his increased workload, Colin had taken it upon himself to try to act as a peacekeeper between his highly stressed colleagues. His efforts went nowhere, however, and eventually he became swept up in the destructive behavior, too. Normally an easygoing person, Colin confessed that he'd "lost it" with his coworkers multiple times, and by the end of the quarter, he was so stressed-out, ashamed, and demoralized that he dreaded going to work.

Now, with workloads returning to normal, Colin described his current work climate as one of "collective amnesia." "Everyone can't wait to forget about what we've just been through," he said, "and no one is willing to step back and reflect on how we've just treated each other." Everyone, that is, except Colin. "I don't want to avoid all this," he told me at our first meeting. "I want to fix it so everyone can go back to normal, and I want to change the culture as fast as possible to make sure this never happens again."

I understood where Colin was coming from. He'd just endured months stuck in an out-of-control, dysfunctional work environment where everyone was, to put it politely, in a state of collective dysregulation. Now he wanted to heal from the micro traumas he'd suffered over the last months, emerge from the moderate-level burnout he was experiencing, repair a lot of damaged relationships, and change the company culture—and he wanted it all to happen immediately! His heart was in the right place, and I applauded his willingness to take care of his mental and emotional health and to address the problems at work rather than ignore them.

But, of course, all of these things would take time, and many were out of his control. As much as we'd all love to wave a magic wand and instantly heal rifts in workplace relationships, or immediately create a culture of support and psychological well-being, these efforts take time, and they take the buy-in of many people working together.

So the first thing Colin and I worked on was recalibrating his expectations by focusing on what he actually *could* control. His expectations shifted from "I want to fix everything today" to "I'll do my part today to help fix this." That mindset shift alone, he said, lowered his stress level from an 8 to a 4, and it left him free to focus on what he could control.

He began with focusing on his and his team members' strengths. This reset his mindset from pessimistic to optimistic and was a great reminder that everyone was so much more than their recent stress-induced bad behavior reflected. He also began a daily practice of looking for three positive things his team members did. At the end of each day, he sent them an email with the subject "here's what I caught today." This practice proved so popular that others took it up, too, and the positive emotions and camaraderie it engendered went a long way in healing relationships that had suffered under the weight of collective stress and anxiety. Finally, instead of beginning team meetings with a "let's get down to business" approach, Colin opened with a reflection question like "What did you learn this week that you're excited about?" or "What's working for us as a team, and what could we improve?" that invited discussion and feedback. His team-centered approach helped improve morale, and for Colin individually, taking some concrete action lowered his stress and made him feel much less like a victim at work, which actually ended up jump-starting his recovery from burnout.

As a matter of fact, experts agree (and my research repeatedly confirmed) that one of the most powerful ways to protect yourself from burnout is to focus on what you can control. Why does that make such a difference? Well, think about the converse: we know that one of the key drivers of burnout is experiencing a lack of control at work, and dwelling on what's *not* within our control can leave us feeling helpless and hopeless. It eats away at our sense of agency, our energy, and our belief that things can change for the better. It amplifies our stress. It can leave us thinking, *Why bother? I can't do anything about that anyway*, or *This is just the way things are, and if I can't deal I must not belong here.* Plain and simple, focusing on what you can't control is inherently stressful, and it's disempowering and self-defeating.

Now, does any of that sound familiar? You've got it—dwelling on what you can't control can produce some of the same symptoms of burnout, including frustration, demotivation, cynicism, inaction, and ineffectiveness, and it can accelerate burnout's development.

But you don't have to purchase this one-way ticket! Actively turning your attention to what you *can* control is one of the first steps in developing the mental fitness and resilience you need to protect yourself from burnout. Let's take a quick look at what's actually in our control, and what isn't.

In my control:

- My boundaries
- My goals
- My values
- My beliefs
- The friends with whom I choose to associate
- What I give my energy to
- How I handle challenges and change
- How honest I choose to be
- How vulnerable I choose to be, and with whom
- My actions, including:
  * Asking for help
  * How I take care of myself (my diet, my mental and physical fitness, my sleep habits and hygiene, my choice of coping mechanisms)
  * How I treat others
  * My reactions to events and other people
  * How I manage and react to my emotions
- My thoughts, including:
  * How I speak to myself
  * My attitude and outlook

Now take a deep breath, and try approaching this next list with an attitude of openness. Bonus points for humor.

Out of my control:

- The past
- (Much of) the future
- What happens around me, with a special shout-out to:

- * Unexpected or unwelcome events (travel delays, layoffs, resignations, supply shortages, power outages, illness, loss, etc.)
- The full outcome of my efforts, and how they'll be received
- Other people's feelings, thoughts, actions, and reactions, including their:
  - * Opinions
  - * Opinions of me
  - * Moods and emotions
  - * Pasts
  - * Futures
  - * Fears
  - * Weaknesses
  - * Strengths
  - * Boundaries
  - * Goals
  - * Values
  - * Beliefs
  - * Attitudes and mindset
  - * Level of energy and what they devote it to
  - * Ability to handle challenge and change
  - * Level of honesty
  - * Willingness to ask for or receive help
  - * Level of vulnerability
  - * Self-care practices, or lack thereof
- OTHER PEOPLE

I think you see the point. To a large degree, what's actually in our control is found within our individual selves. While I stand by my assertion that burnout is an organizational issue more than an individual one (and will continue to proudly sport my "It's not you, it's your job" T-shirt), anchoring into what you and you alone can control is a source of motivation, power, healing, and stress relief. It's a lifeline when it feels like we can't change our work circumstances—or, like Colin, when we can't change them nearly fast enough. Burnout can fool us into believing that we have no control and no options. Yet when we turn inward, we see that each of us has control over our responses to anything life may throw our way.

In this chapter and the next, we're going to examine how the skill of regulation helps us lower stress and take back a sense of control, even when our external circumstances are dysregulated and stressful. We'll first take a deep dive into the physiology and psychology of stress and see how it affects our thinking, our actions, and our physical and mental health—for good and for ill. We'll learn how the skill of regulation can keep us within "the sweet spot" of stress, where we're energized and motivated but can steer clear of becoming overwhelmed and exhausted. Regulation allows us to lean on our own skills and resources to meet stressful moments with more equanimity and effectiveness, and to calm our emotions, minds, and bodies more quickly after stressful experiences. Ultimately, we'll learn how to immunize ourselves from burnout by preventing acute workplace stress from becoming chronic and debilitating.

Understanding and Managing Our Stress Response

If burnout is the result of chronic workplace stressors, we need a solid understanding of just what's happening to our minds and bodies when stress assails us at work. New research has given us a much clearer picture of what's going on emotionally, mentally, and physiologically when we're in the grip of stress—and of ways to actually leverage our built-in stress response for our benefit. So come with me as we take a little behind-the-scenes trip into the mechanics of the stress response, this time with a finer lens than we used in Chapter 2. A grasp of what's happening neurochemically, especially with a few key hormones and neurotransmitters, will be invaluable in learning how to tame and regulate our own stress response, and to spend as little time as possible in a stressed-out, dysregulated state.

As you'll recall, the amygdala triggers the stress response system anytime it perceives a threat, whether that threat is truly dangerous (a hungry grizzly bear) or just *feels* really dangerous (giving a speech). It's all part of the brain's "better safe than sorry" approach to information processing that evolved as part of our survival instinct. Within milliseconds of detecting a threat, the amygdala sends a distress signal to the hypothalamus, which functions as your brain's command center. The hypothalamus activates the sympathetic nervous system (SNS) by sending signals to the adrenal glands, which respond by flooding the bloodstream with two hormones: epinephrine (adrenaline) and norepinephrine. These two hormones work together to increase your heart rate, open your airways, and direct blood to vital organs and large muscle groups, readying your body for quick action. They also increase blood sugar levels and send glucose to the brain to increase alertness and enable quick thinking. In short, these two hormones are responsible for the *fight-or-flight response*, which works splendidly to deal with a short-term threat.

If the threat sticks around, however, the SNS remains activated. The hypothalamus then releases corticotropin-releasing hormone (CRH), which travels to the pituitary gland, signaling the release of adrenocorticotropic hormone (ACTH), which in turns travels to the adrenal glands . . . which trigger the release of cortisol, commonly known as the stress hormone. As the initial surge of adrenaline subsides, cortisol picks up the baton and continues to elevate blood sugar levels to enable quick energy, and in the short term, it suppresses inflammation, which has an immune-boosting effect.

What turns the whole system off? That's the job of the parasympathetic nervous system (PNS). When the brain perceives that the threat no longer exists—which, in the fight-or-flight framework, means you've either subdued the threat or escaped it—it's time for the PNS to hit the brakes. Cortisol levels fall, and the PNS dampens the entire stress response. Within minutes, you're back to normal functioning and off to the pub to celebrate your escape from the grizzly bear, or, more fitting these days, perhaps your successful escape from a round of layoffs.

It's worth remembering that the origins of the fight-or-flight response are found deep within our evolutionary past, at a time when it wasn't so unusual to encounter predators and other imminent threats to our physical safety. If our lives are in danger, we don't have seconds to spare in order to fight a threat or flee from it. The number of lives this lightning-fast response has saved over the course of human existence is truly incalculable.

But as we also saw, there are drawbacks to this approach. Our brains don't always get it right. Sometimes our stress response system has a hair trigger, and sometimes it has trouble turning off. Sometimes our past experiences (things like ACEs or other traumas, or being raised by caregivers who overreacted to stress) can lead to faulty information processing, causing us to see threats everywhere, when in reality the modern world is largely safe.

Today we're also more likely to face stressors of a chronic nature. Just look at Colin for a list of examples: too much work and not enough time and support to do it, ongoing conflicts with coworkers, and organizational dysfunction, just to name a few. These are the kind of stressors that stick around, and when that happens, the SNS has no choice but to remain activated in order to deal with what it's experiencing as an ongoing threat.

And here we have the crux of the problem: as long as the brain continues to perceive a threat, cortisol continues to flow through your body, keeping it revved up and on high alert. Chronic high cortisol has been linked to yet another laundry list of problems, including anxiety, depression, headaches, high blood pressure, gastrointestinal problems, insomnia, weight gain, systemic inflammation, and higher risk of cardiovascular disease and cognitive dysfunction.

Fight-or-flight isn't the only response to stress, though. You've likely heard of the third one, known as the *freeze response*. (In fact, it's now common to refer to the overall stress response as the "fight-flight-freeze" response.) But the freeze response is a little different. It happens when fighting or fleeing just won't work. When there's no time or opportunity to respond to a threat—say you're about to be hit by an oncoming car—our brains respond in the only way that's left, which is to try to numb us to the inevitable pain. This is the classic "deer in the headlights" scenario, and it's a response that occurs in the face of severe, overwhelming, unavoidable stress, or what some refer to as traumatic stress. In this case, rather than the SNS revving up the body and preparing it for action, the PNS effectively shuts the body down. Heart rate and respiration decrease rapidly, you can go cold or numb, and in extreme cases, you can actually pass out.

As part of our hardwired survival instinct, the freeze response does have its advantages. It floods the body with endorphins, a "feel-good" hormone that promotes a sense of calm and blunts our perception of pain, and it provides a buffer between us and the super-scary event that triggered it. But I'm sure you can see some of the difficulties with the freeze response—which is also known as reactive immobility, tonic immobility, or attentive immobility—when it's triggered inappropriately. Though the person experiencing it is fully alert and aware, in its extreme form they cannot move or respond in any way. In other words, their stress is so overwhelming they're temporarily paralyzed. More commonly, we experience the freeze response in milder forms: our mind goes blank, we feel numb or dissociated (sometimes described as being "checked out" or "removed"), we experience sudden, extreme fatigue, or we just feel nonfunctional.

Further, the freeze response is subject to all the same information-processing errors and disproportionate responses as the fight-or-flight response. We can freeze up in situations that don't actually threaten our lives, leaving us ineffective (to say the least!) and incapable of handling the stressor that caused such a strong response. Many people freeze up or go blank when they're put on the spot, for example. And again, this is especially the case if we have a history of ACEs or other trauma. With its "better safe than sorry" approach, the brain learns to become hypervigilant and to respond to every threat it detects with everything it's got.

The bottom line with all three of these stress responses is this: when the stress response system is activated inappropriately, too frequently, or sticks around past its expiration date, it actually causes *more* stress, and long-term, can be severely damaging to our physical and mental well-being.

When it comes to stress *and* to burnout, what sticks around grinds you down.

Better Ways to Respond to Stress

For years, scientists thought that fighting, fleeing, or freezing were our only options for responding to stress. But there are actually two additional responses, and they offer a much different story. Both move beyond sheer survival, enabling us to access certain *advantages* of stress that aren't available otherwise. They are the *challenge response* and the *tend-and-befriend response*, and as you'll see, they also play a key role in building burnout immunity. Let's take a look.

The *challenge response* to stress kicks in when you feel called on to perform or to achieve something. If you're wondering why that doesn't trigger the freeze response, or at least the fight-or-flight response, you're asking exactly the right question. The key difference comes from *how you view the stressor*: it may be challenging and difficult, but you don't see it as life-threatening. And while the challenge response triggers some of the same physiological responses as fight-or-flight—heart rate escalates and you get a boost of adrenaline, for instance—you feel focused, excited, and confident, instead of fearful, angry, or overwhelmed.

Because you aren't anticipating physical harm, explains psychologist and stress expert Kelly McGonigal, your primary goal isn't to avoid a threat, but to go after what you want. In this case the body responds more like it does to physical exercise than it does to a threat:

your blood vessels remain relaxed rather than constricted, your heart has a stronger beat, enabling it to pump out more blood, and you actually gain *more* energy than you do in the fight-or-flight response. And while the challenge response does trigger the release of cortisol, the adrenal glands produce a higher ratio of DHEA, a precursor hormone that offsets cortisol's negative effects. In a nifty little twist, DHEA also increases the brain's capacity to learn resilience from stressful experiences. The overall result of the challenge response, McGonigal says, is increased energy, increased focus, greater self-confidence, and greater motivation. Plain and simple, the challenge response, she says, "gives us the motivation to approach a challenge head-on, and the mental and physical resources to succeed." This is what you want when you have to give a presentation, take an exam, get a project over the finish line, negotiate for better compensation, or perform under pressure, for example.

So unless your life is on the line, you're better off having the challenge response to stress. All of which begs the question: Where can I buy some of that? I'm happy to tell you it's absolutely free, and the source is within your own mind.

Or more specifically, mindset. We're going to take a deep dive into mindset and outlook in Chapter 6, but for now, here's the quick version: research (including McGonigal's) has shown that the most important factor in determining how you respond to stress is *how you think about your ability to handle it*. Don't miss the significance of this statement. The power to determine your best response to stress is in your control, and it depends on nothing more than how you choose to view your ability to manage it. With a little practice, you can learn to shift from a threat response to a challenge response, even if you've lived with an overactive amygdala your whole life. Here's how it works.

The second you face a stressor, your brain automatically begins to evaluate the situation and the resources you have at your disposal to respond to it. (This is the primary and secondary appraisal process we discussed in the last chapter.) Beneath your conscious awareness, the brain begins gathering information: *How hard will this be? Do I have the strength, skills, courage, and the help I need to face this and get through it?* McGonigal's conclusion is straightforward: "If you believe that the demands of the situation exceed your resources, you will have a threat response. But if you believe you have the resources to succeed, you will have a challenge response." This is a prime example of how our thoughts can dictate our reality.

To begin shifting from a threat response to a challenge response—which is to say, to begin believing you have the resources to succeed—try viewing your stress response as a resource. It may feel odd or even impossible at first, but taking baby steps, as long as you keep them up, will get you there. So "try on" the belief that your stress is helpful and enhancing, rather than harmful and detracting. Mindsets are not set in stone and can always evolve.

The next time your stress response gets triggered—your heart pounds, you sweat, you start to worry and doubt yourself—don't try to suppress it or avoid it, which actually backfires by reinforcing your stress. Instead acknowledge and accept it, but tell yourself you'll prevail. *I'm stressed right now, but that's okay; I've experienced stress before and I always get through it.* Or hey, why not go for broke? *I'm stressed right now, but this ain't my first rodeo, and I'm going to kick some ass.* Simply accepting our experience, rather than fighting it or trying to suppress it, can change a threat response to a challenge response. This is how your own mindset and thinking can transform what's happening in your brain and body and help you have a healthier response to stress.

Here are some more quick mindset shifts to try:

- Acknowledge your personal strengths.
- Think about how you've prepared for a particular challenge.
- Recall experiences when you overcame similar challenges.
- Imagine the support of your loved ones.
- Pray, or know that others are praying for you.
- Practice a mantra, like "I've got this," "I can handle this," or

my personal favorite, "This ain't my first rodeo" (I actually wear a T-shirt that says "This ain't my first rodeo" under my suit when I'm giving a big keynote).

There's another beneficial stress response to consider, and this one centers more on our external *behavior* than our internal mindset. The *tend-and-befriend response* occurs when we seek closeness and connection with others in order to reduce stress and help us overcome challenging, difficult situations.

The name comes from a 2000 research paper that noted that females' responses to stress are more marked by tending (protecting and nurturing their young) and befriending (maintaining and strengthening social networks) than fight-or-flight. The thinking goes that, far back in our evolutionary past, there were two distinct roles when it came to caring for offspring: males went out to kill prey and bring back food for family groups, while females remained behind to care for the young. In this system, natural selection favored males who could fight or flee, whereas females stood a better chance of their own *and* their offspring's survival by forming cohesive social groups that worked together to handle challenges and threats. Regardless of how or when this response arose, we know that prosocial behaviors—positive acts with a social benefit such as helping others, volunteering, cooperating, and sharing—occur in all genders, as well as in many animals. (This is just one of the reasons I'm fond of calling this the "giving is relieving" response to stress.)

As with the other stress responses, the hormones and neurotransmitters that are released during the tend-and-befriend response play a central role in mediating its stress-lowering effects. You've already become acquainted with one of them, endorphins, which promote calm and act as a natural pain reliever. Now it's time to meet the other three "feel-good" hormones, or what some refer to as our happy hormones: oxytocin, dopamine, and serotonin.

Kelly McGonigal notes that the tend-and-befriend response increases activity in three systems in our brain: the social caregiving system, the reward system, and the attunement system. The *social caregiving system* is regulated by oxytocin, known colloquially as "the love hormone" due to the role it plays in facilitating bonding and intimacy. When this system is activated and oxytocin is flowing, you feel more empathy, connection, and trust, as well as a stronger desire to bond or be close with others. This network also inhibits the fear centers of the brain, increasing your courage. In addition to social caregiving, oxytocin is released during childbirth, lactation, exercise, sex, and other forms of physical touch such as hugging and massage. It's one of our most powerful natural regulators, able to soothe difficult emotions, promote calm, and help get our brain back online after a stressful experience.

Second, the *reward system* releases dopamine, known as the feel-good neurotransmitter. Activation of the reward system increases motivation while dampening fear. When your stress response includes a rush of dopamine, you feel optimistic about your ability to do something meaningful. Dopamine also primes the brain for physical action, making sure you don't freeze under pressure. It helps regulate mood, learning, and memory, and contributes to feelings of happiness, focus, pleasure, and alertness. Because dopamine is released when your brain is expecting a reward, anything you consider enjoyable could potentially trigger it.

Third, the *attunement system* is driven by the neurotransmitter serotonin. When this system is activated, it enhances your perception, intuition, and self-control. This makes it easier to understand what's needed to meet the challenge before you and helps to ensure that your actions have the biggest impact. Serotonin also plays a role in regulating mood, sleep, appetite, learning ability, and memory. It's hailed as a mood booster and stress reducer, and you can naturally increase your serotonin levels through exercise, exposure to light, and meditation.

Overall, McGonigal concludes, thanks to these powerful hormones and neurotransmitters, the tend-and-befriend response "makes you social, brave, and smart. It provides both the courage and hope we need to propel us into action and the awareness to act skillfully." And here's the thing that really gets me: *"Anytime you choose to help others,"* she points out, *"you activate this state.* Caring for others triggers the biology of courage and creates hope."

How amazing, to have within ourselves the ability to trigger this beneficial and protective state. In a nutshell, choosing a tend-and-befriend response will increase your courage, motivate you to express care and concern for others, and strengthen your social relationships. I think this helps explain the behavior of my research participants with burnout immunity who've told me they have a servant-leader mindset. They describe being very motivated and driven to help others, which in turn gives them courage to handle stress. In a way, it seems to help them develop a kind of mental toughness.

I've experienced this myself. I've had many days in which I've felt overwhelmed and exhausted, and when I look at my calendar and see three student calls and two coaching calls, I dread the thought of hearing people talk about their issues, and I worry that I won't have the energy to support them. This makes me feel a lot of shame, which adds to my stress.

But then I get on the calls, and as soon as we start to connect I forget about my own feelings of stress and overwhelm. I almost instantly feel more empathy, connection, and trust. I also feel more optimistic and confident in my ability to provide meaningful help to my students and clients (which builds my self-efficacy). What's really interesting is this: these are the calls that end up being the most productive, where the students and clients walk away feeling supported and with a greater sense of clarity about what they want and need to do. It's a very meaningful type of connection where, in real time, I'm buoyed by the positive physical and mental effects of endorphins, oxytocin, dopamine, and serotonin—and my clients and students reap the benefits of it.

The best way to choose the tend-and-befriend response is to look beyond your personal to-do list and find ways to help someone else:

- Offer a conversation to a mentee or coworker who's struggling.
- Listen to others with your full attention.
- Give people the benefit of the doubt if you disagree with them.
- Seize every opportunity to express appreciation to others.
- Be generous with your positive feedback.

Having the ability to elicit positive hormonal responses in order to regulate our stress response is an incredibly powerful resource that's fully in our control. We have the built-in ability to choose a better, more productive response to stress in order to help calm ourselves down, think more clearly and intentionally, and make better decisions and actions.

Now, given all the upsides of these four happy hormones, it's pretty clear why we'd want extra portions of them, and relatively little of the stress hormone cortisol. But not so fast! We definitely do *not* want to skip out on cortisol entirely, because in the right circumstances and in the right amount, it helps us feel alert, focused, and ready to deal with the challenging situation we're facing. The goal is to experience just enough stress in just the right circumstances.

The Sweet Spot of Stress

We've seen that when it comes to stress, there is no simple, cut-and-dried conclusion such as "all stress is bad, therefore the avoidance of stress is good." A stress-free existence is not only impossible, it's not even desirable.

What we actually want, for optimum physical and mental health as well as peak performance, is to operate from within a sweet spot of stress, where we experience just enough stress to feel challenged and motivated, but not so much that we feel overwhelmed and ineffective.

Hormesis is a technical term that originated from the field of toxicology, where it describes a dose-response reaction to an environmental agent. At high doses, the agent can be deadly, while at low

SWEET SPOT OF STRESS

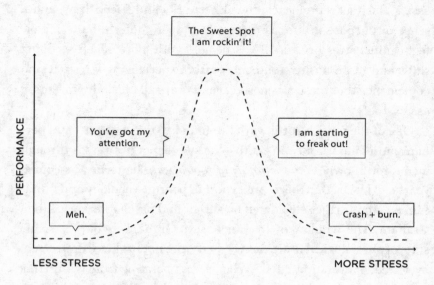

Figure 3.1: The Sweet Spot of Stress

doses, it can actually produce a protective effect. Hormesis is now used in the fields of biology, medicine, and psychology to describe the effect of stress, and the mechanism is the same: at high "doses," stress is toxic, while in low or moderate (and usually, intermittent) doses, it's beneficial. Common examples of hormetic stressors include intermittent fasting, exercise, challenging (though not impossible) cognitive activities, and cold or heat exposure. The idea is that brief exposure to low-to-moderate stressors puts us in the sweet spot of stress: we experience just enough stress to activate a variety of healthy adaptive responses that begin on a cellular level (hormetic stress has been shown to help repair cellular damage, slow cellular aging, reduce inflammation, improve blood sugar regulation, and support the elimination of toxins) and that carry all the way through to improved overall health and greater resilience to future stress. A recent study out of the University of Georgia found that low to moderate levels of stress actually enhance working memory and mental performance. The effects were strongest in those who had access to "psychosocial assets" such as self-efficacy, social networks and friendships, and a sense of purpose in life, as these advantages confer a buffering effect against stressors and are associated with more effective coping skills and more positive outcomes after experiencing stress. It's no coincidence that these psychosocial assets are all burnout prevention assets, too!

One of the most helpful ways I've found to think about—and perhaps more importantly, to get to—the sweet spot of stress is through a concept known as *the window of tolerance*. The term was coined years ago by Dr. Dan Siegel, an expert in neuropsychology and mindfulness, and further elucidated by author and psychotherapist Linda Graham. The window of tolerance, says Graham, is our "baseline state of physiological functioning when we're not frightened, stressed, overtired, or overstimulated." When we're operating from within this state, she says, "we're grounded and centered, neither overreacting to other people or life events nor failing to act at all." It's that desirable, Goldilocks place that's right between too stressed and not stressed enough, between too revved up and too shut down. We're in a state of perfect regulation: calm and relaxed, yet also engaged and alert.

What causes us to slip out of—or in some cases, be knocked out of—the window of tolerance? You've got it: stress. But here's the thing. When our stress response is regulated and healthy—when it responds in a manner that's fitting to the perceived threat—we're able to return to the window of tolerance pretty quickly. Graham cites two big "glitches" that make it difficult for us to return, and they both have to do with a dysregulated, unproductive stress response.

First, our prefrontal cortex operates relatively slowly compared to the amygdala, which is hardwired to detect threats in milliseconds. This means that when we feel threatened, we automatically react in a split second, before having a chance to engage in slower, more regulated and reflective thinking. If you've ever flown off the handle, stormed out of a meeting, or fallen apart when you felt threatened,

	When fear is regulated or absent:	When fear is not regulated:
Sympathetic activation	interest, curiosity, exploration, play, productivity, enthusiasm	fight-flight-freeze response, too revved up, agitation, anxiety, panic
Window of tolerance	Physiological baseline of equanimity: calm and relaxed, engaged and alert	
	When fear is regulated or absent:	When fear is not regulated:
Parasympathetic deactivation	relaxation, reverie, daydreaming, napping, falling asleep after making love	submit-collapse response, fainting, dissociation, numbness

Figure 3.2: The Window of Tolerance from *Bouncing Back*, by Linda Graham, MFT

you know what I'm talking about. Many times, we were conditioned in childhood to respond in this way. "If our earliest experiences did not condition us to regulate our survival responses effectively," says Graham, "the prefrontal cortex may have not fully developed its capacities for self-regulation."

Second, unregulated surges of our old frenemy cortisol can temporarily knock out the functioning of the prefrontal cortex. And considering that part of the prefrontal cortex's responsibility is to regulate the mechanisms that reduce cortisol levels, that leaves us in a real pickle. "When the functioning of our prefrontal cortex is derailed by a stress response, even temporarily," Graham says, "we can remain stuck in a chronic state of alarm, agitation, hostility, rage, panic, or terror—or stuck in numbness, lethargy, or depression for a longer period of time than is good for us."

So how do we get back to our window of tolerance, our sweet spot of stress, when life knocks us about? And how do we remain there as long as we can? Before you dive into the list of recommendations, I want to highlight one more thing that Graham emphasizes: the window of tolerance is our "natural baseline state of equilibrium." It's an innate gift, in other words, the built-in home base from which, in a perfect world, we'd operate all the time. Sure, the world is far from perfect, but I find it deeply comforting to know that no matter the circumstances, the window of tolerance is always there, just waiting for our return.

Here are some "rescue remedies" to use on the fly when you find yourself knocked out of the window of tolerance.

1. **Activate oxytocin through touch**. Oxytocin provides the fastest way to regulate the body's stress response and return to a state of calm equilibrium. To trigger it, seek out safe touch: hugs, holding hands, a head rub, massage, cuddles with a pet, or even massaging your own temples or placing your hand on your heart. To supercharge the effect, gently massage the place where your neck meets the base of your skull. This is the location of the vagus nerve, which is loaded with oxytocin receptors.

2. **Try the tend-and-befriend response**. Reach out to a loved one. If you can be in their presence, all the better, but a phone call or instant messaging will do in a pinch. Feeling supported and connected releases all four of the feel-good hormones, as does helping others.

3. **Treat yourself to a big ol' physiological sigh**. This is a powerful breathing technique in which you complete two inhalations through the nose, followed by one long exhalation through the mouth. According to neurobiologist Dr. Andrew Huberman, the double inhalation "pops" open all the little air sacs (alveoli) in the lungs, maximizing your oxygen intake, while the long exhalation offloads carbon dioxide that has accumulated during the stress response.

4. **Exercise**. The link between exercise and stress prevention as well as stress relief has been firmly established. Find an ex-

ercise you like, or that you can at least tolerate, that gets your heart rate up. Group exercise classes have the extra benefit of social connection. Outdoor exercise gives you the extra benefit of the next rescue remedy.

5. **Spend time in nature**. There is abundant evidence demonstrating that spending time outdoors in green spaces lowers stress, promotes self-regulation, increases attention, and is a significant predictor of happiness and general well-being. The stress-reducing effects occur in as little as ten minutes.

6. **Give it a good cry**. Crying is just as good for grown-ups as it is for babies. Crying releases oxytocin as well as endorphins, and it's a powerful means of self-soothing, mood regulation, and stress reduction.

What Triggers Your Workplace Stress

The bottom line here is simple: if you work in an environment that frequently triggers your stress response, you're going to be more vulnerable to burnout. Everyone has different stress thresholds and different sources of stress, so the trick is to accurately pinpoint the specific events that trigger *your* workplace stress.

Trigger is a word that gets thrown around a lot, but I like psychotherapist and writer David Richo's simple and straightforward definition: "A trigger is any word, person, event, or experience that touches off an immediate emotional reaction." Triggers, he says, incite automatic reactions over which we have zero control. Remember Ben, my coworker from my first job who gaslighted me? Just seeing his name in my inbox or hearing his voice from down the hall automatically made my stomach flip and my heart pound. Even writing about him today, after all these years, makes my skin crawl. These are all physical manifestations of my immediate emotional reaction of fear.

When we're triggered, our effectiveness is compromised, because our logical brain—the area responsible for problem-solving, decision-making, and rational thinking—effectively shuts down. Emotions take over, and we're flooded with adrenaline and cortisol. In this triggered, dysregulated state, we can't see clearly or make sound decisions, and we'll stay in that mode until the trigger has dissipated.

Sounds pretty bad, right? Now consider what happens if you're triggered *every day* at work. While we can weather occasional spikes in stress without much problem—as we've seen, the whole purpose of the stress response is to help us deal with an immediate, short-term threat—it's when stress becomes chronic that we become very vulnerable to burnout. This is why we need to have a clear awareness of what triggers our workplace stress and why. We won't know how to handle our triggers until we can identify and understand them.

One of my CMO study participants was a trauma surgeon before a back injury forced him to turn in his scalpel. He was cool as a cucumber while providing emergency medical care to patients with life-threatening injuries, but in this new leadership role, he was experiencing chronic stress for the first time in his career. "I'm trained for trauma care," he said, "and the outcome is immediate. But budget stuff? Not my thing, and it unnerves me when I can't know the impact of a decision right away." As a seasoned trauma surgeon, he had built up the mental and emotional strength he needed to stay focused and effective in an acute stress environment. As an administrative leader, however, he was significantly more sensitive to the effects of what *for him* was a chronic stress environment.

Or consider the responses from a group of police leaders at the Police Executive Leadership Institute (PELI) when I posed this question: "What makes your stress level jump from a 2 or 3 to a 7+ in a matter of seconds?" I assumed it would be managing an imminent threat, such as an active-shooter situation. Nope! Most of these experienced, well-trained officers said they actually felt calm in that type of scenario. Their biggest triggers coalesced around one of two things: staffing issues when dozens of officers called out with COVID on the same day, or having to deal with misinformation in the media.

Bottom line, an event one person barely registers on a stress scale can be a massive trigger for another. This is why it's vitally important that each of us becomes aware of our unique triggers.

Sometimes triggers are obvious, either because they're vivid and undeniable—your boss yells at you or someone makes a last-minute change to your schedule, for example—or it's a trigger you've lived with for a long time. My biggest trigger has been with me since I was a little girl: witnessing someone use their position of power to attack or disparage another person. Whether the attack is direct or carried out behind someone's back, the mama bear in me immediately surfaces and I want to jump in and defend the person being attacked. Other triggers are subtler and will require more focused attention to identify; still others are entirely unknown to us.

This last group has the potential to be the most dangerous, as we're unaware of how unconscious triggers are influencing our mood, thinking patterns, and behavior. Here's a set of questions that will help you identify what triggers you at work.

EXERCISE: AWARENESS OF YOUR WORKPLACE TRIGGERS

PART 1

1. My stomach lurches when _____.
2. I absolutely cannot tolerate when _____.
3. It makes me want to scream when my boss/coworker/direct report _____.
4. It makes me really angry when _____.
5. I feel unfocused and like my brain is "offline" when _____.

6. I feel out of control when _____.

7. My anxiety skyrockets when _____.

8. It feels really unfair to me when _____.

9. My self-confidence plummets when _____.

10. _____ makes me feel powerless.

11. When my coworker/boss _____ it makes me feel like a child.

PART 2

Did these questions bring any other triggers to mind? If so, write them down here:

1. _____

2. _____

3. _____

PART 3

Sometimes we can identify our triggers by working backward from the *result* of the trigger. Think back over the last few weeks. Look for any occasion that caused an immediate emotional or physical reaction, an abrupt change in your thinking or mental state, or a sudden shift in your behavior. Maybe you suddenly felt sad, irritable, frustrated, numb, or overwhelmed. Or maybe you experienced nausea, muscle tension, shakiness, or pain. Maybe you were overtaken by negativity or an impulse to withdraw. Perhaps you lashed out at someone, became passive-aggressive, or cried.

Any of these automatic reactions is an indication that you've been triggered. Once you identify your triggered state, work backward until you can pinpoint what set you off. There's your trigger.

How I Learned to Regulate My Stress Response

For the first couple of years after my blood pressure issue, I tried a variety of mindfulness strategies to cope—walking meditation, meditation while folding laundry, traditional meditation, yoga meditation, my beloved "beditation." I don't doubt the power of any of these methods, and as I learned to tune in and notice how my body felt when I was stressed—hunched shoulders, a dull pain between my eyes, sometimes a sensation of spaciness or dizziness—I learned to recognize when my cortisol levels and my blood pressure were escalating. For me, this was mission critical. First and foremost, I had to keep my blood pressure under control.

But I also felt like I needed a method to help me calm down by regulating my stress response when I was triggered. Though I was getting better, my stress was still too frequently and too quickly jumping from a level 3 (tolerable) to 7+ (severe or very severe) in response to workplace events. Things like receiving an email from an angry client, being verbally attacked by a coworker in a team meeting, being accused of something that was not what I intended, or learning that I was being reassigned to work in a city that would require significantly more travel were too triggering, and I knew I couldn't rely on Xanax for the rest of my life every time I got stressed out.

It wasn't until I met Dr. Howard Stevenson when I was a doctoral student at UPenn that I discovered a method that immediately worked for me. Stevenson is a clinical psychologist and an expert on how to resolve racial stress and trauma, and he originally developed this method as a "recasting skill" to deal with highly stressful racial encounters. Since then, he's taught it in many different contexts, and he guided our class in how it can be used to manage all types of acute stress situations. It's called the CLCBE Method, and for me, it works every single time to regulate my stress response and get me out of an amygdala hijack. CLCBE stands for Calculate, Locate, Communicate, Breathe, and Exhale. Here's how it works:

- **Calculate**: On a scale of 1–10, with 10 being "worst possible" stress, what is your stress level? If it's 8 or above, you're operating from a state of acute threat and dysregulation. Consider your brain offline.
- **Locate**: Pinpoint where you feel the stress in your body. The more specific, the better.
- **Communicate**: Identify what you're saying to yourself in that high-stress moment. Negative self-talk only makes stress worse. Positive self-talk can help you reach a state of calm more quickly.
- **Breathe**: Breathe in slowly for a count of 4.
- **Exhale**: Breathe out slowly for a count of 7.

"All of this," Stevenson said, "is aimed at reducing stress quickly, ideally within sixty seconds. In threatening moments, people's brains go into lockdown. The more you can relax, the more you can access what you know. When you feel less overwhelmed, your decision-making opportunities become much clearer." Which is an apt description of the entire goal of regulation.

As I increased my awareness skills, I noticed that I needed different regulation methods to control my stress response based on the type of stressor and the acuity level of my stress. For a low-acuity level of stress, like receiving critical feedback on one of my graduate papers, deep breathing was enough to get back to a 2 or 3, and then I was able to think clearly, and remind myself that the feedback was there to help me improve.

For higher-acuity levels of stress, however, I needed CLCBE to keep calm and maintain a professional demeanor, especially on occasions where it wasn't possible or appropriate to deal with my strong emotional reactions right away.

Several months after I learned the CLCBE method, an opportunity to put it into practice dropped right in my lap. I was still doing consulting work during my doctoral studies, and I was brought in to conduct a change management workshop for a health care organization that was about to go through a big, complicated, and very unpopular restructure. My team didn't prep me with any personal details about the attendees—I just knew that the CEO and a dozen or so other top executives and decision-makers would be there.

I took my place at the front of the room, before a big oblong table with execs seated on both sides. At the very end was an empty chair. I assumed it was reserved for the CEO and that either he'd be late or had been called away, so I got started. For twenty minutes everything went really well—the group was engaged and interactive, the conversation was lively, positive, and respectful, and dare I say it, we were even enjoying ourselves in spite of the tense topics of discussion.

Then the door banged open and a harried, heavily sweating, and clearly exasperated guy barged in and plopped down in the empty seat. The energy in the room changed instantly. People sank down in their chairs and the conversation dried up to awkward silences and a few forced interjections, while the glowering CEO sat there with his arms crossed.

My stress rose from a 2 to a 5 or 6, and I consciously lowered my shoulders and slowed down my breathing to keep my stress response in check. That worked until the CEO started yelling.

"I'm sorry, but I don't know why we're here!" he bellowed. "We've been doing this on our own for years, and we don't need change management support." He started pointing at different people around the table. "Who brought her in here?" he said. "Was it you? You? Why wasn't I consulted about this!"

My stress level shot up, and rage was right behind it. (You know how I feel about workplace bullies.) But I was able to mentally run through the CLCBE method in hyperspeed. Calculate: stress level, 9. Locate: stomach: flip-flopping, nauseous. Communicate: I made a conscious effort to anchor into positive self-talk: *You've faced worse, and you did great.* And of course, the breathing. It always, always works, so I focused on breathing as slowly and deeply as possible.

Now remember, this entire routine happened internally, and within seconds. But it was enough to distract me from my impulse to yell back at the rude CEO, to shift my mindset from panic to challenge, and to slow my thinking down. From that calmer, steadier state, I realized that my job in that moment was to bring the emotional intensity down, not fan the flames and make things worse.

So, even though my blood was boiling, I responded with empathy. "I can appreciate how hard this is," I said, "especially in your position. It's a lot of disruption, and I know a lot of people are depending on you." I then looked around the room to make sure the rest of the attendees knew they were included in my sentiments—they, too, were part of the executive team, after all. What I saw on their faces was a mixture of relief, embarrassment, and apology.

I think the calm pause was enough for the CEO to regain a little of his equilibrium, because he suddenly seemed to realize how uncomfortable everyone was. He apologized for his outburst, and then abruptly called the meeting to an end. "Let's regroup and start fresh tomorrow," he said.

The next day, I learned he'd been late because he'd just come from a board meeting where the directors had chewed him out. He'd arrived at the workshop already triggered, stressed-out, and defensive, and his rude and disruptive behavior shut down any chance of having a productive meeting. Dysregulation can come at a high cost.

That meeting marked a turning point in how I learned to regulate my stress response. I saw from the CEO what I didn't want to become. And I was proud of myself for remaining calm and coolheaded despite the intense emotion I experienced.

Today I continue to be diligent about trying to operate from within my sweet spot of stress. It's worth every bit of time and effort, for me and for everyone else at work.

4

The Power and Promise
of Regulation

Remaining Effective in the
Midst of Stress

"Lately I'm either crying in the bathroom or in a quiet rage in the break room. I can't get a grip." —Shireen, nurse practitioner

"I am totally on edge at work. The only way I can unwind anymore is by drinking." —Billie, systems administrator

"I'm in this constant state of dread about my job." —Gil, CPA

"I used to look forward to work, but then we got acquired and the new owners fired half my team. Everyone who's left is overworked and living in a state of fear they'll be next. It feels really hopeless." —Louis, systems administrator

These are quotes from people who were in an active state of burnout when I interviewed them. Their language reflects some of the classic signs of energy depletion and emotional exhaustion that's evident in so many who are suffering from burnout. Thankfully, they've all recovered or are well on their way, but when their burnout was at its worst, none of them believed they'd ever be happy at work again. Everything felt out of their control and beyond their ability to improve or even change. As Louis said, really hopeless.

This sad scenario is all the more tragic considering that each of these employees began their jobs with overwhelmingly positive feelings—they were optimistic, engaged, effective, and took pride in their work. As mismatches between their needs and what their organization provided grew deeper and their stress became chronic and unmanageable, however, burnout eroded their positive feelings and replaced them with feelings of being drained, overwhelmed, and demoralized.

The loss of motivated, happy, high-performing workers and the contributions they make is one of the biggest casualties of burnout. In fact, of the four workers I quoted above, Billie ended up taking an extended leave of absence, and Shireen, who'd been with her hospital for more than twenty years, resigned and joined a telehealth startup.

In the previous chapter, we examined how regulation helps us manage our stress response. Now we're going to look at how it can help us manage our emotions, our thoughts, and our actions at work. To be clear, regulation is *not* an effort to try to tamp down our feelings, police our thoughts, or squash our natural reactions. Neither is it the absence of emotion, strict control of your thoughts (good luck with that!), or being inflexible in your thinking or behaviors.

It *is* the ability to get to a calm, coolheaded state, even when your stress ramps up, and then to operate from a state of focus, clarity, and equilibrium. So I'd encourage you to let go of any notion that regulation is about *restriction*. It actually has far more to do with freedom. Freedom from destructive emotions, out-of-control thoughts, and impulsive actions. Freedom to know your own values and enact them in authentic and purposeful ways. Freedom to be your most authentic self, maintain clarity of vision, and perform at your highest capability, even within high-stress environments.

In this chapter I'll show you how unregulated emotions, thoughts, and behaviors can compound your workplace stress, undermine your

What regulation of emotions, thoughts, and actions means	What regulation of emotions, thoughts, and actions does *not* mean
Working WITH	Working AGAINST
Acknowledging emotions and thoughts	Suppressing or denying emotions
Being aware of our actions and their consequences	Censoring or feeling ashamed about thoughts
Working toward a state of calm equanimity	Becoming rigid and inflexible in our actions
Projecting calm in our actions	Engaging in self-recrimination or punishment
Adopting a stance of self-compassion	Monitoring others' feelings, thoughts, or actions
Self-management in service of our values	

Figure 4.1: What Regulation Does and Does Not Mean

performance, and increase your vulnerability to burnout. But I'll also show you how regulation, practiced with self-compassion, comes to the rescue. Overall, you'll learn how to:

- manage—and even leverage—your emotions instead of living at the mercy of them
- have your thoughts serve your performance and productivity rather than run amok and steal your focus, motivation, or confidence
- identify impulsively reactive behaviors and move toward more intentionally responsive behaviors, and
- behave in a manner that reflects your true values and is most conducive to your personal well-being, as well as the well-being of your coworkers and work culture.

It will take some effort and some practice, but we *can* learn to regulate our emotions, thoughts, and behaviors, even when our stress escalates and things begin to feel out of control. Practiced over time, regulation is one of the most powerful ways to immunize ourselves against burnout and to remain happy and healthy at work.

Regulating Your Emotions in the Midst of Stress

We know that burnout depletes our mental, emotional, and physical energy, lures us into negative thinking, and undermines our effectiveness and overall performance. But one of its most dangerous effects is the emotional exhaustion it engenders. Why? Because our emotions are intimately involved with everything we do. From what we think, to how we react, to how we view our circumstances, to the health of our relationships, to the way we approach and solve problems— even to the way we view ourselves—emotions play an outsize role, whether we know it or not. (Yes, even your super-stoic coworkers are constantly experiencing and processing emotions—they just don't *express* them as explicitly or as frequently as others do.) All of this means that one of the most powerful practices we can engage in, not just to immunize ourselves against burnout but to facilitate our highest well-being in any context, is to learn to regulate our emotions.

In emotional intelligence literature, emotional regulation is referred to as emotional self-control. Both terms refer to the ability to manage our emotions in such a way that we remain effective and in control, even in the midst of high-stress situations. I'd like to expand this concept, however, and add three crucial components. Emotional regulation also entails the ability to 1) be aware of our emotions in all their diversity and multiplicity, 2) understand where they're coming from, and 3) accept those emotions, even the difficult ones.

Let's begin with acceptance, because I want to be clear about what I mean. It does *not* mean that we resign ourselves to a negative or difficult emotional state and do nothing to move through it or address the circumstances that caused it. Remaining stuck in a state of fury, embarrassment, shame, or disappointment, for example, is not only unpleasant, it's unproductive, and long-term, it's harmful. But it *does* mean that we become aware of and truthfully acknowledge the full range of our emotional experiences (point 1 above). In other words, we don't deny, suppress, numb ourselves to, or run away from our emotions, even the uncomfortable or difficult ones.

We do accept that they are present, and that we are experiencing them for a very good reason (point 2). Think of emotions like data. They all provide information. Understanding their source—why we are having a particular emotional reaction to a particular circumstance, in other words—helps reveal who we are, what is important to us, what our values are, and many times, where our boundaries lie and where our unhealed hurts are hidden.

Remember my ragey mama bear, who roars to life when I witness a powerful person attacking an underdog? Part of my process of emotional regulation is accepting that difficult emotional state as part of who I am, being keenly aware of what triggers it, and, certainly, being aware of when it's gathering force, well before it commandeers my thoughts and negatively influences my actions. ("Blind rage" is a real thing!) Without emotional regulation, this trigger will leave me in a state in which my thoughts are unproductive—or maybe I'll be so overwhelmed I won't be able to think at all (the freeze response to stress). And if I'm operating from either of those dysregulated states, I stand the chance of being overwhelmed by strong emotion, leaving my resulting behavior unhelpful at best, or at worst, harmful to those around me.

And let's not forget that there's a *reason* my fury goes from 0 to 60 in two seconds flat. What information does this strong emotional reaction reveal? In this case, it doesn't require a lot of reflection to trace the roots of my rage to early childhood, when I witnessed people in power looking down upon my family. Back then, those in power weren't people with wealth and influence, but ordinary folks who happened to have more than we did. But the experience of being treated as "less than" obviously stuck with me, and, likely because it happened at a pivotal moment in my development, it became one of my biggest triggers.

Without the guardrails of emotional regulation, something with that kind of history and potency has the potential to be very destructive indeed. But *with* emotional regulation, I have the chance to use all the energy and drive and motivation that fury provides to fuel thoughtful, intentional action that can right an injustice. What a powerful force for change! This is part of the reason why, although fury is a very difficult emotional state, I don't want to deny it, suppress it, numb myself to it, or run away from it. I want to welcome it insofar as it's a part of my authentic experience, learn the story it has to tell me, and through the superpower of emotional regulation, use it in a healthy way.

Emotional regulation applies not just to the difficult emotions but also to the full range of our feelings. We humans are feeling-beings, after all, and we often feel before we think—which has a direct impact on our actions, not to mention the people around us who will be affected by them. Emotional regulation allows us to operate from a state of calm equilibrium, where our brain is functioning optimally, our feelings aren't getting in the way of our thinking, and we feel in control and effective.

From my research, I've found that people with burnout immunity are able to use emotional intelligence skills to regulate and stay in control of their emotions, even in the midst of high-stress situations. Here are three powerful strategies I distilled from their experience and that you can learn in order to jump-start your emotional regulation skills and help extend your stay in the sweet spot of stress.

EMOTIONAL REGULATION STRATEGY #1: PEOPLE WITH BURNOUT IMMUNITY VIEW STRESSORS AS PROBLEMS THAT CAN BE SOLVED.
They take a problem-solving approach to stressors, which means they feel they have at least some sense of control over the situation. Perhaps just as importantly, they also surround themselves with other problem-solvers. Think about it: if your attitude is *Hey, this situation is tough, but I know I can problem-solve my way through it, and I've got plenty of people I can lean on for help*, there's very little

chance your amygdala will get hijacked, sending you into a state of emotional uproar where you need to manage your emotions before you can get to effective problem-solving.

Now, if you're already thinking, *Sounds great, but I'm just not built that way—my amygdala gets hijacked at least twice a day!*, hang in there. Any practice you engage in that helps shift your stress response from fight, flight, or freeze (such as mindfulness meditation, deep breathing, physical exercise, journaling, therapy or coaching, being in nature, and so on) to a "friendlier" stress response will bring you closer to starting from a place of emotional regulation. This means you can get right to problem-solving rather than pausing to pour your energy into bringing your emotions under control.

That said, I want to emphasize that first tending to your emotions— what psychologists refer to as emotion-focused coping—isn't some second-class response to dealing with stress. In fact, it can be more effective than problem-focused coping in dealing with stressors that are out of our control. Let's say you learn you're going to be laid off. This is an event that's entirely out of your control—there's nothing you can do to problem-solve a reversal of this corporate decision— and, naturally, you're going to experience a lot of strong emotions in response to such a scary situation. This is exactly the time for emotion-focused coping. You need to accept and regulate your strong emotional response before dealing with the stressor itself. No one can engage in problem-solving when they're melting down.

The trick is not to get stuck there. Emotion-focused coping becomes problematic when it's used as a means of avoidance. If you spend all your time and energy trying to manage or change how you feel about a situation, you delay or maybe even never get around to addressing the stressor that set you off. Further, many of the ways people use emotion-focused coping as avoidance—such as withdrawal, suppressing emotions, denial, giving up, or using substances like alcohol, drugs, or food—come with their own set of negative consequences, which means you further compound your stress.

This brings us back to the folks with burnout immunity. As a group, the differences I noted in them are these: 1) Their general outlook is to view stressors as a surmountable challenge or a problem that can be solved (that is, they take the challenge response to stress). 2) When a stressor hits, they're more likely to turn to problem-focused coping. 3) When they do engage in emotion-focused coping, they tend to spend less time in this response and more time engaged in problem-solving. Put another way, they get to problem-focused coping more quickly.

Bottom line: People with great emotional regulation skills fully experience strong emotions in high-stress situations, but they don't get hijacked by them. They can manage through strong emotion without becoming overwhelmed, enabling them to find solutions to the problem that stressed them out in the first place.

HOW TO PRACTICE EMOTIONAL REGULATION STRATEGY #1

- **Acknowledge and attend to your emotional needs.** When we're triggered and overwhelmed, we can't think clearly or take effective action. So find time to check in with what you're feeling, put a little space between you and the stressor, and take measures to move back into your window of tolerance. Deep breathing, going for a walk, calling a friend, or visualizing yourself in a state of calm equilibrium are all great ways to meet your emotional needs in the midst of a high-stress moment.
- **Ask for help.** Isolating when the shit hits the fan is almost always counterproductive. Reach out for support in managing your emotions and in dealing with the stressor. (Remember, problem-solvers surround themselves with other problem-solvers, and they achieve solutions more quickly.)
- **Assess if the stressor is in your control, even in part.** Especially when emotions are running high, it can feel like you have no agency in a situation and no possibility of affecting an outcome. But look a little further and you may find unexpected solutions. One of my clients panicked when his star

team member quit abruptly. He couldn't convince her to stay, and he assumed the project she led would have to be scrapped. But after he calmed down, he realized that although retaining this employee was out of his control, he could reassign her workload among other team members while working to backfill this key position.

- **Acknowledge what IS in your control and give that your full attention**. Those with burnout immunity don't waste time dwelling on what they can't control; they look to what they *can* control and give that their attention and energy. (Refer back to pages 72–73 for a refresher on what you can and can't control.)

- **Accept what is out of your control**. This can be very difficult, but it's a fact that some things simply aren't in our control and never will be. Once you accept this reality, you can move on to problem-solving for what is in your control. My client couldn't control his star employee's thoughts or actions. But he could control his response, which led to finding a solution to the workflow problem her absence caused. (Which, by the way, alleviated a great deal of his stress!)

- **Adapt your negative or difficult emotions for a positive and productive outcome**. Fury can be repurposed into unmatchable motivation to right an injustice. Anxiety can be channeled into enormous energy for getting a task done. Frustration can help identify what doesn't work and be a galvanizing force for finding solutions. Find the upside to your difficult emotion, and capitalize on it.

EMOTIONAL REGULATION STRATEGY #2: PEOPLE WITH BURNOUT IMMUNITY PROACTIVELY MANAGE THEIR EMOTIONAL INVESTMENT IN WORK.

One of the main causes of burnout is becoming too emotionally invested in your work. Whether you're deeply dissatisfied at work, or you love your job and you're happily giving it your all, a lack of boundaries between work life and personal life can result in the kind of emotional exhaustion and energy depletion that's characteristic of burnout. A few signs that indicate you may be pouring too much of your emotional energy into your work include taking criticism too personally; working more hours than you're required to; working during off hours; your conversations outside of work are frequently about work; your thoughts are dominated by work; you're a people-pleaser; your self-esteem is dependent upon your work performance; or your main source of fulfillment comes from your job.

I've found that those with burnout immunity find ways to put limits on their emotional investment in work. This applies to those who are passionate about their work and willingly put in long hours and lots of mental energy, as well as to those who, for whatever reason, are unhappy with their jobs and feel they don't have the option to leave. Both groups need to take special precautions to protect themselves. See the exercise "When You've Evolved, but Your Organization Hasn't" for more on this topic.

HOW TO PRACTICE EMOTIONAL REGULATION STRATEGY #2

- **Avoid people-pleasing.** That's a job with no quitting time and no end date.
- **Limit your time and your interactions with coworkers who are energy vampires or who have a negative or cynical attitude toward work.** Being around them is its own kind of emotional drain. Try to associate with coworkers who leave you feeling energized and positive.
- **Enact firm boundaries around work.** Block off spans of time in which you're not available, communicate those boundaries, and then stick to them.
- **Create and uphold emotional boundaries.** Take some time

after work—during your commute, for instance—to separate yourself from the events of the day and leave your emotional work baggage at your workplace. When you do have to engage in emotionally draining tasks, reserve time afterward to engage in healthy activities that will renew your emotional energy.

- **Stay grounded in your core identity**. People who over-identify with their work have difficulty separating themselves from their jobs. Who are you and what brings you joy outside of work? Make time for those things.
- **Try not to take things personally**. Remember that what may feel like a personal attack is often not about you but about your role.
- **Be proactive in getting and keeping yourself emotionally centered by connecting with people, places, and experiences that bring you a sense of peace**. A daily meditation or prayer practice, listing your gratitudes, yoga or another form of physical activity, short breaks throughout the workday, taking time off to disconnect from work, and speaking to people you trust are all great options.
- **Counteract negative emotional experiences with positive ones**. One police chief told me her Peloton rides aren't just for the health benefits; she gets pumped from the instructors' positive mental health messages. Another police chief said she turns to uplifting movies and music to boost her mood.

EXERCISE: WHEN YOU'VE EVOLVED, BUT YOUR ORGANIZATION HASN'T

Once you make the decision to work on your regulation skills, it will likely put you in a position where you recognize that you are changing, improving, and evolving, but your organization is stuck in the same old patterns. I've also heard similar frustrations from really experienced and engaged workers who struggle with increasing vulnerability to burnout. They have a high level of self-awareness, their regulation skills are strong, and they clearly see the mismatches between their needs and what their work environment can provide. The problem both groups are facing is that they feel powerless to change their work environment, leaving them vulnerable to burnout.

If you're convinced that your environment can't (or won't) ever change, it's time for some deep, honest self-reflection. Reflect upon: 1) what you are sacrificing for your job, 2) how much longer you're willing to make those sacrifices, 3) what you are absolutely not willing to give up or compromise on for your job, and 4) whether or not you should leave.

What does this reflection-gathering exercise reveal for you? Is your job demanding more of you than you're willing to give? Does your organization's mission, values, and/or culture resonate strongly enough with you that you're willing to make certain sacrifices? For how long? Are the mismatches you detect tolerable? For how long? Are the sacrifices you're making worth your investment of time, emotional energy, and effort?

Only you can answer these questions. But continued commitment to your regulation skills will give you the freedom of peace of mind, and will put you in the best position to make smart decisions about your future.

EMOTIONAL REGULATION STRATEGY #3: PEOPLE WITH BURNOUT IMMUNITY PRACTICE ADAPTIVE EMOTIONAL REGULATION.
Adaptive emotional regulation is something of a catch-all term that refers to proactive responses to stress that are characterized by growth, flexibility, enhanced mental health, and greater well-being. Adaptive emotional regulation practices move you toward health. Examples include problem-solving, planning, acceptance, seeking

help, positive reappraisal (reframing stressful events as benign or even beneficial), and self-compassion.

Contrast that with maladaptive coping practices, which may provide relief in the short term but always increase your stress in the long run. These responses move you away from health and include things like rumination, procrastination, substance use, avoidance, risk-taking behavior, and self-criticism.

There are countless research studies, journal articles, and books devoted to adaptive and maladaptive coping responses, emotional regulation skills, and helpful and unhelpful responses to stress. Here, however, I want to narrow our focus to the adaptive emotional regulation practices that I observed in my research participants and clients with burnout immunity, and that seem to be particularly effective in warding off burnout.

HOW TO PRACTICE EMOTIONAL REGULATION STRATEGY #3

- **Maintain awareness of your emotions in the midst of a stressful experience, and when you're reaching your tipping point**. Each of us has a set of "tells" that indicates when we're about to leave our window of tolerance and move into the distress zone. Rising anger or anxiety, a feeling of numbness or being "checked out," racing thoughts, the inability to think clearly, or bodily sensations such as an elevated heart rate, nausea, or dizziness are all tells that you're heading toward the distress zone. But the folks with burnout immunity are able to pinpoint unique or subtle indicators as well. A graphic designer, for instance, realized that when his stress levels were reaching the tipping point, his creativity suffered. A physician's assistant realized that her bouts of guilt that seemed to hit her "out of nowhere, for no reason at all" were actually associated with spikes in her stress levels. What are your tells?
- **Identify what you need to remain in your window of**

tolerance—and avail yourself of it. At first glance this may seem like an obvious point, but don't discount the massive amounts of self-awareness and presence of mind it requires to advocate for yourself in the midst of a highly stressful situation. When his stress levels threaten to compromise his effectiveness, one of my CMO participants relies on a practice he and his partner dubbed "Grounding on the Grounds." He goes for a walk around the hospital grounds while speaking to his partner for a "grounding" talk. (He does the same when his partner needs a little extra emotional support.) A corporate attorney distracts herself from the trigger that's escalating her stress by looking at family photos she keeps in her office—just a few moments are long enough for her to calm down and recenter herself, and then deal with the stressor with more equanimity and effectiveness.

- **Label your emotions**. Research has shown that simply putting words to our feelings diminishes emotional reactivity, in part because it helps separate us from the transient emotion we're experiencing. People with burnout immunity are able to label their emotions readily and accurately. A coaching client practices emotional labeling by pausing and saying internally, "This is irritation," or "I'm feeling pessimistic now," which helps her see the situation with more objectivity and less reactivity. It's also a reminder that the feeling is temporary; like all feelings, it will pass. To broaden your emotional vocabulary, check any of the online lists of emotions. I'm a fan of Brené Brown's 87 Human Emotions & Experiences and Susan David's Emotional Granularity Umbrellas; both are available for download from their websites.

- **Regulate and positively adapt your emotions during a crisis**. People with burnout immunity seem to be naturally good at this, but we can all learn this skill. One of the more extraordinary stories I heard was from a CMO who told me, "It's not uncommon for surgeons to storm into my office who are of the opinion that I am lowborn, stupid, and not worthy of continued life. And I just wait for them to get that out of their system, and then I say, 'Okay, so tell me your ideas for how we can work together to solve this.' I respond to the situation, not to the attack." That's some pretty serious emotional regulation! For the rest of us mere mortals, take heart: remaining coolheaded under pressure becomes easier with practice. Pausing to breathe deeply before you respond always helps, as does this CMO's practice of focusing on the situation, rather than on his emotions. Depending on the circumstances, you can also briefly remove yourself from the situation until you calm down, speak with a trusted advisor, or write down your thoughts and action plan before you get back to the situation.

- **Understand what triggers your emotional reaction to stress.** With this knowledge in hand, you can prepare ahead of time for situations you know will set you off and leave you vulnerable to an amygdala hijacking. (If you need a refresher, refer back to your answers to the "Awareness of Your Workplace Triggers" exercise on pages 91–92.) Of all the duties of her role, one deputy police chief finds disciplining insubordinate officers to be the most stressful. Ahead of these meetings, she makes sure she gets enough sleep, avoids caffeine, and spends several minutes mentally role-playing the conversation in her head.

- **Understand the underlying reasons you're triggered by certain situations.** Remember the physician's assistant who realized her inexplicable guilt was actually a stress response? Through therapy, she learned that this was a lingering reaction to a traumatic event she'd experienced in childhood. Now that the trigger and the response made sense, she didn't become alarmed and even more stressed when guilt resurfaced, and she was able to respond to herself with self-compassion. One of my coaching clients, an executive director at a nonprofit, was aware that he became unreasonably triggered when he had to meet with his board of directors. He would show up to meetings in a state of emotional dysregulation, feeling defensive, hypervigilant, and expecting the worst. Through some self-reflective journaling, he came to understand that the underlying reason for his emotional overreaction stemmed from his previous job. For years, the CEO would send him into board meetings with very limited information (which alone was stressful), where, frequently, he had to bear the brunt of the board's frustrations. Once he was able to realize that his present feelings had nothing to do with his present work environment, he was able to go into board meetings with a more relaxed, open-minded stance, which led to smoother relationships and greater productivity.

- **Learn to tolerate negative emotions without reacting impulsively.** This is a big one, and we're going to talk about regulating your actions in detail a little later. For now, here's an example. A CMO received news that execs in many fields dread: the board was slashing the budget. In his case, not only would this result in downsizing, it would compromise patient care. Understandably, he was livid. But he recognized that he was so triggered that nothing he said or did while he was in that state would be productive, and in fact could even be destructive. So, instead of firing off a letter of protest to every board member, donor, and leadership team member, he took care of himself first. "It was clear to me that I had to prioritize my emotional state," he said. "Absolutely nothing productive was going to happen if I responded while I was so triggered and pissed-off." So he tabled the situation for the entire weekend. He engaged in activities he enjoyed—hiking and going to the farmers' market and seeing a movie with his partner—and did not sit down to plan his formal response until he was no longer angry.

Regulating Your Thoughts to Maintain Clarity and Calm

One of the most powerful effects that come from regulating your emotions is the ability to slow your *thinking*. When our stress level is at a 7 and above, our brains are pretty much "offline." Researcher and professor Brené Brown defines this state of overwhelm as "an extreme level of stress, an emotional and/or cognitive intensity to the point of feeling unable to function." Brown points out there is an entire body of research indicating that we don't process emotional information accurately when we feel overwhelmed, which leads to poor decision-making. When our stress levels get that high and our hair is on fire, it can be difficult to have enough presence of mind even to figure out what would help.

This is an excellent time to slow your thinking down.

SLOW YOUR ROLL

If you haven't read *Thinking, Fast and Slow* by psychologist Daniel Kahneman, I urge you to do so. There's a reason it became a mega-bestseller and remains one of the top books in decision-making and problem-solving. Its applications also happen to offer a key insight into burnout prevention that many experts have missed. Here's a quick guide to fast and slow thinking to get you started.

One of Kahneman's most important observations is that our brains have two operating systems. Fast thinking, what Kahneman refers to as System 1 thinking, is unconscious and automatic. It happens effortlessly, with little to no sense of voluntary control. Its job is to assess a situation and deliver updates, and it processes information very quickly—so quickly that we're not even aware we're thinking. Slow thinking, or System 2 thinking, on the other hand, is conscious, deliberate, rational, and logical. It requires effort, control, and intention. Its job is to seek information and make decisions, and as its name suggests, it occurs slowly, with our full awareness. System 1

decisions are intuitive and immediate. System 2 decisions are me-
thodical and take some time.

We may like to think of ourselves as rational, System 2 thinkers
who approach decisions with logic and conscious deliberation, but it
turns out that an overwhelming 98 percent of our thinking is System
1, fast thinking. This means that the vast majority of the time, our
mental processes are automatic and unreflective—they're irrational!
But don't panic—this is our brain doing us a favor. Human beings
typically face 35,000 or more decisions every single day, and most
of them are very low-stakes choices such as whether to eat toast or
eggs for breakfast, or whether to turn right or left at the bottom of
the stairs. System 1 thinking puts this multitude of small-stakes decisions on autopilot so we don't have to waste time and energy on
them. We need to preserve our time and energy for the large-stakes
decisions that require System 2 thinking. Fast, System 1 thinking is
the domain of habits and heuristics. Habits are the autopilot routines
that come about from familiar tasks, and heuristics are the mental
shortcuts our brains take in order to speed up the process of making
a decision and reaching an immediate goal.

We couldn't survive without System 1 thinking, but it's not without
its problems. Habits can be counterproductive or harmful, and heuristics can sometimes be flat-out wrong. Think of the problem of bias, for
example. It's incredibly easy—and incredibly common—to make a snap
judgment about someone based upon mere seconds in their presence.
As part of our basic survival mechanism, a snap judgment is useful: we
need System 1 thinking to be able to immediately detect a threat to our
survival. But what if you make a snap judgment about a hiring candi-
date that's wildly off the mark? Or a consequential business decision
that's based on a gut feeling that turns out to be wrong? In a nutshell,
that's the core danger of fast thinking, and it's why we need to become
more practiced at slow thinking, especially when the stakes are high
and we need to make consequential decisions.

This is where Kahneman's research links up with the experience
of burnout. Guess what locks us into fast thinking—what causes us to

make unconscious, emotion-based decisions, rather than conscious, fact-based decisions? Stress. And guess what happens when we make poor decisions that result in poor consequences? You've got it—more stress. Now play out this vicious cycle on an organizational level. If you've got a lot of stressed-out employees suffering from a lot of poor decisions based on fast, unreflective thinking, they'll continue perpetuating stress. Factor in emotional contagion and unrelenting, chronic stress, and you have exactly the kind of psychologically hazardous work conditions that become the breeding ground for burnout.

Now let's zoom in on the individual employee who's stuck in this high-stress environment. Their thinking gets stuck in fast mode, in System 1 thinking, where they're far more likely to commit errors, make decisions based on bias or wrong assumptions, lose the ability to see perspectives other than their own, or lapse into any of the myriad thinking traps (see page 120) we're prone to when we're stressed. A primary example is emotional reasoning, a negative thinking pattern that leads you to believe that the way you feel is an accurate reflection of reality. Emotional reasoning says, "I feel this way, therefore it must be fact." But in reality, the exact opposite is occurring: when we're triggered and our emotions are running high and our thoughts are running amok—in other words, when we're in a dysregulated state—it becomes nearly impossible to see a situation clearly, and thus to be able to make the right decision or take productive action.

Have you ever been 100 percent convinced that a problem at work was unsolvable, or that you absolutely couldn't get through a tough negotiation or see a challenging project through to the end? The situation may feel impossible in the moment, and you may fully believe it to be so, but the reality is that there are very few problems and challenges that aren't solvable, if you receive help and support. That's emotional reasoning at work, and it's the kind of error in thinking that occurs when we're highly stressed and locked into fast thinking.

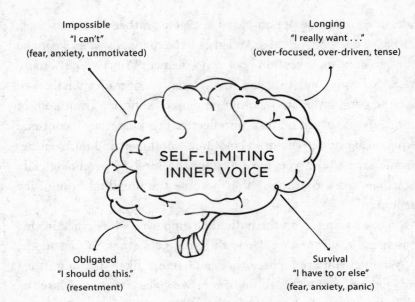

Impossible
"I can't"
(fear, anxiety, unmotivated)

Longing
"I really want . . ."
(over-focused, over-driven, tense)

SELF-LIMITING
INNER VOICE

Obligated
"I should do this."
(resentment)

Survival
"I have to or else"
(fear, anxiety, panic)

STRESS LOCKS US INTO FAST THINKING

Figure 4.2: The Inner Voice of Fast Thinking

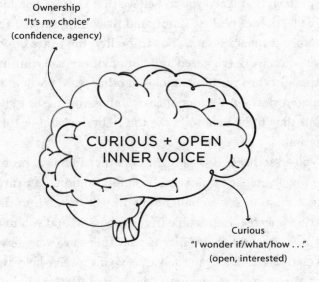

Ownership
"It's my choice"
(confidence, agency)

CURIOUS + OPEN
INNER VOICE

Curious
"I wonder if/what/how . . ."
(open, interested)

SLOW THINKING OPENS US TO POSSIBILITIES

Figure 4.3: The Inner Voice of Slow Thinking

Fast thinking that results from high stress often operates with a self-limiting voice. It says, "I can't," "This must happen this way," "I have no choice," or "I have to do this or else." It skews our vision to a pinpoint, and shuts down our capacity to be creative, open-minded, and empathetic. The inner voice of slow thinking, on the other hand, is curious, open, and full of agency. It says, "I have a choice here," "I'm open to multiple possibilities," and "I wonder what would happen if . . ." It's flexible, adaptable, and able to learn and innovate. People who are able to regulate their thoughts so as to engage in slow thinking are more effective at work, have higher job satisfaction, and are easier to work with than people whose thoughts—*and thus their attitudes and actions*—are in a dysregulated state. They are, bottom line, less vulnerable to burnout.

In the midst of high-stress situations, chronic or acute, how can we regulate our thoughts so we slow our thinking down and regain some clarity? Here are some techniques that work.

1. **Reach for a mantra.** When your hair's on fire and you need relief *right now*, a mantra can help calm your physical and emotional response to stress, and bring clarity to your thinking. In traditional meditation practices, a mantra is a repeated word or sound that helps you focus. Mantras are now used in a variety of contexts, including professional development, therapy, positive psychology, coaching, and mindfulness meditation practices. Find a word, phrase, or sentence that will help you focus on something other than the big, scary stressor in front of you. For even greater calm, link your mantra to your breath. For example, on the inhalation, say or think *peace within*, and on the exhalation, say or think *peace without*. I like to have a handful of different mantras ready to go, so I can arm myself with whatever fits the situation. Here are some of my favorites:

- One step at a time.
- Calm is contagious.

- Breathe in calm, breathe out tension.
- Breathe in confidence, breathe out worry.
- I am in charge of my stress response (*or* emotions, thoughts, or actions).
- All will be well.

2.   **Change your physical location.** You'd be surprised how effective this is in interrupting the stress response and bringing your focus to something other than what's triggering you. If you can get outside, all the better. My coaching client Sara has found a pretty ingenious way to get the same stress-reducing effect when she can't leave her location, though. When she's triggered by a rude email and her anxiety begins to escalate, Sara takes her hands off the keyboard and pushes her chair back from her desk. She breathes deeply until her heart and respiration rates slow, and her emotions and thoughts settle. Not only does this calm her down, but it also prevents her from firing off an email she'll regret later.

3.   **Recall memories that evoke positive emotions.** Research has shown that in an experience of acute stress, just reminiscing over a happy memory has a buffering effect against stress and an immediate positive effect on mood. Not only does recalling the happy memory reduce cortisol levels; it increases connectivity in the brain's prefrontal cortex, an area responsible for emotional regulation. If you need mental cues, create a photo album dedicated to moments when you were relaxed and happy. Pictures of your family, a vacation, or your pet are great things to include.

4.   **Laugh.** Whether it's an LOL or a private snicker, laughter has an immediate stress-busting effect. It lowers cortisol, blood pressure, heart rate, and respiration rate, and triggers the release of endorphins, the body's "feel-good" hormones. So turn to whatever it is that tickles your funny bone—cat videos on

TikTok, your favorite meme account, videos of your favorite comedian, funny movies, or drop by to visit that coworker who cracks you up. I have a short video of my sister Jodi and me "Elaine-style" dancing at my niece's wedding that never fails to make me laugh. I've turned to it plenty of times when I'm feeling tense and need to reset my mood.

5. **Try breathing exercises**. When I first began learning about how breathing can ameliorate stress and anxiety, I was skeptical. My stress, I thought, was no match for a little deep breathing! But wow, was I ever wrong, and I can't tell you how much comfort it brings me to know that we have immediate access to a technique that can stop stress in its tracks. There are a number of breathing exercises available (a quick Google search offers plenty), but one of my favorites is the classic 4–7–8 technique. Simply inhale for a count of four, hold for a count of seven, and exhale for a count of eight. Any type of mindful, diaphragmatic breathing will bring immediate calm and, when you practice it regularly, truly has life-changing potential.

6. **Distract yourself**. Psychologist Gretchen Schmelzer points out that when your emotions are irritated or your thoughts are stuck on an endless loop, sometimes the best thing is to give your overstimulated and stressed-out brain a time to rest and reset. So focus on anything other than the stressor, strong emotion, or thought loop. "Distraction," she says, "can be very healing. It's the emotional equivalent of putting your brain in a sling." She advises her clients to create a list of helpful distractions that will be ready to go the next time stress hits and your brain goes haywire. Change your activity, change your location, put on music, watch a video, be among people, tackle a project, read to your kids, go for a walk. These are all healthy options that can interrupt a cycle of feeling overwhelmed and stuck.

AVOID AND BREAK FREE FROM THINKING TRAPS

Fast thinking leaves us vulnerable to thinking traps. Also known as thought traps, thinking errors, cognitive errors, or cognitive distortions, these are patterns of negative thinking that give us an inaccurate perception of reality.

I sometimes refer to these unproductive, faulty patterns of thinking as self-induced stress traps, because they absolutely do create and amplify avoidable stress. If not managed, they make us even more vulnerable to burnout. A classic example is should statements. This thinking trap occurs when we tell ourselves that things really *should* (or should not) be a certain way, with no exceptions, and with no regard to the actual circumstances. "I should be more like Bob." "I should have known better." "I shouldn't be making mistakes." "They should be able to handle this by now."

Should statements impose a set of expectations on ourselves or others that aren't likely to be met, because they aren't grounded in reality. Is it really possible to make zero mistakes, for instance? Of course not, and believing that you should be flawless sets you up for a lot of self-blame, shame, and guilt. Thinking traps lead us to see everything around us—events, people (and their motivations), our own selves—in a distorted, irrational manner. It's only natural, then, that the decisions and actions we take based on a thinking trap's erroneous version of reality will result in negative consequences, more negative thinking, and, no surprise, more stress.

Researchers have even documented a direct neurobiological link between negative thinking and stress. In a study of people with major depression (which is characterized by negative thoughts, low mood, and loss of interest), researchers found higher levels of cortisol and lower levels of oxytocin. What's more, there was a direct positive correlation between cortisol levels and the frequency and strength of participants' negative thoughts. Put simply, the more often the research participants fell prey to thinking traps, and the more they believed in them, the higher their stress. Left unchecked, thinking traps can lead to or intensify anxiety and depression, make us feel helpless, and result in self-defeating behaviors. At work, they can leave us feeling ineffective and unsure of ourselves, and can impair our ability to problem-solve, communicate effectively, and make sound decisions. And, as always, the longer we remain in the grip of the thinking trap, the worse the outcome, both internally (higher and more prolonged stress, cynicism, self-doubt) and externally (low performance, inefficacy, tunnel vision, poor decisions).

There are many, many thinking traps, but here are the top five that have come up most frequently among my clients, students, and research participants. See if you recognize yourself in any of these. The very first step in breaking free of a thinking trap is to become aware that you've been ensnared.

• **The negative filtering trap**. This one earns my number one spot in the thinking trap lineup because it's a powerful burnout accelerator. When we're caught up in negative filtering, we focus exclusively (and often excessively) on the negative aspects of a situation, rendering us unable to see any positives. When negative filtering gets bad enough, it can trick us into thinking that *we* have no positive qualities. My coaching client Kristin once showed up on a call visibly distraught. Through tears, she launched into a story about getting a terrible performance review, spending the rest of the week dwelling on every line of the tough feedback—and ultimately deciding she wasn't qualified for her job and her only option was to quit. In her shock, disappointment, and panic, all she could see was this single poor review, never mind her otherwise exemplary track record for more than six years at her firm.

This is an example of acute, and quite drastic, negative filtering that was triggered by a painful event. Now imagine the outcomes if negative filtering burrows into your thinking and you *habitually* dwell on the negative at the expense of the positive. (Remember, what sticks around grinds you down.) Negative filtering at work can look like ruminating on difficult feedback, becoming fixated on your co-workers' or employees' weaknesses, becoming fixated on *your* weaknesses, making a small mistake and assuming that the entire project/speech/task was a disaster, or missing a deadline or a detail and assuming that you're incompetent. Not only does negative filtering give us a distorted view of reality, but it escalates our stress and seriously undermines our performance. Getting stuck in this thinking trap often creates a vicious cycle, as negativity begets more negativity, ultimately resulting in the kind of deep cynicism and pessimism that characterizes burnout.

To get free of this trap, examine the actual evidence around you. If you're far into the negativity spiral or, like Kristin, your emotions and thoughts are out of control and your brain is "offline," enlist the help of an objective observer. Does a single poor review *really* negate all your previous exceptional work and indicate that you're incompetent and you should quit your job? Does one bad grade *really* mean you're stupid and you should drop out of school? Of course not.

It also helps to counteract your negative thinking by recollecting all the positive things around you. Again, examining the evidence can help. Kristin, for example, had six years' worth of positive reviews she could examine. If you don't have that kind of hard evidence, make a list of things you're grateful for—and they can be very, very small things. Look around your immediate surroundings and find five things you're grateful for—your favorite pen, the plant on your desk, the socks you're wearing, the sunlight coming through the window, the glass of water within reach—which quickly resets your mood. Research shows that practicing gratitude increases positive emotions, optimism, and self-esteem, while decreasing stress, depression, and cynicism.

- **The "This is impossible!" trap.** When this thinking trap besets you, you convince yourself that whatever is before you can't be achieved or solved. We tend to fall into this trap when we're already overextended and stressed-out, leaving us convinced it's impossible to make any progress. Emotions can run high and fast thinking sets in; those who get caught in the "This is impossible!" trap react to stressors with a sense of overwhelm and defeat. When we're in its grip, we can't have an objective view of the situation or determine a suitable course of action—or sometimes, determine *any* course of action, resulting in paralysis and ineffectiveness.

When things seem impossible, one of the best things you can do is to choose the tend-and-befriend response to stress and reach out to others. This particular thinking trap flourishes when we're isolated. Not only can others help us get a more objective, realistic view of the situation (most work challenges are solvable), but they can help us make progress on our goals. And remember, even micro steps are a powerful antidote to feelings of defeat, cynicism, and resignation. Break your task into very small steps, and act on them one by one. When we take the time to move past our first, automatic reaction of feeling that nothing can be done, and we couple that with reaching out for help, we can break free of this trap and avoid burning out.

- **The unrealistic expectations trap.** Shooting for the moon is okay, but it's easy to fall into this trap when you set expectations so high that you're not giving yourself a fair chance. Maybe you told yourself you'd be a CEO by age twenty-seven, or you'd get a promotion every two years without fail. Maybe you said you'd write that book in three months because your favorite author did it. Maybe the story you've been telling yourself is that true success means retiring by the age of forty.

When we set unrealistic expectations, it can lead us to being too hard on ourselves, overworking, not getting enough time to rest and recharge, and feeling disappointed, frustrated, and self-critical when we don't meet these unreachable goals. Chronically pursuing unrealistic expectations can lead to cynicism, apathy, and ineffectiveness—why keep going when nothing ever seems to work out?

If you fall into this trap, try setting smaller, more attainable goals. Progress is still progress, and achieving any goal means you'll feel less stressed, more confident, and more energized to continue. Nothing feels better than getting items crossed off a to-do list!

It works the same way when it comes to our expectations of others. Like you, they have strengths and things they struggle with. Instead of asking "Why can't they just finish it ASAP?" or "Why didn't they learn this yesterday?" remind yourself that what's easy to you may not come easily to others. Plus, they've got their own workload to deal with, and their priorities may not be the same as yours.

Getting free of the unrealistic expectations trap will require relinquishing a certain degree of control, and becoming aware of our limits. When examining your expectations, ask yourself if you really have the control over the situation that the expectation demands. Is it really within your power to become a CEO by twenty-seven? Can you really expect everyone on your team to outperform their revenue target from last quarter? Can you really expect to write a book in three months when you have a full-time job? Knowing our limits, and realizing when we've been caught in the unrealistic expectations trap, doesn't mean we're unskilled or that we're admitting defeat. It means we're employing a powerful awareness skill that ultimately will lead to greater ease and happiness, and far less stress and burnout.

- **The hero trap.** This thinking trap leads you to believe that things will completely fall apart if you (in your designer superhero cape and tights) don't swoop in and save the day. You may think, *No one else can do this, so I have to*, or *This will never get done unless I do it*. Sometimes, the hero trap comes disguised as conscientiousness: *I need to rescue my struggling colleague*. And let's face it, *all* of these patterns of thinking are rooted in the desire to control things. This path can feel rewarding in the short term—you're being productive, you're helping someone, you feel needed, you feel in control—but as you take on more and more responsibility (and stress!), you risk putting yourself on the burnout expressway.

If you fall into this trap, it's important to remind yourself that you literally *can't* do it all. You need to tend to your own work, and a habit of rushing in and rescuing others guarantees that you'll be spread too thin. Try asking yourself if you're the best person to spearhead that project or task, or if you're even really needed there.

Furthermore, nor *should* you do it all. Remember, when you swoop in and problem-solve for someone, you're depriving them of the opportunity to become more skilled and knowledgeable. If you struggle with delegating, try letting go of control in small steps and eventually working your way up. Let your direct report write the first draft of the memo, for instance, or make yourself available as a guide rather than a member of the delivery team. Remember, big goals require a team effort, and part of a leader's job is to delegate and empower their team. Taking on the burden of executing on every step of the process, or micromanaging every step, can quickly lead to exhaustion, cynicism, and burnout—and it undermines *others'* sense of control, increasing their risk of burnout.

- **The catastrophizing trap.** When we're ensnared by this thinking trap, we're convinced that the worst will happen, even though there's little or no evidence to suggest it. Your boss's request for a one-on-one means you're getting fired, a dip in the market means your 401(k) will be wiped out, the bullet point you left out of a slide means everyone thinks you're incompetent and you'll never get promoted.

Catastrophizing can quickly spiral out of control and lead you to worry about increasingly outlandish scenarios. I once convinced myself that my son, who was fifteen minutes late and hadn't called to explain, had died in a fiery, fifteen-car pileup on the freeway. Where did my mind come up with fifteen cars and a fiery crash? From the sick depths of Anxiety Hell, that's where!

This is the very nature of catastrophizing. The *only* fact I had was that my normally responsible son was late, with no explanation. From there I leapt to the worst possible cause, which, of course, held not a shred of truth. He strolled in moments later, perplexed as to why I looked wild-eyed and red-faced. It was just traffic, and he'd left his phone at his friend's house.

One of the best ways to stop catastrophic thinking is to do whatever you can to get yourself out of your head and ground yourself in the present moment. Gretchen Schmelzer's distraction tip (page 119) is a great example. I also know people who literally say aloud, "Stop!" when they catch themselves in this thinking trap. Do anything that takes your attention away from your spiraling thoughts and keeps your focus on the here and now. Get up and walk around, call a friend, become aware of five things in your surroundings you see, five things you hear, five things you smell, and so on. These grounding activities arrest the catastrophizing, at least for a moment.

Then, when you have a little more clarity and a little less stress, you can try to look at the situation more objectively. Your boss has requested one-on-one meetings plenty of times, for instance. Has that ever resulted in you getting canned? Nope! You're still here, ready to give it a go for another day.

DON'T GET CONNED BY YOUR INNER IMP

Before we move on from our discussion on thoughts, there's one more topic that I want to be sure to address. That is the nearly universal experience of having your own thoughts turn against you. I'm referring to the negative self-talk that chatters away in our minds.

It seems that each of us has an inner critic that just loves to call attention to our flaws, remind us of the embarrassing thing we said ten years ago, compare us unfavorably to others, or point out something hurtful or confidence-killing. There's hardly a quicker way to feel emotionally depleted, disempowered, and discouraged than to buy into these thoughts.

Our inner negative voice goes by many different names. The inner critic, the judging self, the saboteur, the superego, or, as I sometimes refer to it, the inner imp. Whatever you call it, it's a self-destructive force that makes us doubt ourselves or the people around us, focuses our attention on negative (and often cruel) thoughts and self-judgments, and encourages self-defeating behavior. "You're stupid," "you'll never belong," "you're incompetent," and "no one will ever love/accept/hire/appreciate/approve of you" are perennial favorites. The inner critic is expert in knowing how to get us exactly where it hurts, which is a sad reality indeed, as most of the time, its litany isn't even true!

My inner imp's specialty is impostor syndrome. It loves to tell me that I don't deserve my success, or that I don't belong in various places—in college, in grad school, or, these days, teaching at an Ivy League institution or participating in an invitation-only speakers' association, for example. I made a real breakthrough when my executive coach asked me a simple yet powerful question one day after I described how my inner critic had (yet again) stolen my self-confidence: "And how's that working for you, Kandi?" she said. By that point I'd done quite a bit of therapy as well as professional development, and her question was literally all it took for me to snap into awareness and recognize that all of that negative self-talk was doing more harm than good. Now when my inner imp tries to barge its way back in, it's much easier for me to counter its untruths with some good old-fashioned, plain talk: my educational and professional track records speak for themselves, thanks very much, and I deserve to have the opportunities I've worked so hard for.

Here's an important word to the wise, though: don't try to fight fire with fire. Criticizing the inner critic, or speaking to it as harshly as it speaks to you, is one of the fastest ways to get stuck in a negativity spiral—and one of the fastest ways to spike your stress levels. Think about it: if "You're an idiot and you'll never get this" is playing on a loop in your head, you're already stressed and feeling terrible about yourself . . . and then you pile on more self-criticism for being self-critical. Research psychologist and self-compassion expert Dr. Kristin Neff says this renders us "both the attacker and attacked," which creates what we most want to avoid—chronic stress.

Trust me, you're not going to criticize, badger, or shame your inner critic into silence. Really, the most effective way to approach your inner critic is with patience and abundant self-compassion. I know how difficult that can be, but consider the alternative. For years I'd feel even shittier about myself when I realized I'd succumbed to my inner critic's lies. "Jeez, I fell for it *again*," I'd think, or "Ugh, I wasted so much time fretting over this!" It's what I call the inner critic after-party: Rather than stopping to celebrate that I had become aware of my inner critic's mental tricks, I dwelled on the fact that I'd been bamboozled yet again . . . which practically gave my inner critic an exclusive VIP invitation to waltz right back in. It's a vicious cycle of self-recrimination, guilt, and wasted time.

But guess what stops that cycle? Genuine self-compassion. I still marvel over how powerful a force it is. Neff has found that people who approach themselves with self-compassion are much less likely to be stressed, depressed, and anxious, and more likely to be happy, resilient, and optimistic. Extending compassion to yourself actually lowers cortisol levels and increases heart rate variability, an indicator of cardiovascular fitness and higher resilience to stress. It's no coincidence that all of these positive effects are exactly what we need to develop burnout immunity!

Here are five easy ways to start practicing self-compassion today.

1. **Use releasing statements**. When you catch yourself engaging in negative thinking, such as "I really blew it today and this confirms I'm incompetent," try releasing yourself from that feeling with a positive, caring counterthought: "It's okay that I'm upset about this, anybody would be."

2. **Use goal-focused affirmations**. Rather than general positive affirmations, try a more specific, goal-focused affirmation that will motivate you to change (and may be more believable besides). For example, instead of "I love myself just as I am," try "I am learning to practice self-acceptance." Instead of "I am a kind and loving person," try "I will treat myself with the same love and kindness I would use with my closest friend."

3. **Try Kristin Neff's Self-Compassion Break**. You can find full instructions (along with many other self-compassion exercises) on Neff's website, but here's a short version. First, identify a situation that's stressing you out, and take a moment to feel the effects of that stress in your body. Then say to yourself, "This is a moment of suffering." (Feel free to adapt any of these phrases; for this one, you could simply say, "This is stress," or "This is difficult.") Next, acknowledge that everyone experiences difficulty: "Suffering is a part of life," or "Everyone struggles." Finally, extend compassion to yourself: "May I be kind to myself," or "May I be strong."

4. **Practice metta (lovingkindness) meditation**. This is an ancient practice that helps us recognize our common humanity and send lovingkindness to all beings, including ourselves. You can find many metta guides online, along with many variations on the phrases to use, but an extremely simple version can be practiced like this: After taking several deep breaths to center yourself, say (or think), "May I be happy. May I be well. May I be safe. May I be peaceful and at ease." Then repeat these statements with regard to a loved one, an acquaintance or stranger, a person with whom you struggle, and finally, all people or all beings. It's also perfectly fine simply to practice metta for yourself.

5. **Give your self-talk the friend test**. It can be enormously helpful to gain perspective on your negative thoughts by considering their effect on a loved one. For example, would you say, "You're really an idiot and everyone thinks so" to your bestie?

Your partner? Your child? No! Many of us reserve our most cruel judgments and thoughts for our own selves. If your self-talk doesn't pass the friend test, there's no reason you should be subjecting yourself to it.

Regulating Your Behavior Is a Burnout Immunity Superpower

In a way, all the regulation skills we've been learning have been leading to this point: regulation of your actions during high-stress moments. Emotions, thoughts, and actions are inextricably intertwined, and their impact on each other flows in all directions (that is, behavior affects thoughts just as much as thoughts affect behavior). But it's from a regulated state that you have the greatest potential for behavioral change, and your behavior at work is where the rubber meets the road. Regulated emotions and thoughts empower regulated words, attitudes, and actions.

When all systems are flowing optimally—you feel calm, positive, and in control—you also have the greatest chance of immunizing yourself against burnout, and, through the mechanism of emotional contagion, of extending that anti-burnout effect to your coworkers.

FREEDOM FROM IMPULSIVELY REACTIVE BEHAVIORS

There are a million ways that unregulated and unhealthy behaviors show up at work. These impulsive, destructive behaviors are extremely common, and often they're a direct result of being in a dysfunctional system or toxic work environment. Colin, my coaching client we met in Chapter 3, is a perfect example. Normally a very easygoing guy who's capable of regulating his emotions, thoughts, and actions, he reached a breaking point after being stuck in a toxic system. The high-stress conditions made him act in ways that he normally wouldn't, such as raising his voice at his direct reports and blaming others for his mistakes. So while certainly, each of us is responsible for our actions and their consequences, cut yourself a little slack if you find yourself behaving in ways that aren't typical. It's likely the result of the system you're embedded in.

My research uncovered a number of behaviors that constitute unhealthy, counterproductive, or even destructive responses that emerge in moments of high stress. These are what I call **Impulsively Reactive Behaviors**:

- lashing out at someone
- sacrificing your integrity by stooping to someone else's level
- saying something you regret
- taking credit for someone else's work
- copying "all" on a nastygram to show everyone how ticked off you are
- reverting to competitive behaviors when you should be collaborating instead
- making inaccurate assumptions and/or jumping to irrational conclusions
- blaming others to take the focus off you

Not only do these behaviors fail to help us, but they make us feel even more stressed, and sow bad feelings among our teams and organizations. In addition to the original stressor, you now feel bad about yourself, regret your actions, and often feel overcome with shame— all of which spikes our stress levels.

A CMO I interviewed once publicly took credit for someone else's work during a hugely stressful leadership meeting where he felt intense pressure to perform. It wasn't a premeditated act, but rather "a crime of opportunity" that happened when one of the other executive-level leaders assumed the CMO had spearheaded a new initiative— and he failed to correct her. For the remainder of the meeting, the CMO told me, "It's like I was only half there. I kept thinking about how much this was going to hurt the person who designed and launched the program. I spent the rest of the day and all night racked with regret, shame, and guilt."

The next morning, he met with the person whose work he'd taken credit for. "I offered zero excuses," he said. "Internally, I realized I'd been incredibly stressed-out, and that any narcissistic tendencies I have reared their heads in that moment and I failed to rein them in. But to her I just said, 'You're absolutely right. I made a mistake, and I'm going to make this right.' So that's exactly what I did. I emailed the entire leadership team, apologized for my mistake, and gave credit to the right person. I immediately felt better, and I have never made that mistake since."

We've all acted in ways that are out of character when we're under enormous stress and our thoughts and feelings are dysregulated, such as what we saw with my coaching client Colin or this CMO, who was normally a person of integrity.

But we also all have a set of default responses to stress that we fall back on. Usually the origins of these automatic, unconscious responses can be traced to childhood, where we learned them from caregivers. The ones that stuck with us and that we still rely on today were reinforced as we grew into adulthood. In other words, these responses, whether they're positive or negative, constructive or destructive, *worked* to alleviate our stress. Then the brain, ever on a quest for both equilibrium and efficiency, noted the response's effectiveness and will turn to it again the next time stress hits. Deployed enough times, the brain encodes this response as a habit, and voila, you have an automatic, default response to stress.

Now, if your defaults are healthy and have positive effects—say you engage in some deep breathing when stress hits, go for a stroll, or do a guided meditation—that's all well and good, and you can skip on down to the next section. But if the defaults you learned are unhealthy and have negative consequences—substance use, overworking, or avoidance, for example—then it's time to learn a new way to respond.

Getting unstuck from ingrained stress-response patterns is no small task, and many of us will find ourselves resistant to change. It feels good to protect our old ways of doing things, after all—change can be scary and inertia can be a formidable obstacle, not to mention that some destructive default responses are addictive. But remember, even though an unhealthy stress response lessens our anxiety temporarily, the reality is that sooner or later, it will backfire. These responses are often quite self-destructive, and paradoxically, they heighten our long-term stress. And when stress becomes chronic, it raises our risk of burnout.

I want to emphasize that becoming familiar with our automatic, impulsively reactive behaviors should not be a guilt- or shame-inducing exercise. Actually, you should applaud yourself for becoming more self-aware, and for doing the work you need to do to become unstuck, and ultimately, become more effective at work. Treat yourself with as much self-compassion as you can muster. If negative self-talk arises, respond gently, with patience and compassion. And remember: you're engaging in an act of compassion for others as well. When you show up in a state of emotional and mental regulation, and your actions reflect that internal state, you are at your most effective and engaged, the kind of person people love to work with, and who can move mountains at work.

Impulsively reactive behaviors often manifest in what I like to call protective patterns. Here's an exercise that will help you identify your protective patterns, and whether you have a tendency to "rev up" or "shut down" under pressure.

EXERCISE: IDENTIFY YOUR PROTECTIVE PATTERNS

STEP 1

Think about your behavior patterns when under pressure. Which of the following are most like you? Check all that apply to you.

	INTERNALIZE	EXTERNALIZE
APPROACH	I throw myself into work and work longer hours than normal I say yes to new projects or roles even if I don't have the time I have increasingly high expectations of myself and others I can't say "no," even if I want to I perceive other people to be lazy	I turn into a know-it-all If someone disagrees with me, I ignore them or make them regret disagreeing People closest to me agree with me more often than usual I dig my heels in after I make a decision I believe only I have the right plan or answer
AVOID	I retreat: to my office, my work, my thoughts and concerns I start to detach from relationships My communication becomes shorter and more direct I communicate only "essential" information I don't need input from others I feel like other people just get in the way	I overfocus on negative aspects of a situation I wear anger and disappointment as a badge of honor I get annoyed by people who want things to change or have hope I blame the situation or other people for my mood I commiserate and complain with like-minded people

STEP 2

Circle the five check marks that indicate your primary ways of dealing with life and work when you are stressed. These are your protective patterns—they help you defend yourself from your stressors and may inhibit change. The next step will help you unravel the impact of those habits.

STEP 3

List your top five protective patterns and note whether they are linked with approaching or avoiding issues or your emotions, and whether you tend to internalize or externalize your responses.

MY PROTECTIVE PATTERNS:

1. _____
2. _____
3. _____
4. _____
5. _____

For each: Do I approach or avoid? Internalize or externalize?

STEP 4

Write some notes about how your patterns affect you as well as others.

How my protective patterns affect my physical and psychological well-being, my performance, and my ability to learn and adapt:

_____

How my protective patterns affect my team, close colleagues, family, and my organization's culture:

_____

_____

Once we're able to take a big step back to examine our protective patterns and how they are (or aren't!) working for us, we can begin to experiment with more productive and intentional responses. The goal here is to move from impulsive reaction (the default response I'm used to doing) to intentional response (the thoughtful response that would actually help me and others).

CULTIVATE INTENTIONALLY RESPONSIVE BEHAVIORS

Among my coaching clients and research participants with burnout immunity, I observed a number of behaviors that constitute healthy, productive responses they turn to in moments of high stress. These are what I call **Intentionally Responsive Behaviors**. These folks are able to:

- remain in their window of tolerance most of the time, and return quickly when they leave it.
- accept and tolerate negative emotions. It may seem paradoxical that those who can accept and tolerate their negative emotions should experience less negative emotion, but research bears this out. It seems that acceptance helps keep us from reacting to—and thus worsening—our negative mental experiences. The more we use this healthy coping habit, the stronger the protective effect, and the less reactive we are to stress.
- remain calm, composed, and patient when faced with uncertainty or triggered by a stressor. Instead of reacting impulsively to stress (lashing out, backstabbing, gossiping, withdrawing, blaming, etc.), folks with burnout immunity are able to pause before they react, remain coolheaded as they formulate a thoughtful response, and only then respond.
- recognize when their emotional investment in work is becoming harmful, and take steps to curtail it.
- seek to understand other people's perspectives, and not find differences of opinion threatening. This is a valuable skill that those with burnout immunity use regularly, but it becomes especially important when they disagree with someone. Seeking clarity on others' perspectives demonstrates respect, and precludes a great deal of conflict, which is inherently stressful.

- focus on what they can control. Instead of getting hung up on all the things they cannot change, which creates frustration, a sense of helplessness, and negativity, they home in on the things they can change and improve.
- embrace change rather than brace for change. Instead of resisting change, which escalates stress and the risk of burnout, they approach change with optimism and even curiosity. They are highly adaptable and flexible.
- handle conflict with others in a mature and productive way. They do not avoid conflict, but rather see it as an opportunity to bring different perspectives and ideas into the workplace and into productive discussion.
- maintain supportive relationships. People who have high levels of social support are more resilient to stress, gain a calming effect from the oxytocin released during social interactions, and have a greater sense of belonging, which protects against stress, anxiety, depression, and burnout.
- ask for help. Whether it's coworkers, mentors, loved ones, therapists, coaches, managers, clergy, or trusted advisors in other professions, they proactively ask for help when they need it.
- more quickly engage in problem-solving. Rather than getting hung up on frustration, self-pity, anger, or cynicism, they turn to problem-solving and deal directly with the stressor.

I'll add that overall, they make regulation of their emotional, mental, and physical energy a habit, which means they have enough in reserve to take on hard challenges.

I bet you have many things in common with these folks—much more than you realize. The following exercise will help reveal burnout prevention skills and strategies you may not even realize you have.

EXERCISE: ME AT MY BEST UNDER STRESS

Allow 15–20 minutes for this self-reflective writing exercise. Think about a time when you dealt with a stressful work experience really well. Close your eyes and try to imagine yourself in that situation. Recall as many details as you can, and then answer the following questions.

- What emotions were you feeling?
- In what ways were you able to regulate your emotions?
- What were you thinking?
- What thinking traps, if any, did you notice? How did you manage them?
- What was your response to the stressful situation? What, specifically, did you do?
- In what ways were you able to respond intentionally versus react impulsively?
- Who and what was supporting you? How did they support you?

Now, think deeply about your answers.

- What feelings or sensations are you experiencing now, in this moment, as you do this exercise?
- What did you learn about yourself when you were at your best under stress that can be applied to future stressful situations?

How to Fast-Track the Development of Your Regulation Skills

If you find yourself struggling or unable to break free from old patterns of behavior, consider the following support options to accelerate the development of your regulation skills.

1. **Surround yourself with people who are regulation super-**

stars. Not only can you learn from their example, but their positive energy is inspirational and infectious.

2. **Work with a cognitive behavioral therapy (CBT) provider**. All therapy takes time, but CBT is a form of psychotherapy that's designed to be results-driven, and now an option called intensive CBT (I-CBT) can work even more quickly for many issues.

3. **If trauma is keeping you stuck, explore Eye Movement Desensitization and Reprocessing (EMDR)**. This is an interactive form of psychotherapy conducted by a specially trained practitioner that helps you process deeply distressing emotions and memories. It's been shown to be effective in treating a variety of challenging mental health issues, such as post-traumatic stress disorder (PTSD), anxiety disorders, obsessive-compulsive disorders, and major depression.

4. **Work with an executive or leadership coach**. The International Coaching Federation defines coaching as "partnering with clients in a thought-provoking and creative process that inspires them to maximize their personal and professional potential." Coaching has been shown to lessen burnout, in part by increasing clients' self-efficacy and self-determination, and helping them see they have more control over their life circumstances and satisfaction than they typically realize. One of my doctoral students, Dr. Chris Bittinger, found that executive coaching helps clients develop their self-efficacy, improve their emotional intelligence, and enhance their ability to problem-solve their way through and around stressors. What's more, moderate to severe stress levels were *not* highly correlated with burnout—so long as clients were engaged in coaching.

5. **Engage in regular positive self-talk**. Whether you set aside time each day to mentally review positive thoughts or you write them down, make positive self-talk a habit. The key is to come up with self-talk that feels authentic and robust—rather than false, forced, or overly sentimental.

6. **Engage in mindfulness practices**:
* Try Mindfulness-Based Stress Reduction (MBSR), an extensively researched approach to meditation. Created by Dr. Jon Kabat-Zinn, this eight-week mindfulness meditation program has been shown to help alleviate symptoms of anxiety, depression, and chronic pain, reduce stress, and support overall psychological health and well-being. Group classes on MBSR are frequently offered at community centers, hospitals, and schools, and many free courses can be found online.
* Try Howard Stevenson's CLCBE method. Refer back to pages 93–94 for step-by-step instructions.
* Try metta (lovingkindness) meditation. See page 129 for a simple metta practice, or search online for guides.

The Regulation Payoff

When you are familiar with your default responses to stress and gain the ability to shift to the most effective stress response for each particular moment, you can reap the benefits of moderate stress while decreasing your time in the distress zone—all of which strengthens your burnout immunity. When you can calm your own emotions and bring clarity to your own thinking, you can see your environment for what it is, identify the mismatches between you and your organization that accelerate your path to burnout, and make smarter decisions about what you want to do.

But to me, the regulation payoff goes well beyond just protecting yourself from burnout. The ultimate goal of developing your regulation skills is to live a healthier, less-stressed life in which you are happy, fulfilled, energized, and making your greatest contribution. Regulated emotions, thoughts, and behaviors are superpowers when it comes to bringing your vision of your ideal self into being, and to living out your values. People who are living out of the state of calm equilibrium that regulation enables are positive forces who build healthy cultures that team members feel proud to be a part of. They spread good emotional contagion and lower the risk of burnout. They become resilient role models for their team members, their organizations, and their families. One of my biggest motivations to keep up with my regulation skills is to model for my children how to effectively deal with life's hassles, headaches, and hardships.

Ultimately, the practice of regulation is about caring—for ourselves, our coworkers, our organization, and the people our organization serves. It enables us to change our experience from one that is unpleasant, hard, or even horrible to one that helps us feel energized, engaged, and inspired to do our best work.

5

Purpose, People, and Values

The Effective Alchemy of Meaningful Connections

Robert G. Luna is the sheriff of Los Angeles County—the most populous county in the U.S., with close to 10 million residents—and the former chief of the Long Beach Police Department (LBPD). Luna has served nearly forty years in law enforcement, consistently ranked one of the most stressful careers in America. Yet of the many hundreds of people I've interviewed, he was not only one of the most coolheaded and serene (what my boys would call "chill"), he was also one of the most joyful. "I love the job so much," he told me. "I have always had a lot of fun." Likewise, regarding his time with the Long Beach SWAT team—that's Special Weapons and Tactics for you civilians—he told me he "just loved the work."

Luna has known since the age of five that he wanted to be a police officer. "I was always enamored with the idea of putting on a uniform and helping people," he said. "I always wanted to serve, and I wanted to be part of reframing the public perception of police." And after experiencing "bad policing" firsthand while growing up in a heavily patrolled neighborhood in East LA, he knew from a young age that he wanted to bring reform to law enforcement. "I have always had an image of what law enforcement *should* be," he said. "It pushed me to want to change things." When he met resistance along the way, he told me, it only motivated him to move up in the ranks.

When I first interviewed Luna, he was still Chief Luna with the LBPD, a role he'd held since 2014. It was September 2020, still the height of the pandemic, and just months after the murder of George Floyd sparked protests throughout the world against police brutality. "In thirty-five years," Luna said, "I haven't seen anything like it." It was like being on a roller coaster that started dropping in March 2020, he said, and hadn't yet stopped hurtling downward. As a long-time advocate for police reform, he understood protestors' anger and the urgent need for change, but he had "never imagined" the name-calling, the "sustained adrenaline rush" caused by constant media attacks on the police, and having protestors show up at his house while his family was present. To make matters worse, public officials who had always supported the police department were beginning to withdraw their support. "We've been raising our hand, begging for help" for years, Luna said, "and now it feels like no one's listening anymore." His response to my burnout survey indicated a stress level of 9 out of 10 (very severe), though he profiled as fully engaged (not ineffective, not disengaged, not overextended, and definitely not burned-out).

He was smack dab in the most stressful period of his career, and I was eager to understand how he got through it. His response struck me as a mini master class in applied emotional intelligence skills.

"I resist that temptation [to give up]," he said, "by always reminding myself why I wanted this job in the first place." Like many people with burnout immunity, Luna is exceptionally committed to his job—so much so that he experiences it as a sort of calling. His vision to bring systemic change to policing while also making his local community a safer place has sustained him through decades in a high-stress role. "This [job] is much higher than myself," he told me. "It's my job as a police chief to guide my people and my community through it."

To manage his stress, Luna regularly meditates, prays, and works out, adding more exercise as his stress climbs ("more stress, more fitness"). His general attitude is to "hunt for good," a phrase he used to describe how he sees the positives in challenging situations, and he's made a habit of leaving home early enough each day to see the sun come up. "The sunrise makes you really reflect," he said. Likewise, when his stress spikes at work, he turns to nature. "I've learned when I'm really, really stressed, I need to go outside for a walk," he said. "The fresh air, the trees . . . really relieve a lot of pressure. It's very rare that I come home stressed."

I found Luna's awareness of the impact of his stress on others particularly impressive. When he goes home, he reminds himself that he isn't Chief Luna, but a husband and father, and makes a conscious decision to shift to listening more and talking less. This helps him reconnect with his family and protects them from his work-related stress. During stressful moments on the job, he's learned to take a deep breath and "hold his thoughts" before speaking, which prevents poor decisions as well as the spread of stress through emotional contagion. These practices take a great deal of self-awareness, as well as excellent regulation skills.

Just as important, he doesn't hesitate to ask for help. "You've gotta understand yourself and manage your weaknesses," he said. "Asking for help is a sign of strength. You need to have people around you can trust. No matter how bad it gets, I need to rely on other people." Those he turns to most frequently, for advice as well as just to unload, are retired police chiefs and his best friend from seventh grade.

Overall, he said, "the three F's" keep him grounded: faith, family, and fitness. What I would say, after donning my nerdy researcher's hat, is that Luna has been able to remain extraordinarily committed to a high-pressure job without ever coming close to burnout because he's a natural at applying his emotional intelligence. And he is particularly adept at using self-awareness, self-regulation, and relationship management skills to establish and maintain meaningful connections.

My research in those with burnout immunity revealed a variety of meaningful connections that help people manage work-related stress and prevent burnout, but over and over, three key types kept showing up—and Chief Luna happens to embody them all.

Three Types of Meaningful Connections

1. to work
2. to relationships
3. to our values

In this chapter, we're going to explore each of these types of meaningful connections and learn how to avail ourselves of them to navigate through and around stressors and remain within the sweet spot of stress. It's incredibly easy to let high stress steal our full attention, leaving us vulnerable to a dysregulated, unproductive state. This means we need reliable resources we can connect to in order to renew and maintain our mental, emotional, and physical energy, and to help us recover from work stressors that, left unchecked, can chip away at our motivation or even our core identity. For most of us, these resources will come down to the deep, lasting connections we receive from having a sense of purpose, from the warm, supportive people in our lives, and from a set of core ideals we can anchor into. As we saw with Chief Luna, a meaningful connection to work itself and the vision he wants to enact there is key. He's also made a habit of leaning into his relationships for support, and his deep sense of values sustains him, no matter how stressful his job becomes. Whatever your role is, wherever you are in your career, meaningful connections can help you effectively manage work-related stress and keep burnout at bay.

A Meaningful Connection to Work

A student once asked me if having a meaningful connection to work was the same thing as having a connection to meaningful work. We all laughed at what sounded like the beginning of a tongue twister, but this student was highlighting a subtle point that calls for clarification.

Let's start with meaningful connections themselves. Most often, this term refers to relationships with people. But in this book, I'm using the term more broadly, to encompass any of the deep, significant associations we have—with people (pets count, too!), with our purpose or mission, our values, our vision of our ideal selves, and, yes, our work. Meaningful connections imply a bond that isn't casual, quick, or superficial—these are the types of connections that make a discernible difference in our lives, and by extension, the lives of the people we come in contact with.

With this understanding in mind, it follows that to have a meaningful connection to work, your *work itself* must be meaningful. "Meaningful work" is a concept that has come to the fore in recent years and now routinely makes it to the top of many job seekers' "must-haves." Even before the Covid-19 pandemic led nearly two-thirds of U.S. employees to reflect on their purpose in life and nearly half to reconsider the kind of work they do, research found that more than 9 out of 10 workers would accept less money—on average, 23 percent less of their future lifetime earnings—in order to have a job that was always meaningful. Given that up to 70 percent of employees say their sense of purpose is defined by their jobs, and that most adults spend the majority of their waking hours on their jobs, it's no wonder that so many of us are deeply motivated to pursue and engage in meaningful work. And increasingly, we're willing to walk away from jobs or job offers that don't give us that opportunity.

A lot of ink has been spilled on trying to define exactly what constitutes meaningful work, no small amount of it on behalf of employers trying to figure out how to attract and retain skilled employees.

But here's my hot take. Though meaningful work is, by nature, highly specific to each individual, there are a few core attributes we can zero in on. First, meaningful work is work that has intrinsic value to *you*—it's a vehicle of self-expression, it supports your purpose, and/ or it contributes to your own self-actualization. Second, it's work that you perceive to have value to *others*, or what's referred to as prosocial value—you feel that your work helps others or improves their lives in some way, contributes to the greater good, or furthers a cause. Third, meaningful work allows you to feel appreciated, needed, and valued. Whether it's from explicit recognition you receive from your organization, or simply knowing that what you do makes a positive difference to the beneficiaries of your efforts, meaningful work provides you with an opportunity to make an impact and to know that you are appreciated. In short, meaningful work is work that *matters*, to others and to yourself. The closer we are to this ideal, the more meaningful our work becomes.

And, the more protected we *could* be from burnout. I would love to tell you that a meaningful connection to work is the silver bullet that will forever immunize you against burnout. The real story, however, is more complex. On the whole, employees who are engaged in meaningful work *are* less likely to burn out—but only up to a certain point. It seems that as with stress, there's a "sweet spot" when it comes to your connection to meaningful work.

THE BENEFIT OF A NOBLE CAUSE

This beautiful expression comes from a chief medical officer I interviewed for one of my studies on people in high-stress roles. His job requires a delicate balance between ensuring optimal patient outcomes, managing a large staff, navigating the politics of a large organization, and overseeing a complex budget. But he manages it all without succumbing to burnout by connecting with what makes his work deeply meaningful: caring for patients.

"At heart, I'm a clinician," he said. "I always say, 'The patients are our true north,' so I have the benefit of a noble cause. It's really a gift to do something where the output is a giveback." He notes, too, that anchoring into what makes his work meaningful also makes decision-making easier, which alone is a huge stress reliever. When a group is struggling with a decision, he explained, he guides them back to the question of what makes the most sense for their patients. "What we are here to do is deliver care," he said. "That's why I went into medicine, and why I do the CMO role. It's really all about the patients."

A physician who ranked his work-related stress as "very severe" but also found his work highly meaningful had this to say: "I don't feel a ton of stress because I put things in perspective as I walk the halls [of the hospital], and see all these sick people. . . . I know that everybody has stress, but as soon as you walk through that door and you're having patient contact, it's showtime and you've got to come through." What's most fascinating to me about his comment is that although he has an objective awareness that his work-related stress is quite high, he *does not experience it as such* and does not suffer from stress's ill effects. This is a vivid example of how one's subjective experience of stress is transformed by the experience of engaging in meaningful, purpose-driven work. That's the kind of alchemy I can get behind.

When I was a brand-new consultant, I was assigned to supervise a group of hospital financial counselors at four different locations. My objective was to lead the efforts to redesign their work processes and to implement productivity and quality standards, and I threw myself into process-reengineering mode, excited to put my analytical skills to work. But I soon discovered that the best way to learn what the financial counselors actually did, and where their challenges and opportunities for improvement lay, was to follow them around and observe their interactions with patients and their families.

That's when my view of my work changed. The work itself didn't—I would still be creating process redesign documents, workflow diagrams, productivity trackers, and quality improvement spreadsheets, which would make the financial counselors' jobs easier and the organizations run more efficiently. But now I was up close and personal with the people whom all those improvements would ultimately benefit: the patients and their families. Suddenly what was a stimulating intellectual exercise and professional challenge took on deeper meaning and significance.

About four months in, I accompanied a lead financial counselor I'll call Margaret to a patient's room. The patient and his daughter had been in a car accident over the weekend, and now the dad was on life support and the daughter was in critical condition. Their medical bills were already over $100,000, and with multiple surgeries and a long recovery ahead for both of them, their bills would be astronomical.

As soon as the elevator doors opened, Margaret and I heard a woman sobbing from down the hall. It was Mrs. W, the patient's wife. We learned that her husband had recently been laid off, leaving the family with no health insurance. Margaret's job was to help Mrs. W explore potential financial solutions, including COBRA, motor vehicle accident insurance, and, as their income had dropped drastically after the layoff, Medicaid. Mine was to do everything possible to make sure Margaret could do her job quickly and effectively, and to ensure that this family's case took priority. As a result of the new systems and safeguards my team had set in place, the family's accounts were not automatically sent to self-pay collections, and we were able to help Mrs. W apply for and receive Medicaid to cover her family's hospital bills, which ultimately reached more than $1.3 million.

This is just one of dozens and dozens of success stories that arose from that project. Despite often working fifteen-hour days and many weekends in a high-pressure environment, I looked forward to work, was fully engaged, and loved being a part of a team that was providing such meaningful service to patients and their families. Even small administrative tasks felt significant and impactful—because they were. When all was said and done, we were able to secure financial coverage for more than 350 patients and family members above and beyond what the team secured in a typical year. There were many times I was physically tired, and the job could certainly be overwhelming, but I never felt emotionally drained or that my stress was unmanageable. Quite the opposite, in fact; like many who engage in meaningful work, I felt energized by my purpose, and by the impact we had on the families we served. It was one of the most fulfilling experiences of my career.

Studies on meaningful work paint a similar picture. Employees who feel they are doing meaningful work are more productive, more engaged, more resilient, more committed to their organizations, have higher job satisfaction, and enjoy higher well-being overall. These workers are often superstar employees, because they operate from a deep well of motivation, and happily devote themselves to their chosen "noble cause." Organizations and the people they serve benefit by having a motivated, energetic, high-performing, and loyal workforce. There's even evidence showing that meaningful work has a direct positive impact on organizations' bottom line—up to an additional $9,078 per worker per year, along with all the savings generated from avoiding expenses associated with employee turnover.

At first glance, it seems we've struck upon the burnout immunity blueprint: employees engaged in meaningful work are energized, super engaged, and extremely effective—the very opposite of a person in a state of burnout. So, if employees are pursuing work they genuinely love and are willingly going above and beyond while their organizations are enjoying all the benefits that come from having motivated top performers, what's the harm?

As it turns out, there's plenty.

WHEN MEANINGFUL WORK BACKFIRES

It seems that some of the people who are at the highest risk of burnout are those who genuinely love their work and who routinely go the extra mile. Let me be clear that this is certainly no guarantee of developing burnout, as the folks with burnout immunity vividly attest. But it's very important to be aware of the hidden downsides of devoting yourself to meaningful work and to the ways it can potentially backfire.

Perhaps the most common way is that your work life simply becomes unsustainable. Whether it's the relentless pace, the emotional or mental intensity, the long work hours, or a scary combination of all three, becoming subsumed in your job without sufficient time to recharge can put you on the fast track to burnout. If my deeply meaningful yet all-consuming consulting project hadn't had an end date, I have no doubt I would've eventually burned out at that point instead of later in my career. The combination of long hours, high pressure, high intensity—and admittedly, my lack of boundaries around work—would've exacted a high toll.

Researchers have noted a particular vulnerability to burnout in those in the "helping" professions, such as health care workers, social workers, clergy members, counselors, life coaches, and direct care providers. These professionals tend to be deeply purpose-driven and often prioritize the needs of others over their own. Many of them are also vulnerable to a related phenomenon known as empathic distress, a strong aversive response to others' pain and suffering that arises when you spend a lot of time caring for those who are suffering. Empathic distress leads people to withdraw in an effort to protect themselves, resulting in avoidance, cynicism, and reduced motivation—some of the very same signs of burnout. Much the same vulnerability to burnout exists in individuals who are deeply mission-driven and who prioritize their organization's needs and goals over their own. Educators, activists, and nonprofit employees are great examples, as are startup founders, entrepreneurs, small-business owners, and changemakers and disruptors of all stripes.

I met Jenn Richey Nicholas while I was looking for a graphic designer for this book. When I told her the book was about how to protect yourself from burnout, she said, "Oh my god, I desperately needed that book when I was starting out on my career." She agreed to let me interview her, and I was blown away by her story.

Jenn was working for a top-tier graphic design firm on a very high-profile project that would be seen around the world. She had dreamed of being a graphic designer ever since she was in middle school and always loved the idea of being on a highly talented team where she and her colleagues shared a passion for design. The firm's reputation was riding on this project, and it had the potential to be career-defining for the entire team. Everyone was expected to work 120 hours a week or more; many people resorted to sleeping under conference tables and would only go home to shower. Jenn described how "people were dropping like flies from exhaustion," and after one colleague passed out several times, he had to be admitted to the ER. "I was terrified I'd be ruined in the industry if I took a break," she told me. "Fear was the only thing keeping me there."

After months of this grueling schedule where she pushed herself to her physical and mental limits, everything came to a head one day when Jenn went to the rooftop of her office building, stood at the ledge, and thought about jumping. "I just wanted the pain to be over," she said. Her vision blurred as she stood there, and she doesn't remember much more of the episode, except that someone took her back to the office. Incredibly, she managed to go back to work and finish the project. "Walking away was not an option," she said. When it was finally over, she went home and slept for two weeks.

Shortly thereafter, she went to London to visit a friend who was also a graphic designer. Jenn was astonished to see that her friend and her team were working from nine to five—and her friend was astonished to hear what Jenn had just been through. "I gained a lot of perspective on the toxicity I'd been wrapped up in," she said. "That experience made me lose my sense of self. I felt like my body wasn't even mine."

But now she was awake and aware, and she wasn't going back. "Since then," she told me, "I have built myself and my work ethic around never doing that again." Jenn left that firm and worked as a designer at other firms for a few years, while dreaming about launching her own business. Today she runs a successful graphic design firm committed to making a positive social and environmental impact in the world, and where mental health and overall well-being are priorities. "We rarely work more than forty hours a week," she said. "We want to be a model for other studios. Our hope is that, one by one, firms like ours will gradually change the toxic culture of this industry."

When you love your work and consider it a calling, or if you're exceptionally purpose-driven and committed, your job will demand a lot of you. You can often find yourself overextended, because you're so passionate about your cause and care so deeply about improving others' lives, or you're overcommitted to your organization's mission or goals. Without sufficient periods to rest and recharge, the risk is high for exhaustion, depersonalization, and, down the line, a lack of efficacy, as you become increasingly overwhelmed and depleted. When work becomes the central focus of our lives (for any reason), or when our identity gets excessively wrapped up in what we do for a living, we run the risk of making too many personal sacrifices and losing sight of our own self-care, leaving us ripe for burnout.

So, how can you identify and prioritize aspects of your work that are most meaningful to you, without overengaging in work and sacrificing your own personal well-being? How can you continue to engage in chasing your passions and making the world a better place, without becoming drained, discouraged, and burned-out? Here are some tips for both leaders and individual contributors.

What Leaders and Organizations Can Do

1. **Recognize employees' contributions**. Everyone wants to be appreciated, but people who are motivated by helping others and engaging in meaningful work especially need to know that their work *matters*. The effect is contagious, too: research shows that staff who receive frequent appreciation at work are more likely to recognize and appreciate others, which makes them feel valued and has a positive effect on team performance.
2. **Sponsor organization-wide reflection on your mission statement and the specific ways departments and teams are supporting it**. Research from McKinsey found that employees

are five times more likely to be excited to work at a company that spends time reflecting on the impact it makes in the world.

3. **Create a culture that encourages open communication and explicitly prioritizes employees' well-being**. Employees should know that they can go to their managers to ask for accommodations or adjustments to their workload when they feel burnout calling, and that there are options in place—such as "no explanation necessary" days off, access to mental health resources, and wellness initiatives—they can rely on in times of need.

4. **Preserve healthy workplace boundaries**. Build a culture that honors balance between work time and personal time. Encourage employees not to bring work home unless absolutely necessary—and model that behavior. Be proactive in intervening when employees exhibit a pattern of overwork and overcommitment. Do changes need to be made to their workload? Do they need support in managing their time and priorities? Do they need additional resources?

5. **Periodically review workloads**. Is everyone's workload reasonable and fair? If certain employees seem to be taking on the lion's share of the work, get to the bottom of why. Sometimes, passionate, mission-driven individuals willingly take on too much work, and, sometimes, others take advantage of them, assuming they would've volunteered for the extra work anyway.

What Individual Workers Can Do

1. **Communicate and maintain your boundaries regarding work hours**. This applies to the number of hours you're putting in, as well as when you will and will not be available for work (for example, no work after 6 p.m.).

2. **Try setting "intensity boundaries."** Too much of anything, even something you're really enthusiastic about, will eventu-

ally have negative consequences. So find ways to put healthy limits on your efforts and energy. It could be as simple as scheduling regular time away from work or including a "do not disturb" window within your workday, or it could be that you are very strategic about putting guardrails around your role. A teacher in one of my workshops, well aware that she suffered from "shiny object syndrome" and was habitually overcommitted, developed what she called her "phone-a-friend" strategy: she ran every new request by her best friend, who helped to hold her accountable for her boundary management goals.

3. **Release nonessential commitments**. If you're like me, you may need help from an objective party for this one, because *everything* seems essential and high-priority. Go through all of your work commitments and analyze them in terms of priority and need. Some will be unequivocally necessary; others may exist in a gray zone; some can be delegated; and maybe, just maybe, a few of the items on your list can fall away.

4. **Find ways to recharge and rejuvenate outside of work**. Taking breaks during the workday is good and necessary, but we also need restorative practices that take place completely outside the bounds of work. They can give you energy, and help you maintain balance between your work life and personal life.

5. **Broaden your sense of identity beyond your work role**. One of the CMOs I interviewed said that the most important thing that helped her manage stress was never allowing herself to become defined by her work. "I belong to a number of communities and this is one of them," she said. "But it's not the only one."

6. **Allow for and normalize varying "seasons" in your career**. Over a work life that will likely span decades, it's okay to emphasize different primary motivations. Sometimes you'll be mission-driven. Sometimes your job may be strictly

transactional; you're trading your time and energy for money. Sometimes your emphasis will be on skills building and advancement. *All of this is okay.* There really is a time and season for everything, and it's healthy to move in and out of mission-driven work—and to move in and out of periods of rest and rejuvenation—as your needs require.

A MEANINGFUL CONNECTION TO THE PRESENT MOMENT

During those times when stress overwhelms you and it feels like the world is spinning out of control (an amygdala hijack), a grounding counteraction can help bring calm to our overcharged emotions and restore clarity to our thinking. One way to do this is to establish a meaningful connection to the present moment.

Dr. Gretchen Schmelzer, whose distraction tip we learned about back on page 119, offers a powerful practice for becoming connected to the present moment: **Just say one true thing**. "When you are lost in the woods," she says, "what you are supposed to do is slow down—stop and look around. Get your bearings. Pick out landmarks." Saying one true thing about your present experience allows you to "locate yourself in space—[to] find something to stand on—to grab a hold of."

So, find a statement that is true for you, no matter how small. Even "I don't know what to say" or "I feel lost" will do, Schmelzer says, because it prevents you from getting carried away by all the overwhelming feelings stirred up by an amygdala hijack—what Schmelzer refers to as first feelings, or feelings about feelings—and connects you to your *true* feelings about what is happening in the present moment.

I've found that it's just as effective to say one true thing about my *external* circumstances—and again, even the smallest observation works. For example, "The chair I'm sitting in is gray" or "My cup of coffee is half full" brings me back to the here-and-now, and gets me out of the dark wood of my own thoughts. "Your ability to say one true thing," says Schmelzer, "creates the opportunity to move from the experience of lost to the experience of found."

Connecting to the present moment works because it gets us out of our heads, which are frequently consumed with anxious thoughts about the past or the future, and into the only moment that truly exists: the present.

A Meaningful Connection to Relationships

The most extensive and well-researched study on healthy aging is the Harvard Study of Adult Development. Launched in 1938, the study initially focused on 268 Harvard sophomores in the top half of their class, and 456 young men from Boston who grew up in disadvantaged circumstances. Researchers interviewed the original groups every two years, gathering information on their academic achievement and intellectual functioning, personality type and social history, mental and physical health, marital and family life, work life and social network, and dozens of other things. Periodic psychological tests and medical examinations rounded out the data, and over a period of decades, some truly amazing findings emerged. The study's original director and principal investigator, Dr. George Vaillant, famously remarked that after seventy-five years and $20 million, the study's key takeaway was "a straightforward, five-word conclusion: 'Happiness is love. Full stop.'" More recently, psychiatrist Dr. Robert Waldinger, who took over as director of the study in 2005, came to much the same conclusion: "The clearest message that we get from [the] study is this," he said. "Good relationships keep us happier and healthier."

It's well known that humans have a fundamental need for social connection and to feel we belong in a community. But the degree to which we depend on relationships, and the extent to which relationships (or the lack thereof) affect us, is only now coming to light. Our physical and mental health, our happiness, our career satisfaction and earning potential, even our longevity, depend in no small part upon having warm, supportive relationships. In the Harvard study, for example, researchers found that for both groups of study participants, close relationships were the strongest predictor of overall life satisfaction, and a better predictor of long and happy lives than social class, wealth, fame, IQ, upbringing, or even genes. Notably, it's not the quantity of your social relationships, nor is it being in a committed intimate relationship, that makes the difference. The magic ingredient is the *quality* of our close relationships.

"Connection," writes research professor Brené Brown, "is in our neurobiology." It's "the energy that exists between people when they feel seen, heard, and valued; when they can give and receive without judgment; and when they derive sustenance and strength from the relationship." *Those are* the kind of warm, supportive relationships that keep us healthy and happy, and as we'll see, can go a long way in warding off burnout.

You probably already know which relationships in your network meet that criteria, but if you ever need a quick gut check, ask yourself if a particular relationship is *draining* or *invigorating*. Do interactions with this person leave you feeling tired, depleted, used, or anxious? That's a draining relationship that can accelerate burnout by increasing your stress and leaving you feeling exhausted and cynical. As much as you're able, steer clear of these energy vampires. On the other hand, if interactions with someone leave you feeling energetic, inspired, included, or optimistic, that's an invigorating relationship that can actually lessen your stress, help you manage stressful experiences, and lower your risk of burnout. Invest in these life-giving relationships.

Why are positive social connections and supportive relationships such powerful mediators of our well-being? Part of the reason comes from the very way our brains are hardwired. In the book *Primal Leadership*, authors and EI experts Daniel Goleman, Richard Boyatzis, and Annie McKee note that our limbic system, an area of the brain that picks up on and processes emotion, is an *open-loop* system.

Unlike a closed-loop system, which is self-regulating and does not depend on outside stimuli, an open-loop system largely depends on external sources to manage itself. This means, the authors observe, that "we rely on connections with other people for our own emotional stability." Whether we're aware of it or not, our brains are constantly picking up signals from the people around us and responding to those signals. The effect is quite powerful. We already know how emotional contagion influences our feelings and emotional states. But scientists have also found that via the open-loop nature of the limbic system, being in the presence of others can alter our physiology as well, including our hormone levels, cardiovascular function, sleep patterns, and immune function. Goleman and his coauthors cite a study that provides a vivid example: whereas three or more high-stress events in a year (such as financial trouble, being fired, or divorce) *tripled* the death rate in socially isolated middle-aged men, they had *no impact whatsoever* on the death rate in men who had close relationships. That's a dramatic example of the protective effect of close relationships.

But there's more to the story. Close relationships also have a direct effect on our stress. Waldinger of the Harvard Study of Adult Development, which recently began studying its third generation, explains. "What we think happens," he said, "is that relationships help our bodies manage and recover from stress. We believe that people who are lonely and socially isolated stay in a kind of chronic fight-or-flight mode, where, at a low level, they have higher levels of circulating stress hormones like cortisol, higher levels of inflammation, and that those things gradually wear away different body systems." A similar response occurs when we suffer moments of disconnection within our relationships. Feelings of disconnection, Brené Brown points out, "actually share the same neural pathways with feelings of physical pain." This is why ruptures in relationships are so painful, and why chronic disconnection can lead to social isolation, loneliness, and feeling powerless.

A growing body of evidence echoes these conclusions. Loneliness (the painful feeling of being alone, no matter where you are or with whom) and social isolation (a lack of social connection with others) have been linked with a number of negative health outcomes, many of them due to the deleterious effects of none other than our old nemesis, chronic stress. Researchers now know that loneliness and unhappiness accelerate the aging process, and are more hazardous to our health than smoking. Loneliness is associated with an increased risk of cardiovascular disease, metabolic syndrome, functional disability, accelerated cognitive decline, depression, anxiety, poor sleep quality, impaired immunity, systemic inflammation, and suicidal ideation. It seems, in fact, that loneliness and social isolation are such deeply stressful experiences for us that our brains perceive them as a threat. In other words, *our brains register loneliness and social isolation as hazardous to our health*, and launch the stress response in order to deal with the threat. And as we know, when the stress response gets stuck in the On position, it causes systemic problems, in the body and the mind.

It also causes problems at work. Employees who feel lonely or isolated on the job can suffer from poorer performance, lower job satisfaction, and a higher risk of burnout. Take a look at some of the research that specifically examines the effects of loneliness and social isolation on work life:

- People who experience lower connection in the workplace have 73 percent less engagement, 77 percent more stress, 109 percent more burnout, and 153 percent more loneliness than their highly connected peers.
- Social isolation has been connected to poor life satisfaction across all domains, including higher rates of work-related stress and lower job satisfaction.
- Lonely employees are more than twice as likely as those who are not lonely to miss work due to illness and more than five times as likely to miss work due to stress.
- Less than half of lonely employees say they are able to work

efficiently (47 percent) and perform to the best of their abilities (48 percent), compared to about two-thirds of non-lonely employees who are able to perform efficiently (64 percent) and at their peak performance (65 percent).

- Loneliness makes people less effective, and the lonelier the employee, the lower their performance ratings. Why? A study of 672 employees and 114 supervisors found two mechanisms: First, lonely employees felt alienated from and less committed to their organizations, which meant they didn't work as hard or perform as well. Second, they were viewed by other employees as distant and less approachable, which meant they were left out of the loop when it came to workplace communications and interactions.

According to a recent BetterUp study on workplace relationships, people need to have relationships with at least five friendly colleagues to feel connected and supported, and they need seven to feel like they truly belong. Yet 22 percent of people report that they don't have even one friend at work. Not only is this bad for individual well-being (and terribly sad), it's bad for performance, it's bad for collaboration and company culture, and ultimately, it's bad for the bottom line. Socially isolated employees are more prone to disengaging from organizational goals, and are at higher risk of burning out.

Now, think back for a moment to our discussion of the myriad negative effects that can come from ACEs, or adverse childhood experiences. Pop quiz time: What is the single most powerful "antidote" that can stand up to all those scary downstream effects of ACEs, including poor mental and physical health, shortened life span, poorer job performance, and a heightened risk of burnout? Don't worry, I won't make you flip back to Chapter 2. The answer is *social support*. And guess what? The same outsize healing effect of a "social cure" happens here, too: the evidence attests that the positive effects of supportive social relationships are even more powerful than the negative effects their absence causes. They translate into real-life benefits at work.

The BetterUp study on workplace relationships found that employees who put in the effort to establish social connections with their coworkers have 34 percent higher strategic planning skills, 34 percent greater goal attainment, and 27 percent more job satisfaction. And when employees dedicate time to cultivating more friendships at work, they experience 41 percent more personal growth and 48 percent more professional growth.

In an article for the *Harvard Business Review*, researchers and Yale School of Management professors Emma Seppälä and Marissa King point out that research has found a demonstrable link between social support at work and lower rates of burnout, greater work satisfaction, and higher productivity. Not only is having positive relationships with coworkers the most important factor in happiness at work, they write, but workplace social relations that leave workers feeling "valued, supported, respected, and secure" have a direct positive impact on employee engagement. The overall result of feeling socially connected "is greater psychological well-being, which translates into higher productivity and performance."

A doctor I interviewed who recently retired from a job at a large academic medical center said the two keys to managing his high-stress job were the ability to access support and being able to work within a culture that encouraged candid communication. "I was very lucky in that I had a very good support structure at my own level with my team, and then also . . . I was part of a health system that provided a lot of support," he said. The executive team was "very, very approachable. I knew that I could call and talk to them whenever I was feeling stressed, and know that I could have an honest, transparent conversation—and that it didn't make me appear weak. I could just have that conversation, get through it and be done, and then get back to work."

If you don't have the benefit of such an open-door relationship with leadership, or if you'd prefer not to discuss your stressful situations at work, you can assemble or join a group of trusted supporters outside of work. The Major Cities Chiefs Association (MCCA) is an organization that provides a supportive and collaborative forum for police executives from the seventy-nine largest cities in the U.S. and Canada. Their annual meeting provides a rare opportunity for these "top cops," who must protect a significant amount of sensitive information, to candidly share their thought processes and challenges with others who have the experience to understand what they're going through. Several years ago, I began facilitating the MCCA's annual leadership development program, and every year, chiefs tell me how isolated they felt at the top before they joined the organization. In many cases, the relationships that began there evolved into support systems that they rely on regularly. Robert J. Contee, who was on his fourth day on the job as chief of the Metropolitan Police Department of Washington, D.C., when the January 6, 2021, attack on the U.S. Capitol happened, was able to access immediate support through the relationships he'd formed through the MCCA. "Every single chief I called to help with 1/6 said yes," he told me, "and they got here as quickly as they could."

Other people I interviewed relied on faith-based organizations for personal support. When Danielle Outlaw moved from Portland, Oregon, to Philadelphia to become the city's first female African American police commissioner, she knew very few people. A group of local women reached out to her to let her know they were planning to meet regularly to pray for her. "I feel and rely on their genuine love and support," Commissioner Outlaw told me. A CMO joined a weekly prayer group, where he and a small group of confidants took turns listening to each other and offering guidance and encouragement.

Another CMO joined a professional organization that met monthly. "I'm an extrovert," she said, "so I like to bounce some of my problems off of other people and get their inputs and opinions. That helps me deal with stress as well." Members had the expertise to provide informed input on whatever stressful situation she was going through, and because they were not employees of the hospital where she had a leadership role, she could share openly without worrying about confidentiality issues or crossing a professional boundary.

Some people choose to work one-on-one with a trusted advisor—an executive coach, a mentor, or someone in their network. "I've had a coach for a long time," said a doctor who works in family medicine. "In fact, I think if I hadn't had the coach, I would have left the practice. There's a point where you really need perspective about your career, and you need support to help you deal with stress." And of course, there are plenty of ways to access meaningful relationships informally, through friends, family, your network, recreational groups, clubs, associations, and so on. "The key to emotional balance and being able to deal with things is meaningful connections," said one study participant. "No matter what you're doing and how busy you are, if you're doing it with somebody else, or you're getting advice from people, you don't feel isolated. You're going to make better decisions and it's gonna be less stressful."

Supportive relationships have a direct mitigating effect on all three aspects of burnout: exhaustion, cynicism, and reduced professional efficacy. Workers who feel supported and connected are more likely to feel energetic and motivated, have a positive attitude toward their job, and enjoy higher productivity and impact. Strong, supportive relationships just make everything better. I know I've been able to make it through some really tough situations at work because I had a manager or a coworker who believed in me, or who cared enough to come through with a solution at just the right moment. And don't forget, that "solution" can be as simple as a cup of coffee, the right piece of feedback, an expression of gratitude, or a message saying, "You've got this!"

Relationships can also be a source of resilience. Let's take a look at your network to identify your top relational sources of resilience. With a meaningful connection to relationships that leave you feeling valued, respected, secure, and resilient, burnout doesn't stand a chance.

EXERCISE: FINDING YOUR RELATIONAL SOURCES OF RESILIENCE

According to an excellent article in the *Harvard Business Review*, we often think of resilience—the ability to bounce back from setbacks—as a quality we find within ourselves when we're tested. But authors Rob Cross, Karen Dillon, and Danna Greenberg point out that resilience is also heavily enabled by strong relationships and networks, and that we can actually become *more* resilient by connecting with others. People who have shown exceptional resilience, they write, "have cultivated and maintained authentic connections that come from many parts of their life—not only through work but also through athletic pursuits, volunteer work, civic or religious communities, book or dinner clubs, communities of parents they've met through their children, and so on."

They identify eight different relational sources of resilience, which are captured in the chart below. Which of these eight sources have sufficient

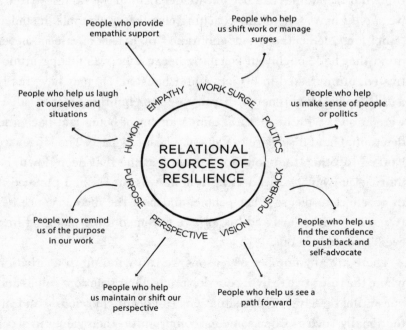

Figure 5.1: Your Top Relational Sources of Resilience

representation in your own network? Where do you need to strengthen existing relationships or seek out new ones to help build new ways of becoming resilient?

A Meaningful Connection to Your Values

If I were to ask you to jot down a list of your top five to ten values, most of us could probably come up with a list without too much effort. But would it capture the full picture? Is it possible that some of those answers don't belong on your list after all, and that others might actually be missing?

The truth is, knowing and understanding our core values takes a high degree of self-awareness and considerable self-reflection. Sometimes our true values can become hidden behind the values we think we *should* have. One of my coaching clients, for example, included "ambition," "dedication," and "endurance" on his list of values—never mind that he'd sought out coaching because he was feeling unmotivated, uninterested in his job, and exhausted. He may have really *wanted* to be a high-energy, driven go-getter, but those stated values were at odds with his natural temperament of being laid-back and deferential, and his desire to work at a leisurely pace. The longer we worked together, the more apparent it became that deep down, he didn't even want the leadership role he was in. He had pursued it in an effort to please other people, and now the incongruence between his true values and his job's requirements was nudging him ever closer to burnout.

There are any number of reasons we can wind up in a situation where the values we're living out don't reflect our true core values and our authentic selves. These situations can occur consciously and intentionally, such as when someone compromises their values in order to gain an advantage (inflating accomplishments in order to land a promotion, for example), or they feel pressured to (lying to cover up a superior's mistake, for example). Or values conflicts can happen incrementally and without our awareness, such as when we're trying to fit in with a particular social group, mold our personal values to the values of our organization, or, like my client, live out other people's dreams and expectations for us. At other times, we simply haven't yet engaged in the kind of honest self-reflection that would reveal our values.

Whatever the reason, few things will propel you into burnout faster than a threat to your core values. So it goes without saying that first and foremost, you've got to have an accurate read on your core beliefs and guiding principles. Knowing what truly matters to you and motivates you, what forms the contours of your purpose and how you go about enacting it, and what you are (and aren't) willing to sacrifice for your job, is all essential information. Further, there's hardly a more potent way to be effective at work *and* to avoid burnout than to gain alignment between your values and the enacted values of your organization.

So let's go on a fact-finding mission to identify your authentic core values. Fair warning: this exercise will ask you to go deep. That's because the stakes are high—but so are the rewards.

EXERCISE: LET'S GO ON A VALUES QUEST

Set aside at least half an hour for this exercise. Approach it with the attitude of embarking on a quest or an exploration—the deeper and more honest your self-reflection, the more effective this exercise will be.

1. Create a quick list of your values—jot down whatever comes to mind, without holding back or censoring yourself.

    - Circle the values that feel really necessary to your identity or your belief system. The ones that if someone said, "You can't do that/ have that/be that," you wouldn't even recognize yourself.

- Circle the values that give you a strong sense of motivation or inspiration, even if you've already circled them.

- Reflect: Are there any values that you've circled twice? Of all the values you've circled, are there any that apply equally to your personal and professional life?

2. Complete these sentences:
   I feel a sense of inspiration at work when _____.
   What I love most about my work is _____.
   I am motivated to be _____ at work.
   I am motivated to do _____ at work.
   Something I would never do at work, no matter what, is _____.
   My work enables me to contribute _____
   _____ [list specific actions, products, services, etc.] so that
   _____[list outcomes for you and for the people you serve].
   I feel most fulfilled and satisfied at work when _____.
   I feel most emotionally engaged at work when _____.
   _____ reminds me of the purpose or meaning in my work.
   (This could be an action you engage in, or it could be a person.)

3. Now let's raise the stakes. List seven things you want to do, be, see, feel, or experience in your professional life before you die.

4. List seven things you want to do, be, see, feel, or experience in your personal life before you die.

5. Review your responses. Are there any values that keep popping up? What do you notice about what you care about and what matters most? What, if anything, surprises you? How do you feel, in this moment, as you reflect on your values?

6. Finally, revisit the list of values you generated for Question 1. Do your core values need an update or an upgrade? Would you cross anything off the list? Would you add anything? If yes to either, do so now.

Beneath your values are motivations that drive you. Notice how your values shine through in the choices you make and in how you spend your time. If your choices and actions do not align with your values, identify changes you can make to gain closer alignment between the core forces that animate and motivate you, and how you're living your life.

THE RELATIONSHIP BETWEEN VALUES AND BURNOUT

As you'll recall from Chapter 2, burnout occurs when there are chronic mismatches between an individual and their organization in one or more areas—workload, control, reward, values, fairness, or community. Values mismatches are especially dangerous, because their effects cut to our core. You could say they threaten us at a level of *being*, rather than one of *doing*. For example, a workload mismatch may leave us feeling exhausted, but a resolution can be reached with a relatively simple process solution, like a redistribution of tasks. But when your values are misaligned, you're being asked to turn your back on something that is fundamental to your identity. That's why values mismatches can feel existentially threatening and trigger a fight-flight-or-freeze stress response, and why resolving them is often a complex, time-consuming endeavor.

Values mismatches always cause inner tension or turmoil and high levels of stress—even if you're not yet fully aware of what your core values are. If you find that you're experiencing symptoms of burnout but you're not sure why, chances are there's a values mismatch percolating beneath your conscious awareness. Getting to the bottom of it will require some soul-searching, self-reflection, and, more than anything, being honest with yourself. The Values Quest exercise may be all you need to identify your true core values, but working with an executive coach, therapist, or mentor can help, too.

On other occasions, values mismatches are blatantly obvious. Being expected to act in ways that violate your moral code, for example, can catapult you right into burnout. "I can deal with the stress that comes from handling a personality conflict or a behavioral issue," an HR manager told me. "It doesn't really bother me at all. But if I need to make a decision because a work task doesn't align with my values, then that is really stressful. It's the most harmful stressor I can see." Working in an environment that allows or ignores unethical behavior such as stealing, cheating, lying, deception, exclusion, or unfairness is inherently stressful, and leads workers to feel overwhelmed, distrustful, cynical, and disengaged. If this describes your workplace, your best solution may be to leave.

Leadership guru Patrick Lencioni once famously highlighted the values of an award-winning company that employed tens of thousands and, at its height, had revenues of over $100 billion: *Communication. Respect. Integrity. Excellence.* That all sounds great—until you realize these were the espoused values of Enron, a company that was engaged in massive accounting and corporate fraud. Even if the discrepancy in espoused and enacted values isn't this extreme, Lencioni points out, corporate values that are empty or dishonest "create cynical and dispirited employees, alienate customers, and undermine managerial credibility." They create distrust. Research has found that employees experiencing values clashes with their organization suffer from poorer performance, lower productivity, and lower well-being all around, and are more likely to quit than employees whose values align with their organization's.

Here's an exercise to help you become more aware of potential values mismatches—and heed the message your values are delivering.

EXERCISE: ARE YOUR VALUES TELLING YOU TO GET THE HELL OUT OF DODGE?

Some values mismatches can be resolved before they usher you into burnout territory and compromise your well-being. Sometimes, though, values mismatches are a warning signal to get the hell out of Dodge. Let's look at these two categories of values mismatches.

GROUP A: GET REAL

You feel **uncomfortable or out of place**.

You feel **disillusioned, disengaged, or disconnected**, and you're not sure why.

You feel that something is **missing, out of alignment, or just "off."**

You feel increasingly or even intolerably **restless**.

You feel inexplicably **unhappy, pessimistic, or unmotivated**.

When something is amiss at work and you can't quite put your finger on why, it's often a clue that your values are out of sync with your organization's. Take the opportunity to get real and assess how well your personal values align with the enacted values of your workplace. If there is a mismatch, can it be resolved to your satisfaction? If not, it may be time to move on.

GROUP B: GET OUT

You feel unsafe. You feel physically or psychologically threatened or abused, or your work environment does not ensure physical safety standards.

You are being treated in an unacceptable manner. You are subjected to disrespectful, unfair, or inequitable treatment. You feel bullied, berated, harassed, or excessively criticized.

You are being asked or feel pressured to compromise your morals. For example: to violate your organization's or your personal ethics; to perpetuate an exclusionary environment; to demonstrate disrespectful, unfair, or inequitable behavior; to ignore or cover up for the ethical violations of others.

If you're in a toxic, abusive, or unsafe work environment, don't waste your time trying to advocate for culture change, hoping that toxic colleagues' behavior will improve, or hoping that self-care strategies will somehow make your job tolerable. Your first and best form of self-care is to develop an exit strategy and then get the hell out of Dodge. Remember Jenn, the graphic designer who suffered an extreme case of burnout because of her toxic work culture? Her advice for people in similar situations is this: "Number one," she said, "just stop. Just get up and go home. Second, imagine there's always something better on the other side."

There always is! Prioritize your health and well-being, taking as much time to recover as you're able to. Get plenty of rest and reconnect with things outside of work—people, places, experiences, and activities—that give you joy and energy.

So, what happens when our values *are* in alignment with our organization's? One result is that we receive the same protective, "alchemical" effect that being connected to meaningful work renders. We may still feel the stress of a high-pressure, demanding job, but working out of a deep sense of our values has a neutralizing effect on toxic stress. Put another way, the work-related stress we experience feels worth it, and it doesn't drain our energy, cause cynicism, or undermine our efficacy. Working out of a deep sense of our core values not only helps us cope with stress; it actually increases energy, promotes optimism, and enhances performance.

In *The Upside of Stress*, Kelly McGonigal recounts a classic study from the 1990s in which researchers had Stanford students keep a daily journal over their winter break. One group of students was asked to write about their most important personal values and describe how their daily activities connected to those values. Another group was asked to describe the positive events that happened to them. The researchers discovered that the first group of students returned to school in better health and in better spirits. They concluded that the students who were asked to see their deepest values reflected in their daily activities experienced a sort of transformation in their perception: "Writing about values helped the students see the meaning in their lives," McGonigal writes. "Stressful experiences were no longer simply hassles to endure; they became an expression of the students' values. . . . [S]mall things that might otherwise have seemed irritating became moments of meaning."

Since then, nearly one hundred studies have reached similar conclusions, leading McGonigal to conclude that writing about your values is "one of the most effective psychological interventions ever studied." In the short term, writing about their values has been shown to make people feel more powerful, in control, proud, strong, loving, connected, and empathetic toward others. It increases pain tolerance, enhances self-control, and reduces unhelpful rumination after a stressful experience. In the long term, writing about values has been shown to boost GPAs, reduce doctor visits, improve mental health, and help with everything from weight loss to smoking cessation and reducing drinking. Incredibly, even writing about values just once, for ten minutes, confers positive effects to our mindset that can last months or even years later.

Why is the effect so powerful and long-lasting? Part of the reason is that it increases our sense of efficacy: Stanford psychologists Geoffrey Cohen and David Sherman found that when we have a deep connection to our values, we're more likely to believe we can improve our situation, either through effort or with the help of others. Such a mindset makes us less likely to adopt avoidant coping strategies like procrastination or denial, and more likely to take positive action. Having a deep connection to our values also makes us more likely to view the adversity we're experiencing as temporary and less likely to assume that the problem reveals something deeply wrong about ourselves. In other words, McGonigal points out, "when you reflect on your values, the story you tell yourself about stress shifts. You see yourself as strong and able to grow from adversity. You become more likely to approach challenges than to avoid them. And you are better able to see the meaning in difficult circumstances." Remembering and remaining connected to your values, she concludes, "can help transform stress from something that is happening against your will and outside your control to something that invites you to honor and deepen your priorities."

Most of the in-depth interviews I conducted with police chiefs with burnout immunity happened to occur during the summer and fall of 2020, in the midst of the Covid-19 pandemic and a rash of violent anti-police protests. I was struck by how many chiefs told me that though it was the most stressful period of their careers, they had never been more motivated to dig in and meet the challenges their departments were facing. "I feel like this was the moment I was born for," said one chief. Another said, "This is what I've been training for for so long." Of the thirty-five chiefs I interviewed during that time, only one contemplated quitting, even though many were eligible for retirement and could have left at any time. "We need strong leadership now more than ever," said one of these chiefs, "and I'm not going to leave my people to figure it out alone."

Chief Bill Scott of the San Francisco Police Department even noted positive effects from this intensely challenging time. "I actually feel energized rather than discouraged," he said. "I have a very positive outlook. We just need to listen—empathy is key. We need to really acknowledge how we impact people, really hear what people are saying to us. Focusing on our values keeps me going when we're criticized."

Focusing on his values also guides his behavior at all times. "It's values that drive how you do what you do," Chief Scott said. So if you are a compassionate person, he explained, your compassion for people will be reflected in your policing. If you respect people and have sanctity for life, those values will be on display in all of your interactions with the people you serve. And during high-stress or emotionally intense moments, he went on, it's especially important to remain firmly grounded in core values such as service, respect, appreciating diversity, and following the policies and laws of the city. "I really do believe that whatever has been instilled in you in your values system will come out under stress," Scott said. So if your moral compass is set and you've been wired to do the right thing, he said, you will always do the right thing instinctively. "I'm here to do a job," he said. "I'm here to serve people. And [my] values really dictate how [I] do that job."

Our values provide us with safe harbor. They're a solid place to land when we're faced with criticism or experiencing stress, when we're weighing the pros and cons of a decision, or when we're just unsure of our next move. They form the scaffolding of who we are, how we want to act, and what we find meaningful.

Vibrant, Engaged, and Effective

I got back in touch with Sheriff Robert Luna in the spring of 2023. It had been two and a half years since we'd spoken, and I was curious how he was handling a new role that I could only imagine was even more stressful than his former job as police chief.

Turns out I didn't know the half of it. After beating seven other candidates in a "very intense" primary election, Luna faced the incumbent LA County sheriff and had to go through all the rigors of fundraising and campaigning—which he found to be a unique kind of stress he'd never faced before. He endured fierce (and sometimes nasty) opposition from his opponent's supporters, including quite a few of the deputies who considered him an outsider and were deeply resistant to change. In the end he won by a healthy margin, but the department he inherited "was in complete turmoil" and mired by scandal, and his commitment to eradicating the deputy gangs that operated within the department earned him plenty of enemies. As if all this weren't enough, Luna had gone from leading a police department of 1,400 to an organization of 18,000, and he was responsible for managing the largest county jail population (around 14,000) of any county in the United States.

The job ahead was so formidable and so high-pressure that Luna's own friends didn't want him to do it. "My best friend in the world said, 'Hey, I'm totally against this,'" he told me. "'I love you and I don't want to see you dead in four years.'" I knew from our previous conversation that Luna had extraordinary emotional intelligence skills—but after hearing about this job? How could *anybody* deal with this level of stress?

"You *have* to be worried about the stress that you're going to endure," Luna said. "Because if you're not worried about it, then you're not doing something about it." He takes a proactive approach with the stress-busting "fundamentals" of regular exercise, eating right, getting enough sleep, and prayer, and he relies on his relationships more than ever for support. "So much has to do with incorporating the right people around you, people that bring you positive energy," he said. "Every time something gets complicated, I talk to my wife, my family, my daughter, my son, my pastors. . . . I make sure I'm processing everything that's going on. I talk to my best friend at least once or twice a week, and a gentleman I used to work with a minimum of once a week. I'm counting on the people that surround me more, and I'm delegating a lot."

And as I observed in him earlier, along with so many other purpose-driven leaders, Luna's deep sense of mission gives him a more expansive perspective when his stress escalates, and reminds him of why he's doing such tough work. Getting into the race to become sheriff of such a large, complex, and troubled organization was inspired by the urgent need for reform. "This was not about me," he said, "and not even just about the sheriff's department. It became a mission to bring the sheriff's department back into the fold of professional policing, and let them be leaders in this country again, as opposed to the road they were going down, which was not good." After hearing about some of the challenges, Luna's best friend, who initially tried to dissuade him from running, fully bought into his sense of mission, and supported his friend throughout the campaign.

"The ultimate goal, at the end of the day, when I pray at night on my own," Luna said, "is to reflect on what we did and what I need to do to be better. A lot of this happened before I got here. What can I do about it now moving forward? And then I have to understand, so I don't stress out myself or stress out the people who work for me, how much control I personally have over what happens, and what process I have in place to make corrections. If I don't, I can start working toward that."

Meaningful connections—to work you believe in, which energizes and sustains you, to the people who surround you, who support and encourage you and keep you accountable, and to your authentic core values, which will always light the way ahead of you—are a burnout immunity superpower. Together they can take the bite out of work-related stress that would've otherwise been horrible or even harmful, and transform it into an animating force that leaves you vibrant, engaged, and far more effective than you could ever be on your own.

6

Four Vital Mindsets for Acquiring Burnout Immunity

How Beliefs Can Make or Break Your Resilience

Each of us experiences and makes sense of the world through a unique lens shaped by our underlying assumptions, biases, and beliefs. This lens impacts our self-perception, our interactions, our values, what we care about, what we are motivated to do or not do, our attitude, our belief in what is and isn't possible, our habits—even our view of reality. It is so central to how we approach life and how we handle life's challenges that it can be the make-or-break factor in everything from learning a new language to growing a business, from recovering from illness to overcoming adversity, from pursuing a new relationship to healing a broken one. Given its involvement in everything we believe, perceive, do, and pursue, it's not an exaggeration to say that it is a fundamental factor in whether or not we have what we consider to be a good life.

What I'm talking about is *mindset*, and it turns out that this intangible, internal set of beliefs we have about ourselves is one of the most powerful forces in determining our life outcomes. Mindset, writes Stanford psychologist Dr. Carol Dweck, "permeates *every* part of your life . . . and profoundly affects the way you lead your life. It can determine whether you become the person you want to be and whether you accomplish the things you value."

With so much at stake, it's vitally important that our mindset is oriented toward positivity and growth, and that it supports our well-being and full potential. Researchers and mental health professionals have long known about the power of mindset, but Dweck brought the issue to the wider public's attention. Her groundbreaking research on mindset is rooted in what's known as implicit theories of intelligence—people's essential, underlying beliefs about where their abilities come from. Dweck observed that there are two overarching types of mindsets that reflect people's beliefs about their abilities. People with a *fixed mindset* believe their abilities are innate and static. Whatever intelligence or talent they're born with is what they have for life. The second group believe their abilities are influenced by their choices and behaviors, and can change over time. Though they may have been born with certain talents and aptitudes, they believe that training, education, and practice can enhance them. These folks are said to have a *growth mindset*.

Now, as Dweck herself points out, these are useful thought categories, but it's important to remember that in real life, people fall along a continuum—it's not as if there's someone out there with a 100 percent fixed or growth mindset, 100 percent of the time. Each of these mindsets is, rather, two points at the ends of a continuum, and it's more accurate to talk about a range within the continuum—for example, fixed, low growth, high growth, or, as I prefer, to speak of people as more or less growth-oriented.

Wherever you are on the continuum, you can see how mindset can dictate behavior, in matters great and small. If you believe you just weren't born with a gift for music and nothing can change that, why bother taking piano lessons? Better to leave that to the lucky folks with natural musical talent. If, on the other hand, you believe you could become a capable pianist through lessons, the guidance of a great teacher, and lots of practice, you could end up playing at home for your friends and family—or, depending on your desire and dedication, for audiences at Carnegie Hall. Or let's say a project comes up at work that piques your interest, but it will require you to learn a new skill. For the person with a fixed mindset, that's an automatic no—learning something new is just too stressful and carries too much risk. The person with a growth mindset, though, will be open to new challenges—even if those challenges feel difficult, stressful, or risky. Now let's up the stakes. Let's say it's not just a project that comes up, but an opportunity for a promotion. A big one, with lots of reward. You can see where this is going. The person with a fixed mindset will be far more reluctant to throw their hat in the ring, while the person with a growth mindset will be more likely to take on this opportunity as a welcome challenge.

Here is where we meet up with the relationship between mindset and burnout. Mindset determines how we take in information and categorize it as stressful or not stressful, and whether or not we believe stress is always harmful or if it has the potential to be helpful. A fixed mindset is one of scarcity—and a life of scarcity is inherently stressful. "Believing that your qualities are carved in stone," Dweck writes, "creates an urgency to prove yourself over and over. If you have only a certain amount of intelligence, a certain personality, and a certain moral character—well, then you'd better prove that you have a healthy dose of them." Operating from an orientation of limitation and lack, and constantly having to prove yourself, is a stressful way to live. It's the kind of stress that will exhaust us, steal our hope, and undermine our effectiveness. In a work context, it's the kind of stress that, left unchecked, will burn us out.

A growth mindset, on the other hand, is one of possibility and potential. "In this mindset," Dweck writes, "the hand you're dealt is just the starting point for development." This doesn't mean, she points out, that people with a growth mindset believe they have the potential to become the next Beethoven if they put in enough effort. It means they do not believe that their full potential is circumscribed by the hand they're dealt. There may be temporary stress involved in working hard or learning something new, but much like a meaningful connection to our work, our relationships, or our values can transform our subjective experience of stress, a growth mindset renders harmful stress into an invigorating challenge rather than a dangerous threat. This kind of stress is short-lived and manageable, and dealing with it actually *reinforces* our energy, optimism, and effectiveness, which alone is a strong dose of burnout prevention.

As you'd expect, people with burnout immunity operate more from the growth mindset end of the continuum. (In fact, I'd go so far as to say that a fixed mindset and burnout immunity are incompatible.) But as I reviewed and coded the data from my burnout immunity folks, I noticed an interesting pattern. Four distinct growth mindset *subtypes*, if you will, kept showing up. These mindsets not only seem to make these individuals exceptionally good at managing work-related stress, they enable these workers to use stress as an advantage. I call these the four vital mindsets for acquiring burnout immunity:

1. the **positive outlook mindset**—helps us see the upside in stressful experiences
2. the **stress-is-enhancing mindset**—helps us see stress as helpful rather than harmful, and to see what we can learn from stressful experiences and how that can be put to use
3. the **servant leader mindset**—helps us focus on why our work matters and to whom
4. the **"aware and care" mindset**—helps us realize it's not enough just to be aware of how stress is affecting us; we also need to care for and about ourselves

In this chapter I'll show you how you can cultivate these vital mindsets for yourself, as well as encourage them in your teams and colleagues. But before we jump in, let me address a concern that always comes up in my classes and workshops: Can you *really* move from a fixed mindset to a growth mindset, especially if you're "way the hell down," as one of my students put it who was "asking for a friend," on the fixed mindset end of the continuum?

You absolutely can—just as you can acquire burnout immunity at any point in your life. Remember, as consequential as mindsets are, when you get down to it, they're just beliefs. Have you ever changed your mind about something you once really believed? We all have. With a little effort, consistently applied, you can do that with mindset, too, and I'll show you practical, high-impact strategies to begin shifting your mindset from one of limitation and scarcity, to one of potential and expansion.

The Positive Outlook Mindset

We're starting with the positive outlook mindset, because perhaps one of the biggest and most consistent findings from all of my studies is the prevalence of a strong positive outlook among those with burnout immunity. And certainly, positive outlook has been shown, time and again, to be a strong protector against burnout.

Let's get clear on what we mean by "positive outlook," though, because this *isn't* about putting on a happy face or being an "eternal optimist." What I'm referring to is a specific emotional intelligence competency that falls under the domain of self-management. According to Daniel Goleman and Richard Boyatzis's emotional intelligence competency model, positive outlook is defined as the ability to see the positive in people, situations, and events, and the ability to persist in pursuing goals despite obstacles and setbacks. The specific emotional intelligence behaviors that people with a positive outlook demonstrate include:

- They see the positive in people, situations, and events more often than the negative.

- They believe the future will be better than the past.
- They view the future with hope.
- They see possibilities more than problems.
- They see opportunities more than threats.
- They see the positive side of a difficult situation.

When it comes to burnout immunity, there are four main elements that fuel and maintain a positive outlook. They are: positive emotions, self-efficacy, optimism, and hope. We're going to explore them one by one, and you'll notice quite a bit of overlap. That's because they each work hand in hand and mutually reinforce each other—which is good news, because applying your energies to any *one* of these elements means you're cultivating your positive outlook all around.

POSITIVE EMOTIONS

A positive outlook is rooted in experiencing positive emotions. Social psychologist Barbara Fredrickson developed a highly influential theory on positive emotions called the Broaden-and-Build Theory, and it has fascinating implications for burnout and how to avoid it. Negative emotions, the theory goes, typically *narrow* our thoughts and behaviors: an experience of fear, for example, draws our entire attention to the threat that's scaring us and focuses our actions on avoiding or neutralizing the threat. In contrast, positive emotions (such as joy, interest, contentment, and love) *broaden* our thoughts and behaviors, allowing access to a wider array of observations and insights, as well as the ability to respond in a more expansive and flexible manner. An experience of interest, for example, "creates the urge to explore, take in new information and experiences, and expand the self in the process." Which is where the *build* portion of the theory comes in. Broadened mindsets, says Fredrickson, build new physical, psychological, social, and intellectual resources—and these resources carry long-term benefits because they stick around long past the positive emotion that prompted them has dissipated. "Through experiences of positive emotions," she says, "people transform themselves, becoming more creative, knowledgeable, resilient, socially integrated and healthy."

Subsequent research on the Broaden-and-Build Theory has also shown that people who experience and express positive emotions cope more effectively with chronic stress, one of the main drivers of burnout, and other negative experiences. They're able to step back from problems and take a broader approach—they can see the problem from multiple angles, in other words, which offers a multiplicity of possible solutions. Researchers also found that positive emotions and broadened thinking influence one another reciprocally, which over time produces "an upward spiral" in which people become better and better at coping, and experience noticeable increases in their overall well-being. Cultivating positive emotions in our own lives as well as the lives of others not only feels good, Fredrickson concludes, but also "transforms people for the better and sets them on paths toward flourishing and healthy longevity."

Already, you can see that we're describing a state that is incompatible with burnout. Workers who are resilient, resourceful, flourishing, and able to cope with stress are not at risk of burning out. Positive emotions provide a way to get to this enviable state. They are invigorating and encourage engagement. They expand our vision and spur actions that make us more effective and more resilient.

Organizations are taking notice. In response to the rising rates of burnout and turnover among health care professionals, the Mayo Clinic launched an initiative to increase joy in the workplace. For them, preventing burnout could actually be a matter of life or death. "Burnout," they noted, "leads to lower levels of staff engagement, patient experience, and productivity, and an increased risk of workplace accidents. Lower levels of staff engagement are linked with lower-quality patient care, including safety, and burnout limits providers' empathy—a crucial component of effective and person-centered care."

So they incorporated joy as part of their organizational strategy. Afterward, not only did they notice a decrease in burnout and an increase in employees' job satisfaction *even during the pandemic,* but their efforts also demonstrated that many of the most effective methods for increasing joy are both simple and inexpensive (or even free). One initiative, for example, encouraged "anonymous acts of kindness." Employees would leave a token of appreciation for people outside their department, along with a note describing how they contributed to Mayo's mission. Another initiative was responsible for creating a roving cart with fresh scrubs for anyone who needed them. Another provided hot coffee to surgeons each Saturday morning. Yet another showed appreciation through "positive gossip": employees began saying positive things about a coworker in someone's ear and allowed that to spread throughout the team.

Among their key insights learned? One was to remove "joy crushers" from work. It's no coincidence that the list of examples they cited happen to be known contributors to burnout: separating people from their values; taking credit as a manager or laying blame; assigning meaningless or pointless work; and not allowing people to have a say in the way they do their jobs. Another key insight is a simple truth that bears repeating: "Kindness is a surefire way to cultivate joy."

A medical researcher I interviewed put it this way: "I think that's how you avoid burnout—it's engaging with others and saying, 'How do I do something with somebody else that's positive?' It doesn't have to be a Nobel Prize–winning thing. Sometimes it's just small things that you do with somebody else. I think as humans, we really do want to connect with each other." Decades of research have shown that being praised or appreciated at work reduces burnout, absenteeism, and turnover. It helps to create cultures where people feel valued and where they want to stick around, and it makes both the giver and the receiver feel good.

SELF-EFFICACY

Reduced professional efficacy is one of burnout's hallmark signs. When we feel we're losing our effectiveness and not performing at our best, it further compounds the emotional exhaustion and negative feelings toward work that come with burnout. It's a vicious cycle that can be hard to escape when you're feeling depleted and discouraged. It's that "Low E" or reduced efficacy state we talked about back in Chapter 2.

Self-efficacy, on the other hand, is Low E's healthy counterpoint. It's the belief that you're capable of handling stressful situations and demands. Call it a High E or "I've Got This!" mindset, self-efficacy is a growth-oriented mindset all on its own. When your self-efficacy is high, you believe you have reasonable control over a situation—that you can, in other words, change it and improve it. The situation can be an inner state—for example, you're able to shift your mood from negative to positive, or you can summon the motivation to complete a task, even if it's something you really don't want to do. Or it can be an external situation—for example, you can build your skills, help to improve your organizational culture, arrange for a better schedule, or switch jobs. Really, it can be anything. The point is that you *can* take action, and you believe that your actions will be efficacious. You have, in other words, agency and autonomy, and you have the confidence to know that you can achieve your goals. When your self-efficacy is high, your outlook is almost guaranteed to be positive.

"I have a core belief that there are always opportunities for positive change," said Chief Bill Scott of the San Francisco Police Department. "And [that belief] always helps me when we're in a cycle of crisis. When you have a positive outlook and stay focused on what's possible, it can make all the difference in how you feel the stress and in the results you produce." Scott's entire mindset is rooted in positivity: not only does he maintain a positive outlook he also starts from the presupposition that positive change is always possible—and the belief that he can make that change happen. That's a High E mindset at work.

OPTIMISM

Like self-efficacy, optimism is something of a growth-oriented mindset all on its own. People who are high in optimism believe that on the whole, life is more positive than negative, and they expect more favorable than unfavorable outcomes. It's not that they don't experience setbacks, disappointments, or even tragedy. But when they do, they believe that things will eventually get better (that is, that negative events and their effects are temporary), and they are more likely to locate the source of a negative event outside of themselves, rather than assuming they're somehow at fault. Their positive outlook empowers them to respond to negative events with more resilience and less stress. Pick any area, from work to health to relationships, and you'll find that optimists fare better than pessimists. Research has shown that having an optimistic attitude can enhance creativity, productivity, stress management, problem-solving, physical and mental health, academic achievement, and overall success and life satisfaction.

Optimism has even been shown to increase life span. One of the largest and most extensive studies on optimism and longevity found that the most optimistic study participants had the greatest chance of achieving "exceptional longevity," or living to the age of eighty-five or beyond (for women the chance was 50 percent greater, and for men, 70 percent greater). Why is this so? To begin with, there is strong evidence demonstrating that optimists engage in healthy behaviors (such as eating a healthy diet and getting enough exercise) and avoid unhealthy behaviors (such as smoking and excessive alcohol consumption). But researchers also identified a number of psychosocial factors that provide a fuller explanation of why optimism has such far-reaching positive effects—and their findings are a burnout immunity gold mine.

Optimists, they observed, have less emotional reactivity to, and faster recovery from, acute stressors. When they encounter difficulties, they have better capacity to regulate their emotions through cognitive means, such as reframing situations as challenges rather than threats, or through changing their behavior, such as resisting immediate rewards in service of longer-term goals. Optimists tend to be goal-oriented and have the confidence to reach their goals, they are more efficacious problem-solvers than pessimists, and they have the ability to adjust their goals when necessary. Emotional regulation, resilience, self-efficacy, a challenge response to stress, cognitive and behavioral flexibility . . . put it all together, and you've got a nearly impenetrable anti-burnout shield.

The work of resilience experts Karen Reivich and Andrew Shatté shows that optimism, resilience, and self-efficacy have a synergistic relationship. "Resilient people are optimistic," they write. "They believe that things can change for the better. They have hope for the future and believe that they control the direction of their lives." That's self-efficacy, born from a growth-oriented mindset. "Optimism is a boon if it is linked with true self-efficacy," they continue, "because optimism motivates you to search for solutions and to keep working hard to improve your situation."

Reivich and Shatté provide a helpful distinction between what they refer to as realistic optimism and unbridled or Pollyanna optimism. "People who harbor unbridled optimism, of the Pollyanna variety," they say, "may not derive any advantage at all. In fact, unrealistic optimism may lead people to ignore real threats for which they need to prepare." For example, if a Pollyanna optimist is diagnosed with a serious illness, they might conclude it's no big deal and they'll be fine, and therefore bypass the medical care they need. But a realistic optimist acknowledges the seriousness of their condition and gets the help they need to recover—and still maintains their hope of a full recovery. But notice that neither the *belief* in the possibility of a full recovery nor the *recovery itself* is possible unless they take action. That's true self-efficacy at work, and it powers resilience. "The key to resilience and success, then," Reivich and Shatté observe, "is to have realistic optimism coupled with self-efficacy."

People always want to know if optimism can be learned. The answer is yes. University of Pennsylvania professor Dr. Martin Seligman is considered the founder of the positive psychology movement. Ironically, his work initially focused on *learned helplessness*, a state that comes about after a person has repeatedly experienced a negative, stressful event, causing them to believe they're incapable of changing their circumstances. Put another way, they're in a state of chronic stress, which nudges them ever closer to the fixed-mindset point on the continuum, where they lose their sense of self-efficacy. But Seligman noticed that although some people face many stressful, adverse events, they retain their optimistic outlook and don't take on this state of learned helplessness. He became curious about how to cultivate that sense of optimism, and his research on *learned optimism* gave rise to a new branch of psychology.

I highly recommend Seligman's classic book, *Learned Optimism: How to Change Your Mind and Your Life*, which provides a wealth of practical advice on how to become more optimistic (and thus happier and healthier), but you can start practicing learned optimism right away. At the core of the method is learning to shift your thoughts from negative to positive. Negative thinking is habitual, so you'll first need to use your self-awareness to notice when a negative thought has taken over, and then use your self-management skills to replace it with a positive thought.

Consider, for example, the incredibly common thought trap of labeling, or taking a single attribute or event and turning it into an all-encompassing attribute or event (for example, "I am a failure" rather than "I failed to finish the test"). Here's the cool thing: the *simple awareness* that you're having a negative thought already begins to shift your mindset from pessimistic to optimistic, which automatically lowers your stress. Thoughts are transitory, and they're not necessarily true. When you realize that this is just a thought, and not a reliable indicator of reality, you open up the possibility for optimism and self-efficacy. Is it really true that not finishing the test means you're a total failure? Nope! What's really true is that you ran out of time, and that's all. This new thought shifts any blame from you to external circumstances, which relieves stress. Now you've got even more room for optimistic thinking: "I ran out of time, but the rest of my answers were accurate." "Sure, I ran out of time, but now I know the format and requirements of the test; I'll do better next time."

"This was just one test, and a single test can't capture whether I'm a success or a failure."

One of the CMOs I interviewed found himself in a spiral of pessimism after managing a series of behavioral issues with physicians. "I began to forget that the other ninety-seven percent of the population is great," he said, "because all I dealt with is the three percent that are bad." So he implemented a positivity practice to begin and end each workday. "I have to make a cognitive effort every day I come into work to make sure to look for the positives of what I do and the people I deal with," he said, "and not concentrate on the negatives. And at the end of every day, I do an inventory: 'What were the positives?'" Learning to become more optimistic does take effort, and consistency. But it pays off, for you and for everyone you work with.

HOPE

Positive psychology researcher and professor Rick Snyder is the creator of hope theory, which consists of three components:

1. **Goals**: Having goals that you feel invested in, such as having a close and loving family or achieving success at your work
2. **Agency**: Believing that you have the ability to achieve your goals and overcome the obstacles that lie along the way (self-efficacy)
3. **Pathways**: Finding multiple potential pathways to achieve your goals and actively committing to pursuing them

Snyder and his colleagues found that having a sense of hope was strongly associated with higher academic achievement, better athletic performance, better health (through illness prevention as well as a stronger ability to recover from illness or injury), a higher pain tolerance, better coping skills, higher confidence, stronger, more supportive relationships, and a sense that life is meaningful. Conversely, those with low hope fare more poorly on each of these measures, and have higher rates of anxiety as well as counterproductive responses such as self-pity, rumination, and avoidance. Hope theory shows us that those who feel a sense of hopelessness are more prone to a perceived lack of agency (that is, low self-efficacy), which contributes to thwarted goals, which in turn triggers negative emotions.

They're also, as you would imagine, more prone to burnout, and this pattern is seen across professions. Doctors who had a high sense of hopelessness also scored high on exhaustion and disengagement, two of the primary components of burnout. A study of child welfare workers—a profession that suffers from high rates of burnout and turnover—found that both hope and resiliency protected against burnout, but hope had the stronger anti-burnout effect. Among competitive athletes, having low hope was found to significantly contribute to all three burnout components. This study also observed that the frustration over unmet goals and the lack of agency that the low-hope athletes felt was a risk factor for burnout, whereas the ability to maintain hope was linked with overall health and well-being.

Hope is so powerful, in part, because it affects our nervous system. When we experience hope, points out author and researcher Annie McKee, the stress response diminishes, resulting in slower breathing, lower blood pressure, less muscle tension, and a stronger immune system. All of these physiological benefits help us manage our emotions. "When we are hopeful," McKee writes, "we are better able to access our knowledge and intellect, use our emotional intelligence, and rely on our intuition. We are more open and willing to consider new and different ways to reach our goals and have the emotional wherewithal to deal with challenges and problems." Further, hope fuels courage, which allows us to take risks. And when those risks pay off, we feel emboldened, and more in control of our own destiny. Hope, McKee concludes, fuels energy, creativity, and resilience, and makes it possible to navigate complexity, deal with pressure, prioritize, and make sense of our lives. It inspires us to reach our potential.

The last thing I want to mention about hope may be the most hopeful observation of all. It comes from Barbara Fredrickson, creator of the Broaden-and-Build Theory: "Although most positivity arises when you feel safe and satiated, hope is an exception," she writes. "Hope comes into play when your circumstances are dire—things are not going well for you, or there's considerable uncertainty about how things will turn out. Hope arises precisely within those moments when hopelessness or despair seem just as likely." Hope is a refuge against despair. It gives us the mindset that we *can* persevere despite difficult circumstances, and the courage and the energy to do so.

HOW TO CULTIVATE A POSITIVE OUTLOOK MINDSET

Having a positive outlook is all about keeping your mindset and attention focused on the belief that things can always get better, no matter how difficult they may be at the moment. Here are several ways you can start cultivating a more positive outlook.

1. **Train yourself to think constructively about the past**. When a negative memory arises, look for the positive. Did you learn something helpful from that experience? Find something you're grateful for as a result of it? Or, is it possible that this negative event gave rise to a strength or a new skill? Whatever the positive, focus on that.
2. **Remember that difficult moments are temporary**. This is just a moment in time, and it will pass.
3. **Intentionally begin your day with positivity**. One deputy police chief learned that the first images he takes in affect his entire day. So instead of immediately turning on the news to see all of the negative stories, he seeks out happy images and videos first thing in the morning. Before big meetings or other stressful events, he shares them with his team, resulting in positive vibes all around.
4. **Inject microdoses of positivity into your workday**. Back in my consulting days, we'd sometimes spontaneously announce that work was over at 3 p.m. and take the whole team out to bowl or play pool. We also did silly little things like creating a system of penalties when someone used one of the many

overused consulting buzzwords—the "winner" had to buy coffee for the team. These small gestures go a long way when everyone is trying to get through challenging phases of a project by alleviating stress and increasing connection, gratitude, and morale.

5. **Get a good laugh**. Humor is a surefire way of increasing positive emotions, so keep those memes and GIFs handy or schedule a lunch with a funny colleague.

6. **Actively plan for a more positive future**. Visualize what you really want, and then write down specific steps that will get you closer to that dream. If you can, include contingency plans for what to do if a step on the journey turns out to be unfeasible. People who plan for a brighter future are far more likely to make that future a reality.

7. **Stay laser focused on what you can control versus what you cannot control**. Dwelling on what's beyond your control undermines hope and optimism. Remain rooted in what you can control—and make sure to follow through, which reinforces your sense of self-efficacy.

8. **Surround yourself with positive people**. Emotional contagion is an excellent resource for cultivating a positive mindset. Positive relationships also help you cope with stress and keep you motivated.

The Stress-Is-Enhancing Mindset

My research revealed that people with burnout immunity have a special relationship with stress. They don't fear, dread, or avoid it, and they don't react impulsively when stressors arrive—as they inevitably will. If I had to sum up their general attitude toward stress, I'd call it *optimistic acceptance*. It goes something like this: "Stress is going to happen, so I might as well try and make the most of it." Some of the folks with burnout immunity even *look forward* to stressful experiences on the job. No, they're not masochists—they just have an exceptionally optimistic attitude toward stress. They have a stress-is-enhancing mindset.

The specific emotional intelligence behaviors they demonstrate include:

- They believe that each new stressor offers an experience to learn, expand, and evolve.
- They actively seek out stretch opportunities they know will be challenging—or even very difficult.
- They value challenges and find them energizing rather than draining.
- They view stressors as challenges, not threats.
- They can handle the discomfort of learning curves and uncertainty.
- They believe that stress will enhance their ability to grow and improve.

All of this will sound familiar, because the stress-is-enhancing mindset shares many similarities with the positive outlook mindset and the challenge response to stress we learned about in Chapter 3. (And of course, it takes a growth mindset to view stress as beneficial and to have an attitude of optimistic acceptance.) But the stress-is-enhancing mindset distinguishes itself in both attitude and effect: people with this mindset welcome stressful experiences because they believe that their most important learning and growth experiences emerge from handling their biggest, hairiest stressors—and with that belief in place, that's just what happens.

More often than not when I lecture about this mindset, someone will push back. Even if it produces good results in the long run, they say, stress is unpleasant at best, and really harmful at worst, so shouldn't it be avoided if at all possible? And if someone is talented and skilled, is stress *really* required to learn and grow and improve?

These are fair questions. Most people don't enjoy stressful experiences, and for good reason. But remember, people with a stress-is-enhancing mindset aren't exactly waiting with bated breath for a stressful situation to arrive, nor are they enjoying themselves in the midst of it. But they don't waste time dreading stress, trying to outrun it, or fretting over when, how, or in what manner it will arrive. Rather, they see stress as full of good potential, and—this is key—they use it productively when it does arrive. Remember, their growth experiences emerge from how they *view and handle* their big, hairy stressors—not because their stress contains some sort of magical positive benefit.

As for whether stress is required for growth, my answer is an unequivocal yes—but with one caveat. To be clear, I am *not* referring to the kind of toxic, chronic stress that leaves you feeling overwhelmed, depleted, or ineffective, and puts you on the fast track to burnout. Avoid that kind of stress like the plague! What we're aiming for is *eustress*, the kind of stress that leaves you feeling motivated, appropriately challenged, and energized.

But here's the wisdom that mindset teaches us: toxic stress aside, it's not that stress *in itself* is either good or bad. The difference lies in how you view stress. Believe it or not, it comes down to this: If you believe stress is harmful, it will be. If you believe stress is helpful, it will be. If there's any magical positive benefit to be found, it's there, in our mindset. Take a look at *how much* of a difference the stress-is-enhancing mindset can make:

- In a study of nearly 30,000 Americans, those who reported experiencing a lot of stress *and* who believed that stress significantly affects health were 43 percent more likely to die prematurely. (This is where I'd include the Face Screaming with Fear emoji if I could.) Meanwhile, those who were experiencing high stress but did *not* view it as harmful were actually the least likely to die compared to any other group in the study—including people who experienced very little stress.

- A study of American veterans conducted over five decades found that the men who reported the most number of daily hassles were three times more likely to die than those who reported the fewest hassles. But it wasn't the stress-inducing events that contributed to their earlier deaths—it was the men's attitude toward them. Viewing everyday stressors (such as cooking or bad weather) as irritating inconveniences, rather than normal or even uplifting experiences, best predicted the risk of death among the men.

- A Stanford study based on over 61,000 found that people who believed they were less active than their peers were 71 percent more likely to die during the follow-up period—regardless of their actual activity levels or other factors that would affect their health.

- In individuals with high cortisol reactivity to stress, having a stress-is-enhancing mindset has been shown to lower the cortisol response, whereas for those who had low cortisol reactivity to stress, it increased the cortisol response. Translation? Having a stress-is-enhancing mindset can help you stay in the sweet spot of stress.

Why is the stress-is-enhancing mindset so powerful? Stanford researcher Alia Crum and her colleagues point to a simple reason: it affects not just how you think and what you believe but also how you *act*. When you believe that stress is harmful, you're more likely to distract yourself from the stressor, try to get rid of the negative feelings associated with stress, turn to alcohol or other substances in order to escape the stress, or withdraw from whatever it is that's causing your stress. And guess what's left behind? Whatever it is that's causing your stress! In contrast, when you believe that stress can be helpful, you're more likely to accept that the stressful event has occurred and is real (that is, you are not in denial), plan a strategy for dealing with the source of your stress, seek out help or advice, take steps to manage the source of stress, and try to make the best of the situation by viewing your stress in a positive way or by using it as an opportunity to grow.

HONKERS, HASSLES, HEADACHES, AND HARDSHIPS

A few years ago, my sister Jodi and I were commiserating about how stressed out we were. For her, it was dealing with the typical headaches that go along with having two teenagers, plus a toddler who she said was "constantly honking" at her. (The laugh I got from that was immediately stress-relieving.) For me, it was also the teenager thing (three of them!), plus I felt surrounded by "constant honkers" at work. At some point in our negativity spiral, we both started laughing at the absurdity of it all and at how good it felt to just vent for a bit.

Then Jodi said something that instantly changed my perception of the stress I was experiencing. "When you think about it," she said, "we're pretty darn blessed. Yeah, we have a lot of people honking at us, we deal with some pretty annoying hassles, and we even have the occasional headaches we need to work through. But thank God we don't have to experience the hardships we went through as kids."

That's when we came up with a stress taxonomy—honkers, hassles, headaches, and hardships—that, to this day, helps both of us keep things in perspective and reminds us of how fortunate we are. Now when I feel the urge to overreact to a stressor, I put it through the taxonomy test. Often I realize that my stressor can be downgraded—what at first appears to be a headache is actually an everyday hassle that is manageable.

The pause also gives me a chance to remember that I've successfully dealt with worse things in my life, and I've always come through having learned something important—about the stressor, about how to manage it, or about myself. The mantra I use in those moments is "I've done hard things before. I'll do it again and get smarter, too."

The stress-is-enhancing mindset encourages a *proactive* response to stress—which alone goes a long way in preventing burnout. Think about it: if you're facing work-related stress head-on and you're learning and growing as a result of it, you aren't emotionally wrung out, you're optimistic and engaged, and your performance and efficacy are improving. The stress-is-enhancing mindset works directly against all three aspects of burnout.

And remember: it can be learned. After completing a training program in adopting a stress-is-enhancing mindset, financial sector employees experienced better health *and* better performance at work with respect to innovation, sustaining focus, engagement, and collaboration. Indeed, I found that my research participants who exhibited a stress-is-enhancing mindset experienced very few symptoms of burnout. "I think I dealt with the stress by trying not to allow myself to become overly emotional," said a systems administrator, "and then channeling whatever anxiety I had into problem-solving." This worker successfully practiced emotional regulation on the job and leveraged his work stress to become more focused, more energized, and more effective. In doing so, he not only brought results to his team, he also eliminated the source of his stress.

The stress-is-enhancing mindset is also a great way to strengthen your resilience, which can prevent or reverse burnout. The American Psychological Association defines resilience as the ability to successfully adapt to difficult or challenging life experiences. Resilience expert Linda Graham defines it as the capacity to respond to pressures and difficulties quickly, adaptively, and effectively. Columbia University professor Dr. George Bonanno defines it as a person's capacity to maintain their core purpose and integrity in the face of dramatically changed circumstances, or the ability to maintain healthy functioning after a highly adverse event. These are all great, and like facets on a jewel, they each highlight an important aspect of resilience.

But my favorite definition comes from positive psychology expert Dr. Karen Reivich: resilience is "the ability to navigate adversity and to grow and thrive from challenges." Simple, straightforward, and accurate—but what really endears this definition to me is the distinct note of hope found within it (which surely reveals something of Reivich's own mindset). The notion of *navigating* adversity gets at the whole journey, and all the inner and outer resources we need to get through it. Perhaps even better, Reivich's definition implies that we're not just dealing with the slings and arrows of life as they come—we're growing and thriving as a *direct result* of those challenges. And with a stress-is-enhancing mindset, we certainly will.

HOW TO CULTIVATE A STRESS-IS-ENHANCING MINDSET

In *The Upside of Stress*, Kelly McGonigal points out that "every moment of stress is an opportunity to transform your stress instincts." Here are McGonigal's tips for transforming discrete moments of stress into positive experiences that increase your energy, confidence, and motivation:

If you feel your heart pounding or breath quickening . . . remind yourself that this is your body's way of giving you more energy.

If you feel tense . . . remind yourself that the stress response enables you to tap into strength.

If you have sweaty palms . . . remind yourself that palms sweat when you're close to something you want.

If you have butterflies in your stomach . . . remind yourself that your digestive tract is lined with hundreds of millions of nerve cells, and this is your body's way of saying, "This matters."

You can do this for any individual experience of stress, and I can attest that it works. When I'm nervous before delivering a keynote, for instance, I use the old trick of telling myself that I feel excited rather than anxious. Both states produce many of the same physiological responses, so why not put a positive, beneficial spin on it, and get myself even more pumped to deliver my best effort?

Now let's widen the lens. Here are more long-term recommendations for cultivating a stress-is-enhancing mindset.

1. **Practice optimistic acceptance of your stress**. If you're accustomed to trying to avoid or suppress stress—or you're still convinced that all stress is harmful—this recommendation will feel really weird. Go into it with the attitude that you'll try it out just for the heck of it. (And hey, this is all just practice anyway.) Baby steps could look like considering a stress-inducing opportunity before automatically saying no; explicitly acknowledging when you feel stressed (a big one for people who love denial); or using an optimistic acceptance mantra when stress arises. Something as simple as "I've handled stress before, I'll handle it again" shifts your attitude from pessimistic to optimistic, and reminds you of your competence and skill.

2. **Seek out stretch roles or experiences—the kind that push you along your learning and growth curve**. In fact, if you start to feel too comfortable in your role or with your skills, treat it as a signal that it's time to stretch yourself and level up.

3. **Recognize when stress signals a win**. Because stress is unpleasant while we're in the midst of it, we can lose sight of the fact that sometimes our stress escalates because, as McGonigal observes, we're getting close to something we want. Maybe your stress is rising because you're up for a promotion, contemplating a new job, or you got picked for a challenging new task. These are all wins, so celebrate them!

4. **Map your stress to your values**. Similarly, stress sometimes rises because an event or experience touches upon our core values. If there's something that always gets you riled up and spikes your stress, see if it's because it's something you care deeply about. If so, use that stress as a deep well of energy and productivity. A former student who excelled at public

speaking became inordinately stressed about delivering a climate-change presentation. What was different about this presentation? The issues she was speaking about *mattered so much to her*. Stress can actually reveal your core values, and when your work springs from those values, it can keep you focused, energized, and motivated.

The Servant Leader Mindset

I wasn't really thinking of servant leadership when I began formulating and carrying out research studies on people with burnout immunity. I was approaching this from the context of emotional intelligence and was on the lookout for specific EI behaviors. Servant leadership simply wasn't on my radar—until a number of my study participants self-identified as servant leaders.

"I live by a 'lead to serve' philosophy," Police Chief Robert Contee of the DC Metropolitan Police told me. "I'm here to do the job I was wired to do." A CMO of a county hospital said, "I really try to think of myself as a servant. I think in the end that I want to feel that I have served the people around me, that their needs are always respected." A CMO of a large teaching hospital said, "When I became a leader, the first thing that struck me was that I'm a servant leader. My responsibility is to make everybody around me better, make things work, and then disappear. And to me, that's very gratifying." Police Chief Jessica Robledo (now retired) told me that since her twenties, she'd known her purpose in life was "to lead with a servant heart."

Well, this required some attention.

First, a little background. The concept of servant leadership was formulated by Robert K. Greenleaf, who expounded its basic tenets in his seminal 1970 essay, "The Servant as Leader." Servant leadership places primary emphasis on the growth, freedom, health, autonomy, and overall well-being of those it serves, rather than on the leader. It thus upends hierarchical "leader-first" models in which leaders command from the top, with everyone below working to help the leader accumulate power, wealth, and influence. Servant leaders instead put their customers, clients, and employees first, and "lead from behind" to empower workers to achieve a vision that mutually benefits everyone. They measure their success not by their individual achievements, but by the success and happiness of the people within their organizations as well as the people their organizations serve.

Greenleaf wasn't creating a new model of leadership so much as he was capturing an ethos that's been around for centuries. But he cogently articulated the tenets of servant leadership for the modern era, and his model became a movement. Research on the personal and organizational outcomes of servant leadership gives us a glimpse into why it's been so enduring. Servant leadership has been shown to encourage collaboration, proactive behaviors (as opposed to avoidance or "passing the buck"), helping behaviors, and corporate social responsibility. Employees who work at organizations led by servant leaders tend to have higher job satisfaction, higher engagement, and higher psychological well-being, and they are more likely to feel they are thriving and engaging in meaningful work. Perhaps not surprisingly, they also tend to have lower levels of emotional exhaustion, cynicism, boredom, and intent to quit. There is also ample research demonstrating that servant leadership encourages creativity, innovation, knowledge sharing, and psychological safety, all of which result in enhanced performance on the individual, team, and organizational levels.

But what does servant leadership actually *look* like at work? How does it play out in specific behaviors and attitudes? Greenleaf's long-time collaborator Larry C. Spears offers this "top ten" set of characteristics of the servant leader:

1. **Listening**—they listen intently to others and try to identify the will of the group.
2. **Empathy**—they strive to understand and empathize with others.

3. **Healing**—they work to "help make whole" the people around them.
4. **Awareness**—they display self- *and* social awareness, allowing them to see situations accurately.
5. **Persuasion**—they rely on persuasion rather than authority to make decisions.
6. **Conceptualization**—they engage in broad, long-term, strategic thinking and are able to inspire long-term vision in others.
7. **Foresight**—they can envision the likely outcome of a situation.
8. **Stewardship**—they hold their organizations in trust for the greater good of society.
9. **Commitment to the growth of people**—they are deeply invested in nurturing the personal and professional growth of everyone in their organization.
10. **Building community**—they actively seek to build community among members of their organization.

I could've been reading a description of my own research participants! Indeed, when I compared Spears's list to the list of emotional intelligence behaviors and characteristics I'd observed in those with burnout immunity (see below), there was so much they shared in common that I realized I'd found another vital mindset for acquiring burnout immunity.

People with burnout immunity . . .

- have a high degree of empathy and genuinely express care and concern for others.
- are focused on serving and fulfilling the needs of other people (employees, patients, customers, clients, community, stakeholders).
- are highly effective mentors and coaches. They are motivated to help others learn, grow, improve their performance, and advance their careers.
- help to create a work environment of psychological safety.

- help to create a work environment that supports the efficacy and best performance of employees.
- are engaged in what their team members are doing.
- are physically and emotionally present for others.
- reward, recognize, and celebrate the efforts of others.
- have a deep belief that their purpose is to help others and to make a positive contribution to society.

But the real question for me wasn't why there were so many servant leaders with burnout immunity—it was why a servant leader mindset seemed to be such a strong contributor to having burnout immunity.

To begin with, there is substantial evidence demonstrating that servant leadership has a protective effect against burnout. One study conducted in a hospital setting credited "five virtues" of servant leadership—interpersonal support, community building, altruism, egalitarianism, and moral integrity—with having a strong anti-burnout effect. Not only did these virtues work directly against all three hallmark aspects of burnout (emotional exhaustion, depersonalization, and a lack of personal accomplishment), but researchers noted that a "spirit of service" in an executive leader can permeate an entire organization. You could say that a servant leader mindset is contagious. In a study of nursing professionals, researchers found that servant leadership decreased burnout and increased job satisfaction—and it did so by conferring "direct buffering effects" against what's known as "hindrance stressors." Here was another piece of the puzzle. Hindrance stressors are the kinds of difficulties that slow us down and impede our performance and effectiveness. They drain our energy and our resilience, and can make people lose trust and confidence in their organizations. They are in direct contrast with "challenge stressors," which, though difficult, actually galvanize growth and achievement. Remember my first consulting job with the group of hospital financial counselors, the one that was so meaningful and fulfilling? It was absolutely *full* of challenge stressors.

Instead of feeling drained or overwhelmed, I was energized, engaged, and effective. And each time I overcame another challenge, my resilience increased.

The "servant leadership effect" plays out across multiple work environments and cultures. A study of hospitality workers found that servant leadership increased employees' work resilience. High work resilience has been shown to increase job satisfaction, psychological well-being, and work engagement—all of which directly lower the risk of burnout. Another study found that mental health counselors in training who are supervised by leaders with a strong servant leadership style experience less burnout as well as less secondary traumatic stress, a phenomenon that arises when a caring and empathic person is indirectly exposed to other people's trauma. A study of university employees found that servant leadership increased employees' work engagement, as well as the trust they had in their leaders—which in turn had a significant impact on achieving better job outcomes.

When all was said and done, I concluded that much of the reason the servant leader mindset prevents burnout *and* contributes to burnout immunity is in its unique stress-busting effects. People who have a servant leadership mindset have a higher tolerance for workplace stress, they perceive stressful experiences as challenging rather than threatening, they are able to tolerate uncomfortable feelings associated with stress, and they are able to productively regulate their emotions, thoughts, and behaviors (which falls under the EI domain of self-management). This last EI skill is really the sine qua non for servant leaders: While they habitually put others first, they do so in a way that doesn't come at a high cost to their personal well-being. In other words, they're able to regulate their emotional, mental, and time investment in others so they don't sacrifice their own well-being in service of others.

And sometimes, the very act of performing their chosen service—that is, of engaging in work they find deeply meaningful and purpose-driven—has a calming effect on workers with a servant leader mindset. "When I'm helping other people get through something," said one CMO, "I don't worry about my own issues quite as much." Another CMO even described seeing patients as his "own personal tranquilizer." "I think getting back to the bedside, getting back to patients, getting back to the families, and connecting to the central *why*—what are we in this whole business for?—is really helpful for me," he said. While the administrative aspects of his role were very stressful, the service aspects were deeply calming. Another CMO described the same personal stress-busting effect when he went on rounds with physicians and got their perspective—and he also high-lighted the positive effects on his team. "It just makes me a much more effective leader," he said. "[The physicians] feel empowered and engaged when they see the CMO out there pulling shifts, seeing pa-tients, using the same EMR [electronic medical records] that they're criticizing, and helping with patients that they're having trouble with. I do that and I feel the same things they do. We get connected. [This] makes you a very effective leader, and it's a very effective antidote to everyone's stress."

HOW TO CULTIVATE A SERVANT LEADER MINDSET

Want to have more of a servant leader mindset or bring more servant leadership practices into your organization—and strengthen every-one's burnout immunity in the process? Try these tips.

1. **Practice giving focused attention to others**. Whether it's clients, colleagues, customers, managers, or teammates, let others speak without interruption. Through eye contact and body language (nods, a smile), convey an attitude of attentive engagement. Ask curious, open-ended questions that invite people to share. Pro tip: Resist planning what you'll say while they're speaking. Even if you're not interrupting, it breaks en-gagement and places the focus on you rather than the other person.

2. **Recognize others' efforts and celebrate wins**. You don't need to wait for performance reviews or formal assessments to

acknowledge others' contributions. Even a quick "Great job!" as you pass someone in the hallway or a Slack message thanking them for something goes a long way in letting others know they are appreciated and that their efforts are meaningful.

3. **Avoid micromanaging**. Allowing others to have ownership over their own work product conveys a spirit of trust and confidence, and boosts their sense of autonomy.

4. **Eliminate hindrance stressors from the work environment**. Remove barriers, bottlenecks, inefficient processes, ineffective tools, unclear work assignments, or other things that could impede employees' progress and elevate their stress.

5. **Create a work environment that exhibits psychological safety**. Employees should have the freedom to learn and grow from mistakes, share their struggles without fear of negative consequences, and have full trust in leadership.

6. **Invest time and energy in others' growth and development**. Whether they're a direct report, a peer, or a student, mentoring others is a great way to help others achieve their potential. You'll notice a reciprocal benefit as they learn from your experience and advice, while you get all the good feels of helping someone who is inspired by you.

The "Aware-and-Care" Mindset

One of the biggest realizations of my burnout recovery process occurred when I was ordered to go on bed rest: this outcome was the impossible-to-ignore *end result* of my long journey toward burnout. My body and mind had surely been sending distress signals all along, but because I was so unaware, and so accustomed to ignoring my basic self-care needs, it took a big, scary wake-up call to grab my attention.

And by the way, the way I was operating is hardly uncommon. Our culture of overwork, constant (and often performative) busyness, and turning a blind eye to our own needs in service of "getting ahead" or bringing more value to our organizations is indeed the norm. The longer you keep the focus on these external goals rather than your internal needs, the more normal it feels—and the more entrenched this harmful mindset becomes in the culture.

A mental and emotional awakening followed my physical wake-up call. And what it came down to was a realization of how much I needed to *be aware and care*. There are a zillion self-care practices and wellness strategies out there that can help protect your physical, mental, and emotional health. But none of them matter if you don't realize you need them (yes, even you, alpha achiever), or if you're not willing to take time away from work to avail yourself of them. So the very first step is to embrace an "aware and care" mindset. You need to realize—and accept—that your well-being matters, and that you are well worth putting some time and effort into caring for yourself.

A PROACTIVE APPROACH

Former Philadelphia police commissioner Danielle Outlaw has worked in high-stress roles her entire career. She began with the Oakland Police Department, where she rose through the ranks to become deputy chief, then went on to become chief of the Portland Police Bureau, and finally, took over as commissioner of the Philly PD in 2020—where she was brought in as an outsider to help reform a department embroiled in scandal. Everyone who goes into law enforcement knows that high stress is part of the job, but Outlaw has had to manage the additional stressors of being a woman in a male-dominated field and being the first African American woman to lead both the Portland Police Bureau and the Philly PD.

When I interviewed her in 2022, she described the pressures associated with being "a first" and having to navigate "many biases," including people's assumptions that she would unfairly show preferential treatment to African Americans, whether in her organizations or in the community. "This job can cause you to feel hypervigilant, hyperstressed, or both," she told me. "There will always be stress, and there will always be things I cannot control or change, so I am very focused and intentional about proactively putting my energy into that which I know I can control."

As we spoke, it became apparent to me that Outlaw's self-regulation is one of her most effective stress management tools. "I am very intentional about what gets my attention—I *choose* what gets my attention," she said. It starts first thing in the morning, with a daily gratitude practice. "During the quiet window before I even open my eyes and am fully awake," she said, "I identify the things for which I'm grateful. I've conditioned myself to start every day that way: to verbally express gratitude for anything that comes to mind, no matter how big or small—and also to be grateful for the amazing things that are *going* to happen today." What a remarkable way to cultivate a positive outlook! She continues that discipline throughout the day, and it applies not just to the big stuff, like maintaining boundaries between her professional and personal life, but to her choice of movies, music, books, and podcasts. She chooses content that will enhance her personal and leadership development, and avoids known stress triggers such as scrolling the department's social media accounts. "I know what drains me, and I work hard to avoid those distractions and protect my energy," she said. "I've learned how to say no—and then I don't let myself feel bad about it."

She's also learned not to take it personally when she receives the kind of criticism that routinely comes with being the public face of policing. "I learned to separate what people were saying about me as a person," she said, "and what was actually strong emotion directed toward my public role—or what I represent in the system in general." She paused to grin. "I'm learning that I need to not give as much of a shit about what others think."

I had a chance to catch up with Outlaw in the spring of 2023, just weeks after she'd returned to work after a back injury. She was as calm and composed as ever, and I wondered if that was simply her natural demeanor. "I've seen it all," she said, "and I'm able to remain calm under pressure. But that doesn't mean that our bodies don't internalize stress. I may look young on the outside, but stress is always affecting you internally, and it will always catch up with you. So I actually made a commitment to prioritize self-care in 2023." For Outlaw, that means taking a long-awaited vacation, pausing to pay attention to how she feels ("If I need to sit down, I sit down"), relying on her team for guidance and support, watching funny movies or stand-up comedy to get her mind off of her work-related stress, and meeting monthly with a group of community spiritual leaders for prayer and fellowship.

Can we just stop and admire for a moment? Not only is Outlaw a purpose-driven individual who has willingly taken on more stress with every promotion, for more than two decades she's been able to thrive in a high-stress career because of her proactive approach to stress management. Instead of waiting to respond to stress when it strikes, she gets ahead of it with great intention, keeping her mind and body healthy and ready to handle the formidable stressors of her job. That's emotional intelligence and burnout immunity at their finest.

It's also an example of a fully formed "aware-and-care" mindset. This mindset says that deep self-awareness, the kind that must be practiced with careful intention, is a necessary part of the job. It says that self-care is not optional—it, too, is a basic job requirement. It says that to *do* your very best, you must *be* your very best, and that takes a daily commitment to investing in yourself. Perhaps the biggest gift of the "aware-and-care" mindset is that it boldly asserts our own worthiness: we are worth whatever time, energy, intention, and community it takes to bring our best selves into being and offer our best efforts at work.

Another police chief I spoke with eloquently captured this sentiment. "I'm a worthwhile human being that deserves help when I need it," he said. "There isn't any one person that can manage all of this on their own. You need to have a team of people who are supporting you and, frankly, you probably need coaching and/or counseling. When you're in a situation where you feel like, 'Okay, I've reached the limit of my ability to cope,' you really need to have the self-esteem, the self-awareness, and the belief that you're a worthwhile person that deserves help."

It's this kind of mindset that will enable you to remain in a high-stress job you love. The "aware-and-care" mindset informs all your actions and choices, from your overall leadership style and ethos to how you manage your work-related stress, and, ultimately, how you avoid burning out. "It takes a lot of intention," Outlaw said, "but I've always felt like I was prepared to do great things, especially through adversity." With her support system and her proactive approach to self-care and stress management, she will continue to do so.

HOW TO CULTIVATE AN "AWARE-AND-CARE" MINDSET

You are worth your own time and attention. Here are some practical tips for beginning to cultivate an "aware-and-care" mindset.

1. **Notice when and how you are slipping out of your sweet spot of stress**. Take a pause and do whatever you need to do to move out of the distress zone and back into the window of tolerance.
2. **Add renewal activities to your routine**. While comfort activities like overeating or drinking too much can provide short-term relief from stress, the relief is always short-lived, and your stress may be worse afterward. Renewal activities, on the other hand, facilitate deep connection to things and people we love outside of work, and provide sustained stress relief. Some examples include being in nature, hobbies, art, community service, exercise, and travel.
3. **Work with an accountability buddy who can help you prioritize your self-care**. Several of my research participants have running partners who help them get in their weekly miles. Others have teamed up with work friends who remind each other to take breaks.

4. **Stop yourself from overworking**. Plain and simple. No further explanation necessary.

5. **Set and protect your boundaries**. This includes workload and work hours, physical boundaries that help you feel safe, and emotional boundaries with others.

6. **Proactively surround yourself with support** *before* **you need it**. When stress escalates, and certainly if a crisis occurs, you don't want to scramble to find support.

7. **When you make mistakes, respond with an attitude of self-compassion, rather than self-criticism**. Research has found that responding to one's own pain and failure with a non-judgmental attitude and an acceptance that this is just part of being human protects against burnout. Bonus feature? Self-compassion has also been shown to improve sleep and promote higher job satisfaction.

The Power of a Growth-Oriented Mindset

Mindset shows us that our perception influences our experience. Mindset changes our subjective experience of stress. In a fixed or negative mindset, everything looks and feels worse—and therefore everything *is* worse. But in any of the growth-oriented mindsets, the opposite effect occurs: everything is better because you're viewing and experiencing life from a place of positivity, optimism, high efficacy, and hope. You believe you are able to change your circumstances for the better—and therefore you can, and you do. When you encounter a difficulty, you believe that it is temporary and that you can overcome it. That's the power of a growth mindset.

We'll close with an exercise that shows you how you can begin shifting your mindset away from the fixed end of the continuum and toward growth. Remember that progress is rarely sudden or quick, so give yourself abundant self-compassion and lots of credit as you take on this important work. Meaningful change is often more powerful, and longer-lasting, when you take smaller steps applied consistently.

EXERCISE: FIVE POWERFUL PRACTICES TO SHIFT YOUR MINDSET TOWARD GROWTH

By shifting your mindset away from the fixed end of the continuum and toward growth, you can better:

- manage your emotional response to triggers
- think more positively about stress and
- develop new, more productive coping habits.

Here are five practices (left column) that can help you adopt a more growth-oriented mindset. For each one, begin by answering the set of key questions (right column). You might want to revisit this exercise on a regular basis—for example, each quarter—to gauge your progress and ensure that you're making continual steps toward growth.

Practices to shift your mindset	Ask yourself these key questions
1. Challenge your assumptions and beliefs.	What assumptions and beliefs do I have about the current situation? How are those assumptions and beliefs helping or hindering my ability to accurately understand the problem? How are those assumptions and beliefs helping or hindering my ability to address the problem?
2. Face your fears.	What do my fears have to tell me about my ability to deal with the situation? How are my fears holding me back from focusing on what I can control?
3. Put things in perspective.	On a scale of 1–10, how important is this to me relative to my values? How are my assumptions and beliefs impacting my ability to accurately assess the relative importance of this issue?
4. See things from different perspectives.	If I were to pick three very different people who have slightly nuanced views on this, how would they describe the situation? If I "tried on" their perspective for a bit, what would that look and feel like? How might their perspective shift my perspective and/or my actions?
5. Focus on what you have to learn.	What is possible for me and others in this situation? How can I learn and grow from this particular experience/situation? What will this experience teach me about myself? What will this experience teach me about my ability to handle stress? What competencies and capabilities will I develop through this experience?

7

3Rx

The Recover, Reconnect, and
Reimagine Prescription

Years ago, when I first read Christina Maslach and Michael Leiter's *The Truth About Burnout*, this passage leapt off the page: "Burnout is the index of the dislocation between what people are and what they have to do. It represents an erosion of values, dignity, spirit, and will—an erosion of the human soul. It is a malady that spreads gradually and continuously over time, putting people into a downward spiral from which it's hard to recover."

Appearing just after a section titled (in all caps, no less) "THE EROSION OF THE SOUL," the authors already had my attention. But what really got me was the urgency of the passage—and how familiar it felt. My younger self, the Kandi who was eager to please and to prove herself, who played through the pain and who'd barely heard of boundaries much less upheld them, would've dismissed Maslach and Leiter's pointed words as overblown. The Kandi who had lived through the downward spiral of burnout, with its slow erosion of my health, happiness, and effectiveness, recognized their truth.

Metaphysical discussions of the soul aside, burnout does affect us in a deep place, and it brings consequences that extend far beyond physical and mental exhaustion. It's not just an experience of extreme fatigue, of having too much to do and not enough time or support to do it, or of being so fed up you want to quit. It can't be cured by starting (or intensifying) a self-care routine, taking a vacation or even a sabbatical, receiving coaching or therapy, or, heaven forbid, further "professional development" or "strengths training." (Trust me, you cannot bootstrap your way out of burnout, and piling on more when you're already past capacity only worsens matters.) Each of these things can *help* prevent or heal from burnout, but on their own, they are no panacea. Nor do they address the environmental factors at work that are causing your burnout in the first place.

This is why we really need to reframe the way we conceptualize and approach burnout, especially if we have any hope of truly recovering from it. It does little good to think of burnout as a temporary setback or a rough spot in your career, as job dissatisfaction on steroids, or as something that occurs because of a flaw or deficiency in the worker. Burnout is actually more akin to suffering from a prolonged illness or complex injury. Think about what's required to fully heal in those cases. You need adequate time to rest and recuperate, medical care from trained professionals, medications or other therapies that address your specific symptoms and diagnosis, and, once you recover, lifestyle changes that can prevent a recurrence. Burnout is no different. It's a multifaceted condition that requires a multifaceted response—and that response will depend on many factors, including the severity of your burnout, its specific symptoms, the work stressors that are causing it, and how long you've been in its grip. In all its iterations, there is no question that burnout can compromise your health, steal your happiness, and kill your career. So, no, Maslach and Leiter's observations are not overblown, and the sooner you can get on a path to recovery, the better.

In this chapter, we're going to look at a variety of ways that people have recovered from burnout or have prevented full-blown burnout once they realized the severity of their workplace stress. But before we dive in, I want to take a cue from Maslach and Leiter and spend a little time looking at a couple of deeper issues connected to burnout. To begin with, let's get clear about what recovery from burnout even means. What it does *not* mean is getting *just well enough* to "get back in the game" and continue in the same working conditions that burned you out.

In just the past six months, three different HR leaders have contacted me with requests like this: "Kandi, we need your help. We know we've been asking a lot of our people with all the changes from the pandemic, and now everyone's trying to get back to a new normal. They're all overworked and some are complaining of burnout. The problem is that things aren't going to get any easier around here. If anything, we're going to ask even more from people. Can you come in and help them develop their resilience?"

To which my "inside voice" answer is, Hell no! I don't want to be in the business of helping you develop a bunch of boiling frogs.

Now that's no knock on resilience, of course, and I have no doubt that resilience training could help some of these workers become better equipped to handle work-related stress and other adversities. But it's only part of what calls for a much broader solution, and again, it's only temporary, because it does not get at the root of the problem: the workplace circumstances that are burning out these workers in the first place. You can't formulate a solution if you're focused on the wrong problem, and neither can you heal in the same environment that's making you sick.

I also don't want to support a work culture that doesn't prioritize the well-being of its employees. In recent years we've made great strides in supporting employees with things like flexible work schedules, wellness initiatives, employee resource groups, and expanded mental health benefits. But let's face it, those advances aren't available to everyone, and in many capitalist economies jobs are still characterized by hustle culture—aka burnout culture. We're talking about "always-on" work cultures that glorify the grind, require or reward excessive hours, ignore boundaries, foster unhealthy competition, see asking for help as a weakness, and discourage the use of PTO or even taking breaks. Too often, workers who (understandably) struggle in this kind of toxic environment shoulder the blame for its ill effects. They are told, in so many words, that they can't cut it, don't belong, or are lazy or deficient in some way. Most of the time these messages are conveyed implicitly, but I had one client whose manager actually said, "This is an up-or-out culture. It's your choice—up or out? Let me know what you decide." More often, it's condescending, exclusionary comments like these: "Maybe you'd be more comfortable in a less demanding role." "Don't feel bad—very few people can handle this level of intensity." "Not everyone has what it takes to keep up with our pace."

Especially in the wake of the pandemic, however, there are indications that workers across industries and generations are rejecting and resisting soul-eroding work cultures. They are leaving organizations that take advantage of them and that encourage cutthroat behaviors. They are saying no thanks to job opportunities that don't square with their values. They are quietly quitting jobs that demand too much and reward too little. Some are revenge job hunting or rage applying to positions that will catapult them out of an environment where they aren't valued or respected. Some are launching their own businesses or embarking on freelance careers in order to have more autonomy and flexibility. Some are taking early retirement. Still others are unionizing to advocate for better working conditions. Post-Covid, the number of union-organizing campaigns among medical residents tripled. "It was a massive wave," said Sunyata Altenor, communications director for the Committee of Interns and Residents, "and we anticipate that it will continue to grow."

The common thread that runs through all of these post-pandemic work responses is that workers are tired of being treated as agents of profit and productivity, and they are tired of not having their values, dignity, spirit, and will respected. Dr. Vivek H. Murthy, the U.S. surgeon general, put it this way: "The pandemic . . . sparked a reckoning among many workers who no longer feel that sacrificing their health, family and communities for work is an acceptable trade-off." The doctoral program at UPenn where I teach began receiving record numbers of applications in the summer of 2020. The students I've spoken with described how the pandemic forced them to reevaluate their relationship with work or get out of a bad work experience and finally pursue a dream they'd harbored for years.

Empowered employees are reconsidering their worth, their purpose and values, what they're willing to sacrifice for work, and how work fits into their lives, rather than the other way around. They are saying yes to a host of better options and brighter paths. Their message is this: Work life really doesn't have to be this way. Life is too short and the cost is too high to devote so much of our time and energy—our best hours, days, and years—to a role, an organization, or a work environment that does not support the full development of our best and happiest selves.

Which really is the ultimate aim of recovering from burnout or advocating for yourself before you reach full-blown burnout. We're not getting better just to jump back into the pot of boiling water. We're getting better to be able to be our best selves and pursue the career of our dreams, the one that supports our values, enables us to enact our purpose, and puts our unique skills to optimal use. Ultimately, recovering from burnout is a gift to ourselves, our coworkers and loved ones, and to the people we serve through our work. Think about the void your absence would cause. Could your team get by without you? Your clients? Your customers? Your community? Your patients? Your passengers? Your students? Your shareholders? Your staff?

What would the world look like without the contributions that only you can offer?

In this chapter, we're going to examine what I call the Three-R prescription for healing from burnout—or 3Rx for short. The three R's stand for Recover, Reconnect, and Reimagine.

As for the first R, I want to acknowledge a certain painful irony that comes along with recommending tips and strategies for making a full burnout recovery. The ultimate responsibility for burnout recovery (and certainly prevention) lies with the employer, not the employee. While there's plenty about our individual experience that's within our control, if we're not a member of the executive leadership team it's unlikely that we'll have much control over the structural, systemic, or cultural forces that are contributing to our burnout. (Indeed, in cases where workplace changes are simply not possible, or if you're in a toxic or unsafe work environment, recovery can't begin until you leave.) That said, we can and certainly *must* act on what is within our control to protect ourselves, and there are plenty of coping strategies and protective measures that can prevent burnout, stop it from worsening, or promote the healing process and aid in our full recovery.

With the second R, reconnect, I'll show you how reconnecting with the things outside of work that bring you joy and vitality—things like people, hobbies, downtime, and group activities—can help mitigate your work stress and keep burnout at bay. As can reconnecting with your values, your vision of your ideal self, and the contributions you want to bring to the world through your work.

Finally, the third R will usher you into a new reimagining of what your life can look like, post-burnout. Together we'll reimagine your ideal self, a new and healthy relationship with work, and maybe even a new way of doing work that will keep your values, dignity, spirit, and will in alignment with the work you are made to do.

Rethinking Recovery

Just as we need to reframe the way we think about burnout, we need to hit Refresh on the way we think about recovery. First of all, let's not use recovery only as a last resort, when illness or exhaustion has forced us to slow down and recuperate! So much burnout, with its myriad ill effects for individuals and for organizations, could be prevented if we took a proactive, preventive approach and *regularly and consistently recovered from our work stress*. Athletes engage in regular periods of recovery throughout their training—not just when they sustain an injury or have no gas left in the tank. Their rest days are actually the key to preventing a great deal of injury and exhaustion. Like athletes, we owe it to ourselves to start treating recovery as an essential component of professional training and top-level performance. Honestly, we need to treat it as an essential component of work and use it as a preventive strategy rather than strictly as a cure. Bottom line: regular *work-stress recovery*—or what many researchers and HR leaders refer to simply as *work recovery*—can prevent much of the need for *burnout recovery*. It can, quite simply, immunize us against burnout.

Every worker needs to regularly recover from work-related stress (and below we'll look at ways to do so), but it's especially critical for workers in high-stress roles and environments, and those with others' lives in their hands. Pilots and flight crew members, for instance, must meet federally mandated rest requirements, and they receive detailed fatigue education and training in order to prevent fatigue-related errors, which can have deadly consequences. Truck drivers are also subject to federal "hours of service" requirements, which regulate how long they are on duty and ensure they get adequate breaks. In contrast, there are few regulations for health care professionals—a sad truth for clinicians and for those they treat.

The research linking health care worker fatigue with medical errors is striking. One study found that 82 percent of preventable medication errors and near misses (errors that are caught before they harm the patient) occurred as a result of fatigue, which is associated with reduced cognitive performance, diminished attention and vigilance, poor performance, and decreased patient safety. Another study found that surgical residents were fatigued nearly half the time they were awake and actually *impaired*—that is, functioning at less than 70 percent mental effectiveness—more than a quarter of that time. Overall, fatigue levels increased their risk of medical error by 22 percent.

The effect becomes even more pronounced once burnout sets in. A number of studies have found that physician burnout is associated with a decline in patient safety, and in medical units with higher burnout scores, researchers have observed less effective teamwork among clinicians, along with an increase in unfavorable patient outcomes, patient dissatisfaction, and patient and family complaints. One study even found that patients cared for by burned-out nurses had a higher likelihood of developing a urinary tract or surgical site infection during their hospital stay. Researchers noted that if the proportion of nurses with high burnout could be reduced from an average of 30 percent to 10 percent, some 4,160 infections could have been prevented.

Now, I linger on this point not to pick on health care professionals, but because there is a clear correlation between a lack of work-stress recovery—a prime contributor to exhaustion and burnout—and negative outcomes for both patients *and* providers. More to the point, this cautionary tale is hardly limited to the health care industry. *No one* is at their best physically, mentally, or professionally when they're denied the opportunity to decompress, rest, and recharge.

And really, how could they be? Chronic stress is destructive. The stress response, which puts us on high alert and floods our bodies and brains with adrenaline and cortisol, is meant to deal with a short-term threat. When work life presents us with a constant stream of stressors—anything from job uncertainty to unreasonable work demands to a toxic coworker to the unrelenting accumulation of everyday hassles—the brain responds by constantly launching the stress response. That wouldn't be so bad if the stress response reached its natural point of completion—in other words, if we had the chance to unwind and return to our baseline, pre-stressed state. But if we have no opportunity to recover, the stress response gets stuck in the On position, and our bodies and brains are constantly revved up and awash in cortisol. That's when we find ourselves on the fast track to burnout.

The same strategies you can use to recover from day-to-day work stress and *prevent* burnout can also be used to help you *heal* from burnout. Remember: what sticks around grinds you down. Work recovery strategies bring us back to baseline after a stressful experience, ensuring that stress doesn't stick around. When these strategies are practiced regularly, they're a burnout immunity superpower. If, however, you're already burned-out or are heading there rapidly, you can rely on these work recovery practices to get you on the road to recovery.

One word of caution: there is no one-size-fits all approach, so resist the temptation to compare yourself to others or give yourself a deadline for recovery (I wish it worked that way but it doesn't). This will only cause more stress and stall the healing process. The fact is, no one path to recovery will look exactly like another, because there is enormous variation among individuals (personality, temperament, mindset, stress tolerance, etc.), one's unique experience of burnout (the severity, duration, and prevalence of symptoms), what's causing the burnout (for example, a mismatch regarding workload or values, a lack of autonomy, toxic colleagues, insufficient downtime, etc.), and, as it turns out, how committed you are to your organization and what's motivating that commitment.

Organizational psychologists John Meyer and Natalie Allen developed the Three Component Model of Commitment to describe the psychological states and motivations driving employees' commitments to their organizations. If you have an *affective commitment*, you are motivated by genuine affection for your role and your workplace. You have positive feelings for your job, alignment with your organization's mission and values, and a sense of purpose at work. Even if your work-related stress is high or you're in a state of full-blown burnout, you're more likely to stay because you are strongly motivated by the purpose, meaning, and satisfaction you derive from your work. You stay at your job because you want to.

Those with a *continuance commitment* are motivated by a fear of loss. The loss could be financial (salary, benefits), professional (seniority or role-specific skills), or social (friends or associates, or perhaps you stay because you don't want to move your family). Many burned-out physicians I spoke with, for example, were choosing to stay because they had hundreds of thousands of dollars of student loan debt to repay. Others didn't want to start over after having spent the last seven-plus years training to be a doctor. Whatever the reason behind a continuance commitment, you stay at your job because you need to.

Finally, if you have a *normative commitment*, you're motivated by a sense of obligation. You remain with your organization because you feel it's the right thing to do. Maybe you feel you owe your organization loyalty because they invested in your professional development or took a risk on hiring you. Or maybe you feel a strong sense of loyalty to your colleagues or staff, or you feel that the people your organization serves will suffer if you leave. In my interviews, I heard the normative commitment reflected in comments like "If not me, then who?" and "I can't leave my people to figure this out without me." Whatever the particular factors are, you stay at your job out of a sense of duty.

I'll add a fourth kind of commitment—or rather, the lack of one. I know there are plenty of you out there who have zero commitment to your organization and plan to quit at first opportunity. Believe me, I've been there, and we're going to talk about this experience, too.

Whatever kind of commitment you have to your organization—from "This is my dream job and I'll never leave, no matter how exhausted I am" to "Take this job and shove it" and everything in between—will help determine your unique path to healing. As you read the following self-care strategies, keep in mind what kind of commitment is motivating you and how it could impact your recovery.

SELF-CARE STRATEGIES FOR RECOVERING FROM WORK STRESS *AND* BURNOUT

You may have little to no control over big-picture work conditions (such as a "rise and grind" culture or unfair systems), but you have nearly limitless control over how you respond to your work environment and its stressors, and how you recover from the day-to-day work stress that can lead to burnout if your stress is not managed. These strategies are thus focused on the ways you can protect yourself and recover from work stress and burnout.

Organizational psychologists distinguish between *at-work recovery* and *off-work recovery*. The distinction is pretty self-explanatory, but it underscores that certain forms of recovery are necessary when you're at work and in the midst of wrangling your job demands, while others happen when you're off-site and away from work demands. We're going to examine a variety of both types, with options that can be deployed in a snap during a busy workday, as well as ongoing strategies you can lean on throughout your career. Remember, the key is consistency. Day-to-day work stress must be managed regularly in order to prevent burnout, and recovering from burnout can be a long process that needs a comprehensive cure.

1. **Take micro breaks**. Taking ten-minute breaks throughout the workday has a powerful stress-busting effect precisely because it interrupts the accumulation of work strain and stress. In other words, it helps to prevent stress from becoming chronic. Research has shown that shorter, more frequent breaks are more effective than one longer break at the end of the day—or saving up a big break for a vacation. Try to schedule a micro break every hour or two. You can use the time in whatever (healthy) way you like. Step outside and get some fresh air, do a mini meditation, walk around the block, chat with a colleague, grab a snack, listen to your favorite music, drink some water, close your eyes, and just relax. It may not seem that these small steps are any match for your stress, but remember, their effect is cumulative.

2. **Have some fun**. Author Catherine Price says that *true* fun materializes when we experience the confluence of three psychological states: playfulness, connection, and flow. Playfulness is a quality of lightheartedness that allows you to do things just for the pleasure of it. Research shows that playful people are better at managing stress. Connection is the feeling of having

a special, shared experience with someone, which helps us be more resilient during stressful times. And flow is the state of being fully engaged and focused. Importantly, Price points out that flow is an *active* state—it's not binge-watching Netflix. This echoes other organizational and behavioral psychology research that finds that more effortful, active forms of activity, such as cardiovascular exercise, and mastery experiences that require effort, such as learning a new language, are more effective for work recovery.

3. **Maintain your social connections**. Everyone I've ever known who's recovered from burnout has been vulnerable enough to let others in to help. Lean on loved ones for support and to help you see a path forward; work with a coach, mentor, or therapist; delegate tasks or ask to share your workload; reach out to all your relationship sources of resilience (see Figure 5.1 on page 165 for a refresher); surround yourself with positive, optimistic people and draw on their energy; work on developing stronger relationships with coworkers. Social connection increases our resilience to stress and keeps us physically and mentally healthier, and isolation is known to be a direct causative factor of burnout.

4. **Establish and maintain boundaries**. This oft-cited recommendation never gets old. All of us need boundaries between personal and professional life that protect our downtime and allow us to mentally detach from work, physical boundaries that ensure our safety and best working conditions (Don't you love it when the office chatterbox leans over your desk for an impromptu chat? Yeah, me neither), emotional boundaries that defend against negative emotional contagion, and professional boundaries that keep our workload manageable and prevent exhaustion. Boundaries are safeguards that limit your exposure to many of the factors that cause burnout, such as overwork, mental fatigue, saying yes to every request, unrealistic expectations, and time spent with negative colleagues who

drain you of energy and optimism. If you're already in a state of burnout, boundaries are imperative for your recovery.

5. **Try an anti-stress diet**. Did you know it's possible to lower stress and mitigate the harmful effects of stress through nutrition? Foods that are rich in omega-3 fatty acids, such as fish and seafood, chia seeds, and flax seeds, and fermented foods such as yogurt, kefir, kimchi, sauerkraut, kombucha, miso, tempeh, and apple cider vinegar, have been shown to reduce anxiety and lower the harmful inflammation associated with high stress and anxiety. Foods that are high in dietary fiber, such as fruits, vegetables, nuts, seeds, and whole grains, can also decrease the body's inflammatory response.

6. **Get proper sleep**. Scientists have noted a bidirectional relationship between sleep and burnout: insufficient sleep is one of the main risk factors for burnout, and burnout can also trigger or worsen insomnia and other forms of disturbed sleep. On the positive side, getting sufficient sleep (seven to nine hours per night for healthy adults) eases burnout symptoms and is a key factor in a full recovery. Good sleep boosts mood and energy levels, and makes it much easier to face stress with a problem-solving mindset.

7. **Access your organization's mental health and wellness resources**. A recent survey of 800 employee benefits and HR leaders and 800 employees found that while 61 percent of respondents accessed their organization's health care benefits, only 19 percent accessed their mental well-being benefits. All the wellness programs, ERGs, EAPs, and employee benefits are for naught if employees aren't using them. Educate yourself on what your company offers and maximize your use of these crucial resources.

8. **Take time off**. Likewise, take advantage of whatever paid time off is available to you. Studies show that PTO programs actually result in fewer unplanned absences, and one reason could be that workers are reducing their stress and boosting

their health by enjoying downtime and renewal. We all need to mentally detach from work. That includes clocking out after a normal workday (no checking email after hours!) as well as planned time away to devote to rejuvenation and mental self-care. Though days off can result in reduced output in the short term, workers who have had time to truly detach and decompress return to work with improved mood, more energy, and greater productivity.

9. **That goes for vacations, too.** Did you know the U.S. is the only advanced economy that doesn't require employers to offer paid vacation time? Even when organizations offer paid vacation days, many employees are reluctant to use them. Recent data from the Pew Research Center attests that nearly half of American workers don't take all the paid time off (vacation and sick days) their employer offers. Their reasons include not feeling the need for more time, worry that they'll fall behind, feeling badly about coworkers having to take on additional work, fear of compromising their chances for advancement, and fear of losing their job. A little more than 10 percent say their manager actively discourages them from taking time off. Workers who don't take the opportunity to rest, recharge, and recover from their daily work stress are more at risk for mental and physical exhaustion, cynicism, and lower performance—they are more at risk for *burnout*. And while vacation alone cannot cure burnout, it can give you recovery time to regain energy, give you a new perspective, catch up on sleep, restore your positive mood and creativity, and mentally detach from the stressors of work.

10. **Take a sabbatical or leave of absence.** If your burnout is severe, you may need more than a few days or weeks away from work. Like a vacation, a sabbatical cannot cure burnout, but it can give you radical detachment from work and its stressors, extended time to recharge and renew—and perhaps even spark a transformation. Business professors and researchers

Kira Schabram, Matt Bloom, and DJ DiDonna conducted research on professionals who took sabbaticals for various reasons. One group took a sabbatical in order to work on a passion project, while another left to travel and find adventure. But it was the third group—who were turning to sabbaticals to escape unsustainable expectations and toxic work cultures—that experienced the most dramatic positive transformations. "Exhausted and burned out," the researchers wrote, "[this group's] sabbatical was a last resort because continuing on their current path was untenable." Once on sabbatical, these workers "started slow" because they needed "extended time to heal." They slept more, ate healthier, and reconnected with friends. As they began to recover, their energy and excitement levels rose, they became more adventurous and less risk-averse, and they gained new perspectives. Then they began exploring new forms of work and career paths, earned new certifications, and expanded their networks. Their pattern, the researchers said, went "from recovery to exploration to putting that learning into practice." At the end of their sabbaticals, not surprisingly, most of this group did not return to their former jobs that were burning them out.

11. **Lavish yourself with self-care and renewal activities**. It's never a bad time to invest in your own well-being, but it's mission critical when you're burned-out. Up the frequency of whatever activities and experiences you engage in to help you feel renewed, restored, and recharged. Don't be afraid to try something new. One of my clients forced himself to join a tai chi class at a point when he was so demoralized and exhausted he didn't even want to leave the house. He's now been practicing consistently for three years and cites it as a key factor in his recovery from burnout.

12. **Try meditation**. Mindfulness meditation—the practice of tuning in to your experience and accepting it without judgment—has been shown to reduce stress and burnout by decreasing

self-judgment and overidentification with negative experiences, and by increasing resiliency, compassion, and emotional regulation. Instead of overidentifying with and overreacting to negative experiences or difficult emotions, mindfulness meditation trains you to simply note your experience (whatever it may be) and then gently let it go. Researchers believe it is effective because it tames the stress response and allows us to be less reactive when stress occurs.

13. **Manage your mindset**. Do you believe you can and will get better? Then in all likelihood you will. On the other hand, if you believe it's impossible to get better, then you're stuck. Amazingly, mindset is just that simple—or more correctly, just that powerful. Resetting your mindset can be especially helpful when you feel stuck in a job that's burning you out. Rarely are assumptions 100 percent true, so shift your thinking from "I'll never be able to leave" or "I'm stuck in this job forever" to "I can't quit *for now*." You may indeed be unable to quit right now, but you *will* be able to someday. Now try this one: "I'm *choosing* to stay for now." This mindset emphasizes your agency and autonomy. It's empowering. Burnout has a way of eroding your sense of control. But you do have control over your own choices, and for many people, Step 1 in leaving a job that's burning them out *or* advocating for workplace changes that will mitigate their burnout is believing that they have a choice, and that they can create better options for themselves. Refer back to Chapter 6 for specific tips on cultivating a positive, optimistic mindset.

14. **Keep negative self-talk in check**. One surefire way to keep your stress revved is to buy into the words of your inner critic. Recently I had one of those days where writing was like pulling teeth. After a day of writing, deleting, and rewriting, I'd only managed to produce two paragraphs. My inner critic went on a rampage of heckling and catastrophizing: you aren't as sharp as you used to be, this shouldn't be so hard, you'll never get this done, you're all washed up. I sheepishly confided my self-talk

to a friend, who immediately reframed it for me: *This was really, really hard, but I didn't give up and I produced two well-researched and well-written paragraphs.* You know what? She was right! I persevered in spite of the difficulty, and the result is polished writing that also got me that much closer to the book that's now in your hands.

15. **Ask for change**. Speak to leadership to see what changes can be made to your work conditions. Can you cut back on hours or workload, work from home at least part of the time, extend some deadlines, or reprioritize your duties? Do you need to be reassigned to a different team or department? Do you need to receive more feedback, recognition, or better compensation? Do you need to rein in a job that's crept past the original job description or moved you out of alignment with your values? Have a candid conversation with leadership about what changes you need to reconnect with your health, happiness, and productivity.

A SPECIAL CASE: RECOVERING FROM EMPATHIC DISTRESS

Empathic distress is an especially potent and painful burnout trigger. It can both cause burnout and accelerate its development. It's also one of the more common career killers in the health and human services fields, leaving many burned-out and even traumatized workers in its wake.

Empathic distress is a strong aversive response to others' pain and suffering that causes you to withdraw in an effort to protect yourself. People who work in environments where they are frequently exposed to others' suffering, such as health care workers and mental health providers, are especially vulnerable to empathic distress, but really, it can happen to anyone who is very sensitive to others' emotions and experiences. (There's also evidence that those who experienced early life adversity are more prone to empathic distress.) If you're the type of person who easily absorbs and vicariously experiences the feelings of others, and your daily work exposes you to others' pain and suffering, your odds of having an empathic distress response are high, which puts you at very high risk for burnout.

First, let's get clear on the differences between compassion and empathy, because there's a tendency to use these terms interchangeably, when in reality, they're quite different. The first, baseline distinction to know is that compassion is feeling *for*, and empathy is feeling *with*. Research from social and developmental psychology posits that empathy actually precedes compassion. It works like this: An empathic response to someone's suffering results in two kinds of reactions—compassion or empathic distress. Compassion is characterized by feelings of warmth, concern, and care for the person who is suffering—and importantly, it's accompanied by a strong motivation to move *toward* the person and help alleviate their suffering. On the other hand, an empathic response to another's suffering means you're actually sharing their feelings of distress, grief, fear, or pain. The natural reaction in this case is to move *away* from the source of suffering. In other words, as opposed to compassion, which is other-focused, empathic distress is self-focused and accompanied by a strong motivation to protect oneself by withdrawing. Not surprisingly, those experiencing empathic distress have a higher risk of depression, anxiety, poorer health, nonsocial behaviors, and burnout.

For years, people used the term *compassion fatigue* to describe a kind of secondary trauma caused by an overidentification with the suffering of those they help through their work. But newer research reveals that compassion fatigue may be a misnomer. According to this new science, compassion is psychologically and neurologically *energizing*. Compassion increases activity in the brain involved in releasing the "feel-good" hormones dopamine and oxytocin, and generates positive emotions that actually counteract the negative effects of empathic distress. It's empathic distress, not compassion, that drains us, generates negative feelings, increases our stress, and raises our risk of burnout.

Professor of veterinary sciences Trisha Dowling gives a perfect illustration of how one can respond with empathic concern

Empathy	
Compassion	**Empathic Distress**
Other-related emotion	Self-related emotion
Positive feelings: e.g., love	Negative feelings: e.g., stress
Good health	Poor health, burnout
Approach and prosocial motivation	Withdrawal and nonsocial behavior

Figure 7.1: Two Reactions to the Suffering of Others

and compassion without crossing the line into empathic distress. She writes: "While empathizing with my client making a euthanasia decision [for their terminally ill pet] invokes my own feelings of sadness, moving to compassion for my client's situation results in sympathy, empathic concern, and positive emotional feelings that counterbalance my sadness and cause me to take action to help my client. Instead of withdrawing and rushing through the procedure in self-defense, compassion enables me to slow down and be present with my client without experiencing distress."

When we can respond with compassion rather than empathic distress, not only are we protected from secondary suffering and increased stress but we also enjoy positive feelings and strengthen our resilience. And, very importantly, we're able to be present and help the person (or animal!) who is in need of help, rather than withdraw because we are overwhelmed, leaving them alone in their suffering.

Fortunately, there is abundant research demonstrating the efficacy of compassion training in increasing compassion toward oneself and others, and in promoting self-awareness, resilience, positive affect, prosocial behavior, and a nonjudgmental attitude, all while lowering stress and anxiety. Most of the research has been conducted on mindfulness meditation programs like Mindfulness-Based Stress Reduction (MBSR), present moment awareness, body scans, breathing exercises, and metta or lovingkindness meditation. I have several clients who swear by Transcendental Meditation, including this school superintendent who memorably described the effect of his twice-daily TM sessions: "There's a sense of calmness, a stillness, a fondness for everything that descends on you. I can literally feel the tension in my muscles and this whole sense of stress just drain away. . . . I am shocked by how many problems that seemed impossible get resolved—you get up and it's like either it doesn't matter or you found a solution to it." Classes and online guides to mindfulness meditation are widely available, and through apps like Insight Timer, Headspace, and Calm.

Reconnect

Months into my own burnout recovery, I began to see the process of healing in a new light: I was on a journey of slowly but steadily reconnecting all the ties that burnout had weakened or severed.

Burnout had, after all, become a major interruption in my good health, my performance, in my planned career trajectory, and even in my self-perception. I was not the invincible, indefatigable worker who always turned in an A+ performance and who took for granted a steady rise to the storied pinnacles of success (whatever that was . . . the goalpost was always moving). I realized I never *had* been that person—no one is—and moreover, I didn't even want to be!

Burnout, if nothing else, is clarifying. Once you experience it, you know what does and does not work for you, and what you're willing to sacrifice for work and what you are not. Even if you don't hit bottom like I did, burnout insists that you face what you can no longer ignore, deny, pretend, or put off: something must change.

Retired Chief Jeri Williams of the Phoenix Police Department reached that point in the spring of 2022. Over a career in law enforcement that spanned more than three decades, she'd endured many high-stress events, including death threats, bomb threats, protests staged and shots fired at her own home, being physically extracted from a Pride parade because of concerns she would be kidnapped or killed, and having to manage the grim aftermath of police-involved shootings. But it was "a series of unfortunate events" that occurred in 2021 that marked the most stressful—and most hurtful—period of Williams's career.

In August the U.S. Department of Justice announced an investigation into the Phoenix PD after officers arrested protesters on gang charges, and Williams was sued by some of her own officers after she reassigned them. "It felt like it went from business to personal," Williams told me, "and that's when I started reevaluating my own mental health and my own self-worth." Every time the phone rang, she said, she felt "a jolt of panic" and braced for more bad news. By the spring of 2022, she was "emotionally and physically and mentally exhausted" and made the tough decision to speak to her boss about resigning. "Once I said it all," she said, "it was literally like I had a four-thousand-pound weight released from me."

At the same time, she felt a tremendous obligation to the city and to the department, so she and the city manager came up with an exit strategy that would keep her in place until an interim police chief could take over. During that time she began envisioning what her life would look like post-burnout, and since her retirement in October 2022, she's been providing mentorship and guidance to other police chiefs across the nation. Beyond that, she's not interested in the details. "A lot of my recovery," she said, "is just releasing the notion that I have to be in control of everything. My entire life has been planned, and now I am *so* okay with not having a plan."

Williams, after a thirty-three-year career, was ready for retirement. But if you're going to continue working post-burnout, the first order of business is to change the work stressors that led to your burnout, to whatever extent you're capable. The next steps are self-focused, and this brings us back to reconnection, which to me is one of the best parts of recovery. It's time to reconnect with what *really* matters to you and to whatever healthy conditions and practices keep your stress low and your happiness and vitality high.

Go into this phase of the healing journey with an attitude of anticipation. This is a time of renewal, of refreshment, of rejuvenation. A chance to reknit connections that burnout has frayed, a chance to rekindle your excitement and engagement. I found that the more I trusted in the image of healing as reconnection, the more hopeful I felt. My mindset became *Everything gets better from here.* And it did.

RECONNECTION FOR RESTORATION

The Colorado Resiliency Arts Lab (CORAL) at the University of Colorado's Anschutz Medical Campus is an innovative program that was launched in response to the escalating numbers of health care professionals suffering from burnout and psychological distress. Part research lab, part creative arts program, CORAL offers various art therapies to facilitate stress reduction, positive coping skills, connection to one's purpose at work, and connection to one's peers—all of which help participants recover from burnout, work-related stress, and even trauma.

CORAL's first published study, which divided 146 burned-out health care workers into four art therapy groups (creative writing, visual arts, music, and dance) and one control group who received no treatment, found that those who received arts therapy no matter the discipline saw a 27.8 percent drop in anxiety, a 35.5 percent drop in depression, a 25.8 percent drop in PTSD, and an improvement in all three components of burnout, especially emotional exhaustion (11.6 percent reduction). Further, their positive affect score increased by 28 percent while negative affect dropped by more than 23 percent, and their intention to quit fell by 10.1 percent. A recently published follow-up study produced similar results: once again arts therapy alleviated participants' symptoms of burnout and promoted overall healing and stronger resiliency.

These are really striking results, and when you peek behind the scenes, you begin to see the magic in the CORAL program's methodology. In the original study, participants were divided into cohorts of 40–60 people who met weekly for ninety minutes for twelve consecutive weeks. Each session followed a standard protocol that was designed to create a sense of psychological safety, invite vulnerability, and integrate participants' experiences within the community—in other words, to establish deep connection. The first four sessions used creative ways to introduce group members, establish expectations, and promote trust and authentic emotional expression. The middle four sessions encouraged vulnerability among participants as a means to promote resiliency, and the final four sessions were devoted to art making—both individual work as well as the creation of a team project.

CORAL director and cofounder Dr. Michael Moss believes the program's success is due to the combination of group therapy and creative practice. Participants are able to candidly share both the highs and lows of their work life, process their high-stress experiences and their negative emotional states in a safe and supportive environment, connect with people who offer energy and support, and release their stress through a creative means of expression. It provides participants with an opportunity to connect with others who get where they're coming from and to reconnect with their ideal vision of themselves, before high stress and burnout left them exhausted, cynical, and less effective, or perhaps even traumatized.

We may not all have access to a structured arts therapy program, but there is no reason we can't take a page from the CORAL method and embark on our own reconnection-inspired recovery. If, like me, you're not an artsy person by any stretch of the imagination, that's okay. First of all it's the process, not the product, that counts.

Second, it need not be art per se; any leisure activity, hobby, or pastime that helps you detach from work and decompress after a stressful day will help. Ideally, it's an activity that inspires a flow state. Here are some examples from my research participants and clients: gardening, napping, crosswords, scuba diving, dining out, classic car restoration, being a member of a bowling league, playing chess, driving, hiking, fishing, reading, volunteering, travel, quilting, competitive running, dancing, cooking, spending time with pets, writing poetry, and needlework. I love how one of my clients, an avid woodworker, beautifully describes how his favorite pastime releases his stress: "It's taking that chaos and bringing it back together in a new form—taking a blank piece of wood and making a cabinet, for example—that does it for me. Having a creative outlet is the escape that really sets me back on track."

If you're not currently involved in any such activity, think back to what you enjoyed doing before you were burned-out, and see if you can reconnect with it. Or is there something you've always wanted to try but never got around to? Trust me, don't delay any longer. Everyone I know with burnout immunity or who has recovered from burnout is intentional about creating a meaningful life outside of work, in which they prioritize doing things they love that bring them joy.

Finally, don't forget that perhaps the most important part of reconnection is that it takes a village. Recovering from burnout is never a solo endeavor. CORAL and any other burnout recovery interventions don't work without the power of social connection. We need others to help relieve some of the burden of our stress by listening to us, to help us see new ways to solve problems, to help us process the negative emotions associated with work stress, and to help us feel less isolated. Especially when the stressors of our job can't change or can't change quickly enough, we need supportive people around us. Who's on your relational sources of resilience team? Who will listen to your work experiences with openness, compassion, and confidentiality?

The Mayo Clinic sponsored a study of an internal program called COMPASS, which stands for COlleagues Meeting to Promote And Sustain Satisfaction. (Translation? Physicians who periodically get together for lunch.) In the study, one group of doctors met for lunch and conversation every other week for six months, while a control group went about their regular routines. The lunch group was assigned a topic of discussion, but beyond that, their meetings were entirely self-directed; no facilitator or leader was present.

Six months after the study concluded, participants reported a 12.7 percent decrease in burnout, a 12.8 percent decrease in depressive symptoms, and a 1.9 percent decrease in intention to quit. Meanwhile, all of those symptoms *worsened* in the control group, especially regarding intention to quit, which increased by 6.1 percent over the course of the study.

The positive results were so striking that Mayo expanded the program. Such is the power of simple human connection! No expensive or elaborate means are necessary—just listening and being listened to by a group of your peers. Currently more than 1,700 physicians and scientists participate in the COMPASS program, meeting biweekly to discuss common work challenges and issues, and enjoy the camaraderie of connection.

Reimagine

We have now arrived at the point we've been heading toward all along, where you get to reimagine and recapture a vision of your ideal self—and then move forward to bring it to life. Reimagining is the ultimate exercise in optimism and the ultimate vote of yes for yourself.

Even if you're still in the midst of burnout, you can start reimagining the self you'd most like to be and the life you most want to lead. In fact, there may be no better time. It will give you something to aspire to, and it will give you deep motivation for healing. It will give you hope.

In the field of psychology, the ideal self has a specific meaning and is part of our self-concept. Your self-concept is your overall image of who you are. It's your beliefs and perceptions about yourself, which are influenced by biological, social, and environmental factors. It's the answer you'd give to the question, "Who am I?"

Your ideal self, on the other hand, is the self you wish to be. It's the answer you'd give to the question, "Who would you be, if you could be exactly who you wanted?"

Our ideal self encompasses our dreams and images of a desired future, our passions, and the deepest expression of what we want in life. Not surprisingly, jobs that lead us away from our ideal self increase our risk of burnout, whereas jobs that are in alignment with our ideal self help to immunize us against it. In the best-case scenario, your job even helps to bring that ideal self into being. If you were exactly who you wanted to be, doing exactly what you wanted, what would that self and that life look like?

The concept of the ideal self really hit home for me when I was a doctoral student. By that point, I had recovered from the physical effects of burnout, and I had made major positive changes to my self-care practices. I'd even started to pursue a lifelong dream of furthering my education and preparing for a big career shift. But I didn't yet have a deep, guiding vision of who I really was at my core and what contributions I wanted to make in the world. I knew that someday I wanted to teach and that I probably wanted to be an executive coach. I figured it would all work out one way or another, and I'd just see what came up after I graduated.

That began to change after I became acquainted with Richard Boyatzis's intentional change theory, which presented a more nuanced idea of the ideal self. In Boyatzis's model, the ideal self is made of three components: 1) an image of your desired future, 2) hope (which encompasses self-efficacy and optimism), and 3) a comprehensive sense of your core identity. Boyatzis and his colleague Kleio Akrivou see the ideal self as the primary motivator of any intentional change we make to get closer to our desired future. (They also note that intentional change is really hard work, which I found inordinately reassuring.) When our efforts at intentional change fail, it's because we lack sufficient drive and the proper intrinsic motivation. It's only when we have a fully developed notion of our ideal self that we can make the kind of intentional change that brings that self into being. Thus the ideal self acts as both an organizing principle and an activating force that propels us ever closer to becoming the person we really want to be and who is doing work that aligns with our noble purpose.

My vision of my ideal self started to become clearer during a leadership class facilitated by my dissertation chair, Annie McKee. For two full days, we did visioning exercises, leadership development lessons, small group discussions, and lots of deep self-reflection. It was intense! Our homework was to create a detailed visioning exercise for our future, based upon our notion of our ideal self. I poured my heart and soul into it, detailing not just the career goals and personal milestones I wanted to achieve but also the kind of lifestyle I wanted, how I wanted work to fit into my life, the contributions I wanted to make, and how I wanted to support other people's development. That work gave me clarity about my ideal self and what I wanted, and enabled me to create a tactical plan to get there. It allowed me to take control of my future, rather than let my life unfold on autopilot.

Month by month, year by year, I followed that plan and watched my vision come to life. I got my doctorate, started teaching, took on big research projects, and got my coaching certificate. Every now and again, I would look at that original visioning exercise and marvel over how it was all coming to fruition. Looking back now, I can see that intentional change theory was the biggest thing that propelled me forward after I started to recover from burnout. Because from that point onward, every major decision I made was proactive, intentional, and deliberate. Having a vision of my ideal self lent specificity and urgency to my aspirations. It gave me the energy to change and led me to create a game plan to keep myself on track and make that change happen. It marked the beginning of living my life fully aware and fully awake. Ultimately it helped me pursue meaningful work in service to my values and my highest purpose—to facilitate transformational experiences that inspire people to lead with their values and embody their unique purpose—without sacrificing my physical or mental health, or my time with family and friends.

And that, my friends, is how after years of work I finally acquired burnout immunity.

Your Ideal Self and Work Environment

Now it's your turn. How do you want work to fit into your life, and not vice versa? How can you pursue the dreams and goals that emerge from your unique ideal self, and that align with your values and purpose? We're going to do a series of exercises that will help you gain clarity on your ideal self and your ideal work environment, and then we'll put it all together in a visioning exercise that will help you reimagine and revive your best self at work. These are longer exercises that require deep self-reflection, so you may want to complete them over a few sessions.

EXERCISE 1: MY IDEAL SELF INVENTORY

These questions are meant to spark self-reflection, so if any don't resonate with you, simply skip them and go on to the ones that do. Let's start envisioning your ideal self. This is the self you'd most love to be, your "wildest dreams" self. Go big and don't censor yourself! Allow yourself to imagine your very best you.

PHYSICAL

- Picture yourself at your healthiest, most attractive, and most capable. What conditions are contributing to this optimal physical state?

EMOTIONAL

- Picture yourself at your happiest, most grounded, and most confident. What conditions are contributing to this optimal emotional state?

SOCIAL/RELATIONAL

- Let's think about the people surrounding you in your ideal life. Are you part of a large friend group or a small, closely knit circle?

- Are you in a long-term partnership, a mingling single, or a solo artist?
- Is your ideal self a parent? If so, how many children do you have?
- What's your family like? How often do you interact with them, and what are those interactions like?
- What's your ideal balance of social interaction and alone time?

BEHAVIORAL

- What kind of leisure activities do you participate in? How often?
- If you could design your ideal schedule (sleep/wake times, hours worked per week, periods of downtime and leisure, etc.), what would it look like?
- Are you involved in any sort of volunteer activity? If so, describe it.

INTELLECTUAL/CREATIVE

- What sort of ongoing learning opportunities are you involved in? This could be anything from formal education to being a member of a book club to attending lecture series and webinars.
- How do you see yourself sharing your knowledge, expertise, creativity, or talent with others?

SPIRITUAL/MEANING MAKING

- Are you engaged in a faith practice? If so, describe it.
- Are you involved in a religious or spiritual community? If so, describe that.
- Do you have any spiritual practices, traditional or nontraditional, that keep you centered and connected to a sense of something larger than yourself? What are they?
- Overall, how do you, as one of my clients memorably put it, "assemble your own spiritual well-being"?

PROFESSIONAL

- We'll get to the specifics of your ideal job in the next exercise, but here let's dream big. What are you doing professionally that brings your unique purpose to life? You can use this prompt to spark your thinking; adapt it however you like:
I [provide/create/catalyze] [products/services/solutions] to [clients/customers/audiences] so they can [outcome].

A couple of my favorite client responses are "I create magical and life-changing adventures for reluctant travelers who've always wanted to follow their bliss" and this one, written from the perspective of looking back over a successful career: "I designed, built, and gifted a beautiful, functional home to every unhoused person in LA." Is this realistic? No, but that's not the point. This person captured his deepest desires in his ideal professional life, and guess what he does now? He left his architectural firm to join a nonprofit that builds affordable housing for unhoused and low-income individuals and families.

EXERCISE 2: MY IDEAL WORK ENVIRONMENT INVENTORY

Now, with that dream job in mind, let's get more specific about your ideal work environment.

PHYSICAL

- We'll work from the big picture to the granular. First, where do you work in the world? (It's okay to name multiple countries and continents!) What type of area is it (urban area, small town, neighborhood, rural area, etc.)?
- At your specific location, what are your ideal physical working conditions? For example, is your ideal self in a sprawling, open-concept office, an executive suite, your home office, the

great outdoors, on the road, or not tethered to any specific location? Do you want to go into an organization every day, have a hybrid schedule, work fully remotely, or be a digital nomad?

- Now, how about the energy of your workspace. Are you in a bustling, high-energy environment or cozied up in your home office? Something in between or a little of both?

SOCIAL/RELATIONAL

- Roughly how many coworkers do you have? What are they like?
- To what extent do you interact and collaborate with your colleagues while you're on-site? To what extent, if any, do you interact with them outside of work?
- How do you communicate with leaders? If you are a leader, how do you communicate with teammates and staff?

BEHAVIORAL

- In terms of autonomy, flexibility, and the control you have over your work processes, what are your ideal conditions for how you get your work done?
- What's your ideal PTO and vacation policy?
- What are your boundaries between work and nonwork time? In your ideal vision, how are those boundaries honored?
- To what extent are you involved in decision-making, setting an agenda, or developing a mission or vision?
- What sort of feedback do you need in order to do your best work? What is the best way for you to receive this feedback?

EMOTIONAL

- What are the emotional boundaries that enable you to do your best work, and how are those boundaries honored?

- What resources and safeguards are in place to support your mental and emotional health? What is your ideal way of accessing them?
- How does your work culture invest in and protect your emotional and mental health? How open are people regarding their emotional and mental health? What kinds of support and care are available to you?

VALUES

- What values do you hold that inspire and motivate you to do your best at work?
- How does your ideal work environment enable you to enact them?
- How do your values align with your organization's mission?

REWARD

- What's your ideal compensation? Name your number, but also think beyond monetary reward. Do you want equity, for instance? Do you want to own a company or a business? Do you want to do gig work so you can maximize your flexibility? Do you want to do something completely outside the system, like bartering? Remember, this is dream time.
- How would you like to be recognized for your efforts?
- How would you like to be thanked for your efforts?
- How would you like to know that you're having an impact and being effective?

GROWTH AND ADVANCEMENT

- What sort of training, continuing education, professional development, or mentoring options are you taking advantage of in your ideal work environment?

- What sort of opportunities exist for promotions and career advancement?
- When you reach the end of your career, where would you like to be? What would you like to have achieved?

EXERCISE 3: VISIONING: REIMAGINING YOUR IMPACT

Using all the rich self-reflection you just generated, answer the following questions about the experience and the impact you want to have through work:

1. When I go to work, I want to feel _____.
2. At the end of the workday, I want to feel _____.
3. The impact I make with my work is _____.
4. The people who benefit from my work are _____.
5. If I could accomplish one thing in my life, it would be _____.
6. I want to be remembered for _____.

As you reflect on your answers, what patterns do you notice? What conditions will help you to rise above your current circumstances and establish a vision and a plan that will provide the energy needed to achieve the impact you want to make?

The Good Stuff

I know I've thrown a lot at you in this book and that this is not easy work, especially if you're burned-out or at risk of burnout, or if you're engaging in a lot of deep self-reflection and perhaps facing some painful realities for the first time. But trust me, it is all worth it. I promise! I'm not one of those lucky people who was born with burnout immunity, and I'm not exactly known for my serenity under pressure. That's why even today, after all the strides I've made to recover from burnout and heal my relationship with work, I still work at my EI skills on a daily basis. Which is to say, I've made a commitment to continually getting better at living my life in a way that's centered on my values, my purpose, and my vision of my ideal self. Every day, I see that person a little more clearly, and if anything at work threatens to lead me away from that healthiest, happiest version of myself, I say no. I don't want to live that way, and neither should you. *This* is the great reward of recovering from burnout, learning skills to protect yourself from burnout, or simply learning better ways to manage your work-related stress. You're now free to focus on the good stuff, the stuff that makes life meaningful and worthwhile.

I'm reminded again of the Harvard Study of Adult Development, and how, after so many decades of research and so many millions of dollars spent, the study's conclusions came down to simple truths about love, happiness, and warm relationships. Recently, study leader Dr. Robert Waldinger was asked about his definition of "the good life." His reply was refreshingly straightforward: "Being engaged in activities I care about with people I care about."

Are you living this kind of good life? Are you engaged in meaningful work you care about, with colleagues and customers and clients you care about? When you are away from work, are you doing enjoyable things with people you love? *This* is why we do the work to get better. It means we now have the physical, mental, and emotional wherewithal to go for the life we want, the one that's worth getting healthy for. A life that may be stressful from time to time, or even much of the time, but one that is fulfilling, effective, impactful, and on the best days, brings you and others genuine joy.

And that, dear readers, is my hope for each one of you!

Acknowledgments

Truth be told, I had no idea researching and writing a book would be so darn fun. Like many of my friends who got their doctorate, I thought I may never want to write again after my dissertation. Apparently, post-doc writing trauma is a thing—and boy did I experience it! I also didn't know if I was capable of unlearning the academic writing skills I had worked so hard to develop in order to write a book about my research in a way that wouldn't put people to sleep.

But if there's one thing my life experiences and research have taught me, it's that what we're capable of is directly impacted by the relationships we surround ourselves with. The epitome of that is the relationship I've developed with my writing partner, Catherine Knepper. It's an understatement to say that both this book and my life are immeasurably better because she is in them. From the minute we met, I knew that Catherine got me. She has an eerie sense of knowing what I want to say and how I want to say it, often before I do. She helped me find and bring my voice to the page and pushed me to be vulnerable, even when it felt cringey and uncomfortable. Not only did she save me from a few bad ideas but she also brought her own wicked smartness and creativity to the writing. I'm so incredibly grateful for her friendship and her massive contributions to *Burnout Immunity*, and I look forward to collaborating on future projects.

With my deepest sense of gratitude, I also wish to thank a number of other people who contributed to this book and were (and continue to be) important sources of resilience.

My literary agent, Jill Marsal of the Marsal Lyon Literary Agency, believed in this project from the get-go. I knew I had the makings of a dream team when she agreed to take me on as a client. Her guidance and encouragement throughout the process have been invaluable.

My editors at HarperCollins—Kirby Sandmeyer and Hollis Heimbouch—immediately understood my vision and saw the potential in this project. They also saw ways this book will have an impact that go beyond my wildest dreams. I'm grateful to them for validating my vision and ideas, and for the editorial excellence they provided that strengthened the quality of this work.

My public relations team at Fortier PR—Mark Fortier and Mallory Campoli—provided the expertise and guidance needed to position this book for maximum visibility and impact. I especially appreciate Mark's advice on the book title, which accurately and authentically captures the essence of my research findings.

When I wrote the section on meaningful relationships in Chapter 5, there were several people who were consistently on my mind.

My family—Erick, Spencer, Colsen, and Sawyer Hernandez—consistently remind me that a stressful life is a meaningful life. I've sacrificed a considerable amount of time with them to be able to focus on my research and writing, and not once did they make me feel guilty for it. They showed an interest in my work and gave me the patience and space I needed to focus on doing what I love. It means the world to me to see the boys grow up to be the resilient role models Erick and I believe they will be.

My dad, Robert Wiens, is the most resilient role model I've ever met. His role modeling was perhaps the single biggest reason for my interest in resilience literature. His life experiences would have resulted in dire consequences for most people, but his mental strength and emotional stability saved his life (and probably mine, too). I am so incredibly proud to be his daughter and feel an overwhelming sense of gratitude for his presence in my life.

My stepmom, Cindy Wiens, has shown a keen interest in my work for years. Her support and encouragement along the way have been an inspiration during some of the toughest days.

My sister, Jodi Fellman, has been my biggest cheerleader. When I experienced moments of self-doubt or overwhelm during the book-writing process, her daily Snapchats gave me just what I needed to recalibrate and regain my focus. And, when it felt like all hell was going to break loose, she FaceTimed me to show me her latest dance moves, a surefire way to get me to put things back into perspective.

My good friend Dr. Darin Rowell continually reminds me that optimal performance and resilience are about relationships. For the past ten years, he has helped me gain clarity and take focused action on my values and goals. And, throughout our doctoral program as well as the writing of this book, he provided the support and encouragement I needed to put my best effort into my research and writing while keeping my burnout immunity high. I'm also especially grateful to him for providing feedback on early drafts, codesigning some of the exercises, and for helping me parlay my research into several coauthored *Harvard Business Review* articles

My team at the University of Pennsylvania—Dr. Don Boyer, Dr. Anna Weiss, Dr. Jay Mehta, Dr. J. P. Orlando, Nyssa Levy, Jessica Hall, and April Coleman—have been my village throughout this journey. I'm thankful for their support and encouragement, which have been major antidotes to my stress.

My mentors, Dr. Annie McKee and Dr. Nigel Paine, taught me what it means to be a scholar-practitioner who cares deeply about examining the lived experiences of research participants. Through our many personal conversations and my time in their classes, they fueled my passion and curiosity for what it takes to be an effective leader in today's demanding world. They taught me that it's about self-compassion, a deep connection to a noble purpose, and a commitment to lifelong learning.

My colleagues and research mentors, Dr. Dana Kaminstein and Dr. Sharon Ravitch, helped me cultivate a researcher mindset and develop the skills needed to conduct rigorous academic research. Long before I knew qualitative research was a thing, I had a deep sense of curiosity about other people's life experiences. But it wasn't until I took research methods classes with Dana and Sharon that I was able to shift my identity to one of a scholar-practitioner.

My friends Dr. Gretchen Schmelzer and Dr. Peter Loper were frequently there to geek out with me on all things related to healthy human development. I hope that what I've learned from them is accurately captured in these pages. They were also both instrumental in providing feedback on early drafts and helping me think through and design a couple of the exercises.

My doctoral and master's students at the University of Pennsylvania, my coaching clients, and my workshop participants provided the perfect laboratory for me to test out many of the reflection questions and exercises found in *Burnout Immunity*.

Finally, and perhaps most importantly, I wish to thank the hundreds of people who participated in my research projects. I'm incredibly grateful for the richness of their stories and their willingness to share their time with me.

The Burnout Risk Assessment

One of the first and most important steps to protecting yourself from burnout is becoming aware of your risk level. Where does your risk level fall? Answer the questions below, and then tally your score at the end using the numbers in parentheses. If you prefer a digital version, you can access the assessment online by using the QR code below, which will give you access to additional tools and tips for addressing your experience of burnout.

My stress level over the last three months has been . . .

Very mild (1)
Tolerable (2)
Distressing (3)
Severe (4)
Worst possible (5)

I concentrate my energy on what I can control.

Strongly disagree (5)
Disagree (4)
Neutral (3)
Agree (2)
Strongly agree (1)

I feel comfortable asking others for help when I am stressed out.

Strongly disagree (5)
Disagree (4)
Neutral (3)
Agree (2)
Strongly agree (1)

I'm experiencing a lot of conflict with other people at work.

Strongly disagree (1)
Disagree (2)
Neutral (3)
Agree (4)
Strongly agree (5)

I view stressors as problems that can be solved.

Strongly disagree (5)
Disagree (4)
Neutral (3)
Agree (2)
Strongly agree (1)

My work culture feels toxic.

Strongly disagree (1)
Disagree (2)
Neutral (3)
Agree (4)
Strongly agree (5)

I am working longer and harder than I want to.

Strongly disagree (1)
Disagree (2)
Neutral (3)
Agree (4)
Strongly agree (5)

There's way more to my identity than my work.

Strongly disagree (5)
Disagree (4)
Neutral (3)
Agree (2)
Strongly agree (1)

My stress level does not feel sustainable.

Strongly disagree (1)
Disagree (2)
Neutral (3)
Agree (4)
Strongly agree (5)

Over the last three months, I have considered leaving my job.

Strongly disagree (1)
Disagree (2)
Neutral (3)
Agree (4)
Strongly agree (5)

I have the support I need to be effective at work.

Strongly disagree (5)
Disagree (4)
Neutral (3)
Agree (2)
Strongly agree (1)

I have a bad attitude about work right now.

Strongly disagree (1)
Disagree (2)
Neutral (3)
Agree (4)
Strongly agree (5)

I feel emotionally exhausted at the end of the workday.

Strongly disagree (1)
Disagree (2)
Neutral (3)
Agree (4)
Strongly agree (5)

I feel a sense of purpose in my work.

Strongly disagree (5)
Disagree (4)
Neutral (3)
Agree (2)
Strongly agree (1)

I feel like I am good at my job.

Strongly disagree (5)
Disagree (4)
Neutral (3)
Agree (2)
Strongly agree (1)

I have a hard time telling others "no."

Strongly disagree (1)
Disagree (2)
Neutral (3)
Agree (4)
Strongly agree (5)

I always make time for the people and/or things I love outside of work, regardless of my busy schedule.

Strongly disagree (5)
Disagree (4)
Neutral (3)
Agree (2)
Strongly agree (1)

In times of high stress, I focus on the positive impact I can make on what happens next.

Strongly disagree (5)
Disagree (4)

Neutral (3)
Agree (2)
Strongly agree (1)

I am making too many personal sacrifices for work right now.

Strongly disagree (1)
Disagree (2)
Neutral (3)
Agree (4)
Strongly agree (5)

I focus on what is most important to me in life.

Strongly disagree (5)
Disagree (4)
Neutral (3)
Agree (2)
Strongly agree (1)

Results

20–40 points = Low Risk

Your stress level is most likely at a point that you can reasonably manage with your current support system. You may be feeling a sense of harmony with work and life, and generally have a good deal of energy to get things done. Setting and holding boundaries may be working for you, too. To keep your resilience skills sharp, reflect on the mindsets, behaviors, and people that are supporting you. When you're heading into a difficult project or busy time of year, lean on those supports and double down on your self-care practices. If you keep up your healthy habits, you can keep burnout at bay.

41–70 points = Moderate Risk

You may have days where you feel depleted and burned-out and other days when you feel energetic and engaged. Do you feel less creative, innovative, collaborative, or more closed-minded about changes at work? Do you feel like you're working harder and at the same time feel less effective than normal? Do you sometimes feel numb, overwhelmed, or have thoughts of escaping your current situation?

First, don't panic! A moderate risk of burnout doesn't necessarily mean that you're in a hopeless situation. In fact, knowing where you are on the burnout risk scale is a major first step in making some meaningful changes. It's time to take a look at the workplace triggers that are increasing your stress, as well as the patterns in your thinking and behavior that may be contributing to your stress.

Next, pay close attention to when and where you most often feel stressed or anxious. What do you notice about your stress triggers—are they connected to certain times of day, people, activities, or experiences? Reflect on the impact of these feelings and thoughts on different aspects of your life. How is your escalating stress affecting your ability to learn new things, your relationships, your performance at work and home, and your physical and psychological health? Keeping a close pulse on how you are feeling during the workday as well as how you respond to stress will be key to mitigating further risk of burnout.

Finally, continue focusing on the positive impact you can make, even when things are really tough. Be kind and forgiving to yourself and others when mistakes are made. And don't forget how great it feels when you make time for people and/or things you love outside of work! Engaging in meaningful connections and activities outside of work is one of the most powerful protective forces against burnout.

71–100 points = High Risk

You may feel like you've lost your energy, enthusiasm, and confidence. Burnout can come in many different forms and have various effects, depending on the person. Physical illness, a lack of hope, impatience, irritability, a decline in work performance or the quality of relationships, and a sense of apathy or indifference toward your job are all signs of burnout. However you're experiencing it, know that burnout is not your fault, and it is reversible.

You may want to start by examining the organizational issues that are causing you stress. Which ones are in your control and can be changed? Which ones are not? Stressors that are out of our control tend to make us feel emotionally exhausted and increase the risk of burnout. Step up your self-care practices and request time off. Seek help from the sources available to you: friends, family, mentors, colleagues, managers, your organization's ERG or wellness program, an executive coach, or a therapist.

Notes

Chapter 1: Breaking Free of Burnout

10   Goleman defined EI: Daniel Goleman, *Emotional Intelligence: Why It Can Matter More Than IQ* (New York: Bantam Books, 1995).

11   by three things: Departmental News, "Burn-out an 'occupational phenomenon': International Classification of Diseases," World Health Organization, May 28, 2019, https://www.who.int/news /item/28-05-2019-burn-out-an-occupational-phenomenon-international -classification-of-diseases.

13   Domains and Competencies: Daniel Goleman and Richard E. Boyatzis, "Emotional Intelligence Has 12 Elements. Which Do You Need to Work On?" *Harvard Business Review*, February 6, 2017, https://hbr.org/2017/02 /emotional-intelligence-has-12-elements-which-do-you-need-to-work-on.

20   a chilling conclusion: Carmen Allison, "Intense Workplace Pressure: Exploring the Causes and Intrapersonal Effects of Pressure on Executive Leaders" (EdD diss., University of Pennsylvania, 2023), https://www.proquest .com/docview/2811838428.

20   *part of success*: "Asana Anatomy of Work Index 2022: Work About Work Hampering Organizational Agility," Asana, April 5, 2022, https://investors.asana.com/news/news-details/2022/Asana-Anatomy-of -Work-Index-2022-Work-About-Work-Hampering-Organizational-Agility /default.aspx.

Chapter 2: Case Study: YOU

24   more-profitable companies: Tasha Eurich, "What Self-Awareness Really Is (And How to Cultivate It)," *Harvard Business Review*, January 4, 2018, https://hbr.org/2018/01/what-self-awareness-really-is -and-how-to-cultivate-it.

25   collaborate more effectively: Lauren Landry, "Why Emotional Intelligence Is Important in Leadership," *Business Insights* (blog), April 3, 2019, https://online.hbs.edu/blog/post/emotional-intelligence-in -leadership#:~:text=Leaders%20who%20excel%20in%20social,more%20 effectively%20with%20their%20peers.

25   success by *half*: Tasha Eurich, "Working with People Who Aren't Self-Aware," *Harvard Business Review*, October 19, 2018, https:// hbr.org/2018/10/working-with-people-who-arent-self-aware.

26   Tasha Eurich concluded: Ibid.

26   their EI competencies: These results are based upon eighty- five clients' multi-rater assessments.

27   "equal-opportunity international crisis": Edward Segal, "New Surveys Show Burnout Is an International Crisis," *Forbes*, October 15,

2022, https://www.forbes.com/sites/edwardsegal/2022/10/15/surveys
-show-burnout-is-an-international-crisis/?sh=5343e2867cf7.

32   "needs to change": Michael P. Leiter and Christina Maslach,
*The Truth About Burnout: How Organizations Cause Personal Stress and
What to Do About It* (San Francisco, CA: Jossey-Bass Inc., 1997), 21.

32   with the mine: "Understanding Job Burnout," IT Revolution,
February 18, 2019, https://itrevolution.com/understanding-job-burnout
-christina-maslach/.

32   on the job: Ibid.

32   of these areas: Michael Leiter and Christina Maslach, "Six
Areas of Worklife: A Model of the Organizational Context of Burnout,"
Journal of Health and Human Services Administration 21 (1999): 472–89.

33   of their work: Ibid.

34   Flexible scheduling: Axonify, "Axonify Releases Annual
Global State of Frontline Work Experience Study," PR Newswire, October
14, 2021, https://www.prnewswire.com/news-releases/axonify-releases
-annual-global-state-of-frontline-work-experience-study-301399564.html.

34   here is simple: Leiter and Maslach, "Six Areas of Worklife."

35   cynicism and withdrawal: "The U.S. Surgeon General's
Framework for Workplace Mental Health & Well-Being," Office of the U.S.
Surgeon General, 2022, https://www.hhs.gov/sites/default/files/workplace
-mental-health-well-being.pdf, 24.

35   in the past year: Ibid., 25.

35   "to manage stress": Ibid., 26.

36   write Maslach and Leiter: Leiter and Maslach, "Six Areas of
Worklife."

37   healthy organizations need: Ibid.

38   to burn out: Ben Wigert and Sangeeta Agrawal, "Employe
Burnout, Part 1: The 5 Main Causes," Gallup, July 12, 2018, https://www
.gallup.com/workplace/237059/employee-burnout-part-main-causes.aspx.

38   "incompatible with burnout": Leiter and Maslach, "Six Areas
of Worklife."

39   *mentally and spiritually*: Ruchika Tulshyan, "The
Psychological Toll of Being the Only Woman of Color at Work," *Harvard
Business Review*, September 20, 2022, https://hbr.org/2022/09/the
-psychological-toll-of-being-the-only-woman-of-color-at
-work?utm_medium=email&utm_source=newsletter_daily&utm
_campaign=dailyalert_notactsubs&deliveryName=DM217219.

42   "important external stakeholders": Michael Housman and
Dylan Minor, "Toxic Workers," Working Paper 16-057, Harvard Business
School, 2015, https://www.hbs.edu/ris/Publication%20Files/16-057
_d45c0b4f-fa19-49de-8f1b-4b12fe054fea.pdf.

42   suffer for it: Amy Gallo, "How to Manage a Toxic Employee,"
Harvard Business Review, October 3, 2016, https://hbr.org/2016/10/how
-to-manage-a-toxic-employee.

42   within three to six months: Jacqueline Brassey, Erica Coe,
Martin Dewhurst, Kana Enomoto, Barbara Jeffrey, Renata Giarola, and
Brad Herbig, "Addressing Employee Burnout: Are You Solving the Right
Problem?," McKinsey & Company, October 7, 2022, https://www.mckinsey
.com/mhi/our-insights/addressing-employee-burnout-are-you-solving-the
-right-problem.

43   becoming toxic yourself: Housman and Minor, "Toxic Workers."

44   a full year: L. Bonnesen, S. Pihl-Thingvad, and V. Winter,

"The Contagious Leader: A Panel Study on Occupational Stress Transfer in a Large Danish Municipality," *BMC Public Health* 22, no. 1874 (2022), https://doi.org/10.1186/s12889-022-14179-5.

44   lead to burnout: S. G. Barsade, "The Ripple Effect: Emotional Contagion and Its Influence on Group Behavior," *Administrative Science Quarterly* 47, no. 4 (2002): 644–75, http://dx.doi.org/10.2307/3094912.

45   each other frequently: Devon Price, "Burnout contagion: Managing and reducing socially-transmitted burnout," CQ Net, April 25, 2018, https://www.ckju.net/en/dossier/burnout-contagion-managing-and-reducing-socially-transmitted-burnout.

46   not be tolerated: Sigal Barsade, "Emotional Contagion," Wharton@Work newsletter, https://executiveeducation.wharton.upenn.edu/wp-content/uploads/2018/03/1102-Emotional-Contagion.pdf.

47   to life experiences: https://psychcentral.com/health/temperament-and-personality#temperaments-influence.

53   learn from experience: Linda Graham, *Bouncing Back: Rewiring Your Brain for Maximum Resilience and Well-Being* (Novato, CA: New World Library, 2013), 4, 11.

54   to new experiences: Ibid., 4.

54   quickly, adaptively, and effectively: Ibid., xxv.

54   "anything at all": Ibid., 5.

55   into future generations: "Fast Facts: Preventing Adverse Childhood Experiences," Centers for Disease Control and Prevention, last reviewed June 29, 2023, https://www.cdc.gov/violenceprevention/aces/fastfact.html.

55   conserve metabolic resources: https://www.ncbi.nlm.nih.gov/books/NBK541120/.

56   use of the car: "ACEs and Toxic Stress: Frequently Asked Questions," Center on the Developing Child, https://developingchild.harvard.edu/resources/aces-and-toxic-stress-frequently-asked-questions/.

57   down the line: C. A. Nelson et al., "Adversity in Childhood Is Linked to Mental and Physical Health Throughout Life," *BMJ*, October 28, 2020, https://www.bmj.com/content/371/bmj.m3048.

57   federal poverty level: Marilyn Metzler, Melissa T. Merrick, Joanne Klevens, Katie A. Ports, and Derek C. Ford, "Adverse Childhood Experiences and Life Opportunities: Shifting the Narrative," *Children and Youth Services Review* 72 (2017): 141–49, https://doi.org/10.1016/j.childyouth.2016.10.021.

58   risk of burnout: Peter Yellowlees et al., "The Association Between Adverse Childhood Experiences and Burnout in a Regional Sample of Physicians," *Acad Psychiatry* 45, no. 2 (April 2021): 159–63, https://pubmed.ncbi.nlm.nih.gov/33409937/.

58   burnout and depression: Gloria McKee-Lopez, Leslie Robbins, Elias Provencio-Vasquez, and Hector Olvera, "The Relationship of Childhood Adversity on Burnout and Depression Among BSN Students," *Journal of Professional Nursing* 35, no. 2 (2019): 112–19, https://doi.org/10.1016/j.profnurs.2018.09.008.

58   to experience burnout: Eric M. Brown, Kristy L. Carlisle, Melanie Burgess, Jacob Clark, and Ariel Hutcheon, "Adverse and Positive Childhood Experiences of Clinical Mental Health Counselors as Predictors of Compassion Satisfaction, Burnout, and Secondary Traumatic Stress," *Professional Counselor* 12, no. 1 (February 7, 2022): 49–64, https://doi.org/10.15241/emb.12.1.49.

58   *lifelong positive results*: Elizabeth Crouch, Elizabeth Radcliff,
      Melissa Strompolis, and Aditi Srivastav, "Safe, Stable, and Nurtured:
      Protective Factors Against Poor Physical and Mental Health Outcomes
      Following Exposure to Adverse Childhood Experiences (ACEs)," *Journal of
      Child & Adolescent Trauma* 12, no. 2 (May 25, 2018): 165–73, https://doi
      .org/10.1007/s40653-018-0217-9. Emphasis added.
59   "body breakdowns": A. Michel, "Embodying the Market: The
      Emergence of the Body Entrepreneur," *Administrative Science Quarterly*
      68, no. 1 (March 2023): 44–96, https://doi
      .org/10.1177/00018392221135606.
60   later in life: Graham, *Bouncing Back*, xxv–xxvi.
60   "navigate stressful situations": Dr. Peter Loper, interview with
      the author, October 7, 2022.
60   high in neuroticism: L. S. Varghese, A. P. Rogers, L.
      Finkelstein, and L. K. Barber, "Examining Mentors as Buffers of Burnout
      for Employees High in Neuroticism," *Human Resource Development
      Quarterly* 31, no. 3 (2020): 281–300, https://doi.org/10.1002/hrdq.21390.
60   associated with ACEs: J. M. Grusnick, E. Garacci, C. Eiler,
      J. S. Williams, and L. E. Egede, "The Association Between Adverse
      Childhood Experiences and Personality, Emotions and Affect: Does
      Number and Type of Experiences Matter?" *Journal of Research in
      Personality* 85 (April 2020): 103908, doi:10.1016/j.jrp.2019.103908.
61   a foreign city: Elizabeth Hopper, "Understanding Self-
      Efficacy," ThoughtCo., August 11, 2021, https://www.thoughtco.com/self
      -efficacy-4177970.

Chapter 3: Put Your Stress to Good Use

75   entire stress response: "Understanding the Stress Response,"
      Harvard Health, July 6, 2020, https://www.health.harvard.edu/staying
      -healthy/understanding-the-stress-response, accessed January 9, 2023.
77   actually pass out: Melanie Greenberg, *The Stress-Proof
      Brain: Master Your Emotional Response to Stress Using Mindfulness and
      Neuroplasticity* (Oakland, CA: New Harbinger, 2016), 21.
78   angry, or overwhelmed: Paula Davis, "What Is Your Stress
      Response Style?" *Psychology Today*, August 17, 2018, https://www
      .psychologytoday.com/us/blog/pressure-proof/201808/what-is-your
      -stress-response-style, accessed January 10, 2023.
79   cortisol's negative effects: Kelly McGonigal, *The Upside of
      Stress: Why Stress Is Good for You, and How to Get Good at It* (New York:
      Avery, 2016).
79   "resources to succeed": Ibid., 109.
80   "a challenge response": Ibid., 113.
80   praying for you: Ibid.
81   challenges and threats: S. E. Taylor et al., "Biobehavioral
      Responses to Stress in Females: Tend-and-Befriend, Not Fight-or-Flight,"
      Psychological Review 107, no. 3 (2000): 411–29, https://doi
      .org/10.1037/0033-295X.107.3.411.
82   increasing your courage: McGonigal, *The Upside of Stress*,
      137.
82   freeze under pressure: Ibid.
82   the biggest impact: Ibid.
83   "and creates hope": Ibid., 139.
85   or heat exposure: M. P. Mattson, "Hormesis Defined," *Ageing*

Research Reviews 7, no. 1 (January 2008): 1–7, doi: 10.1016/j
.arr.2007.08.007.

86   after experiencing stress: Assaf Oshri et al., "Low-to-
Moderate Level of Perceived Stress Strengthens Working Memory: Testing
the Hormesis Hypothesis Through Neural Activation," ScienceDirect,
November 5, 2022, https://doi.org/10.1016/j.neuropsychologia.2022
.108354, accessed January 27, 2023.

86   "act at all": Linda Graham and Rick Hanson, *Bouncing Back:
Rewiring Your Brain for Maximum Resilience and Well-Being* (Novato,
CA: New World Library, 2013), 191.

86   engaged and alert: Ibid., 194.

87   The Window of Tolerance: Ibid., 201.

87   "for self-regulation": Ibid., 207.

87   "good for us": Ibid., 206–7.

88   "state of equilibrium": Ibid., 196.

88   with oxytocin receptors: Ibid., 210–12.

88   the stress response: Holly MacCormick, "How Stress Affects
Your Brain and How to Reverse It," *Scope* (blog), Stanford University
School of Medicine, October 7, 2020, https://scopeblog.stanford.
edu/2020/10/07/how-stress-affects-your-brain-and-how-to-reverse-it/
accessed January 16, 2023.

89   as ten minutes: Kirsten Weir, "Nurtured by Nature," Monitor
on Psychology, American Psychological Association, April 1, 2020, https://
www.apa.org/monitor/2020/04/nurtured-nature, accessed January 16,
2023.

89   and stress reduction: A. Gračanin, L. M. Bylsma, A. J.
Vingerhoets, "Is Crying a Self-Soothing Behavior?," *Frontiers in Psychology*
5, no. 502 (May 28, 2014), doi:10.3389/fpsyg.2014.00502.

89   have zero control: David Richo, *Triggers: How We Can Stop
Reacting and Start Healing* (Boulder, CO: Shambhala, 2019), 1.

90   trigger has dissipated: Anne Grady, "Handle Your Stress
Better by Knowing What Causes It," *Harvard Business Review*, June 21,
2017, https://hbr.org/2017/06/handle-your-stress-better-by-knowing
-what-causes-it.

94   "become much clearer": Juliana Rosati, "Facing the Moment:
Professor Howard Stevenson on Managing Racial Conflict Through Racial
Literacy," *Penn GSE*, April 14, 2016, https://www.gse.upenn.edu/news
/facing-moment-professor-howard-stevenson-managing-racial-conflict
-through-racial-literacy, accessed January 9, 2023.

Chapter 4: The Power and Promise of Regulation

113   poor decision-making: Brené Brown, *Atlas of the Heart:
Mapping Meaningful Connection and the Language of Human Experience*
(New York: Random House, 2021), 6–7.

118   for emotional regulation: M. Speer and M. Delgado,
"Reminiscing About Positive Memories Buffers Acute Stress Responses,"
Nature Human Behavior 1, no. 0093 (2017), https://doi.org/10.1038
/s41562-017-0093.

119   overwhelmed and stuck: Gretchen Schmelzer, "In Praise
of Distraction," January 19, 2023, http://gretchenschmelzer.com/blog-
1/2015/2/5/in-praise-of-distraction.

120   higher their stress: Susan Jennifer Thomas and Theresa
Larkin, "Cognitive Distortions in Relation to Plasma Cortisol and Oxytocin

Levels in Major Depressive Disorder," *Frontiers in Psychiatry* 10 (2020), https://doi.org/10.3389/fpsyt.2019.00971.

128   chronic stress: Kristin Neff, "Why We Need to Have Compassion for Our Inner Critic," Self-Compassion, https://self-compassion.org/why-we-need-to-have-compassion-for-our-inner-critic/, accessed December 27, 2022.

128   resilience to stress: Kristin Neff, "The Physiology of Self-Compassion," Self-Compassion, https://self-compassion.org/the-physiology-of-self-compassion/, accessed December 26, 2022.

128   "anybody would be": Catherine Moore, "How to Practice Self-Compassion: 8 Techniques and Tips," PositivePsychology.com, June 2, 2019, https://positivepsychology.com/how-to-practice-self-compassion/, accessed January 27, 2023.

129   "my closest friend": Ibid.

129   "May I be strong": Kristin Neff, "Exercise 2: Self-Compassion Break," Self-Compassion, December 13, 2015, https://self-compassion.org/exercise-2-self-compassion-break/, accessed January 27, 2023.

136   are to stress: B. Q. Ford, P. Lam, O. P. John, and I. B. Mauss, "The Psychological Health Benefits of Accepting Negative Emotions and Thoughts: Laboratory, Diary, and Longitudinal Evidence," *Journal of Personality and Social Psychology* 115, no. 6 (2018), doi:10.1037/pspp0000157.

139   "personal and professional potential": "ICF, the Gold Standard in Coaching: Read About ICF," International Coaching Federation, August 18, 2022, https://coachingfederation.org/about, accessed January 30, 2023.

139   they typically realize: G. Gazelle, J. M. Liebschutz, and H. Riess, "Physician Burnout: Coaching a Way Out," *Journal of General Internal Medicine*, U.S. National Library of Medicine, December 20, 2014, https://pubmed.ncbi.nlm.nih.gov/25527340/, accessed January 30, 2023.

139   engaged in coaching: Chris Bittinger, "The Influence of Executive Coaching on Executive Leaders' Ability to Manage Stress and Mitigate Burnout" (EdD diss., University of Pennsylvania, 2023).

Chapter 5: Purpose, People, and Values

146   work they do: Naina Dhingra, Andrew Samo, Bill Schaninger, and Matt Schrimper, "Help Your Employees Find Purpose—or Watch Them Leave," McKinsey & Company, April 5, 2021, https://www.mckinsey.com/capabilities/people-and-organizational-performance/our-insights/help-your-employees-find-purpose-or-watch-them-leave, accessed March 7, 2023.

146   was always meaningful: Shawn Achor, Andrew Reece, Gabriella Rosen Kellerman, and Alexi Robichaux, "9 Out of 10 People Are Willing to Earn Less Money to Do More-Meaningful Work," *Harvard Business Review*, November 6, 2018, https://hbr.org/2018/11/9-out-of-10-people-are-willing-to-earn-less-money-to-do-more-meaningful-work, accessed March 6, 2023.

146   by their jobs: Dhingra et al., "Help Your Employees Find Purpose."

150   with employee turnover: Achor et al., "9 Out of 10 People."

153   on team performance: "The U.S. Surgeon General's Framework for Workplace Mental Health & Well-Being," Office of the U.S. Surgeon General, 2022, https://www.hhs.gov/sites/default/files/workplace-mental-health-well-being.pdf, 26.

154   in the world: Dhingra et al., "Help Your Employees Find
       Purpose."

156   "experience of found": Gretchen Schmelzer, "One True Thing,"
       November 6, 2022, http://gretchenschmelzer.com/blog-1/2022/11/6/one
       -true-thing, accessed February 19, 2023.

157   amazing findings emerged: You can find the full results at
       https://www.adultdevelopmentstudy.org/.

157   "Full stop": Scott Stossel, "What Makes Us Happy, Revisited,"
       Atlantic, February 19, 2014, https://www.theatlantic.com/magazine
       /archive/2013/05/thanks-mom/309287/, accessed March 5, 2023.

157   "happier and healthier": Melanie Curtin, "This 75-Year
       Harvard Study Found the 1 Secret to Leading a Fulfilling Life," *Inc.*,
       February 27, 2017, https://www.inc.com/melanie-curtin/want-a-life-of
       -fulfillment-a-75-year-harvard-study-says-to-prioritize-this-one-t.html,
       accessed March 5, 2023.

158   "strength from the relationship": Brené Brown, *Atlas of the
       Heart: Mapping Meaningful Connection and the Language of Human
       Experience* (New York: Random House, 2021), 169.

159   had close relationships: Richard E. Boyatzis, Annie McKee,
       and Daniel Goleman, *Primal Leadership: Unleashing the Power of
       Emotional Intelligence* (Boston: Harvard Business Review Press, 2013),
       6–7.

159   "different body systems": Emine Saner, "Forget Regret!
       How to Have a Happy Life—According to the World's Leading Expert,"
       Guardian, February 6, 2023, https://www.theguardian.com
       /lifeandstyle/2023/feb/06/how-to-have-a-happy-life-according-to-the
       -worlds-leading-expert, accessed March 5, 2023.

159   and feeling powerless: Brown, *Atlas of the Heart*, 171.

160   health than smoking: Fedor Galkin, Kirill Kochetov, Diana
       Koldasbayeva, Manuel Faria, Helene H. Fung, Amber X. Chen, and Alex
       Zhavoronkov, "Psychological Factors Substantially Contribute to Biological
       Aging: Evidence from the Aging Rate in Chinese Older Adults," *Aging* 14,
       no. 18 (September 27, 2022): 7206–22, https://doi.org/10.18632
       /aging.204264.

160   suicidal ideation: L. C. Hawkley, "Loneliness and Health,"
       Nature Reviews Disease Primers 8, no. 22 (2022), https://doi.org/10.1038
       /s41572-022-00355-9.

160   highly connected peers: BetterUp Insights Report—2022, The
       Connection Crisis, BetterUp, https://grow.betterup.com/resources/build-a
       -culture-of-connection-report, accessed November 9, 2022.

160   lower job satisfaction: R. Clair, M. Gordon, M. Kroon, et al.,
       "The Effects of Social Isolation on Well-Being and Life Satisfaction During
       Pandemic," *Humanities and Social Sciences Communications* 8, no. 28
       (2021), https://doi.org/10.1057/s41599-021-00710-3.

161   peak performance (65 percent): "The Loneliness Epidemic
       Persists: A Post-Pandemic Look at the State of Loneliness Among U.S.
       Adults," https://newsroom.cigna.com/loneliness-epidemic-persists-post
       -pandemic-look.

161   communications and interactions: Sigal Barsade, "No
       Employee Is an Island: How Loneliness Affects Job Performance,"
       Wharton IDEAS Lab, https://ideas.wharton.upenn.edu/research/how
       -loneliness-affects-job-performance/.

161   of burning out: BetterUp Insights Report.

162   more professional growth: Ibid.

162   "productivity and performance": Emma Seppälä and Marissa
       King, "Burnout at Work Isn't Just About Exhaustion. It's Also About
       Loneliness," *Harvard Business Review*, June 29, 2017, https://hbr
       .org/2017/06/burnout-at-work-isnt-just-about-exhaustion-its-also-about
       -loneliness.

165   your top relational sources of resilience: Rob Cross, Karen Dillon, and
       Danna Greenberg, "The Secret to Building Resilience," *Harvard Business
       Review*, September 17, 2021. https://hbr.org/2021/01/the-secret-to
       -building-resilience, accessed March 11, 2023.

170   "undermine managerial credibility": Patrick Lencioni, "Make
       Your Values Mean Something," *Harvard Business Review*, January 30,
       2023, https://hbr.org/2002/07/make-your-values-mean-something,
       accessed March 8, 2023.

173   "in difficult circumstances": Kelly McGonigal, *The Upside of
       Stress: Why Stress Is Good for You, and How to Get Good at It* (New York:
       Avery, 2016), 71.

173   "deepen your priorities": Kelly McGonigal, *The Upside of
       Stress*, 75.

Chapter 6: Four Vital Mindsets for Acquiring Burnout Immunity

178   "things you value": Carol S. Dweck, *Mindset: The New
       Psychology of Success* (New York: Random House, 2006), ix, 6.

179   "dose of them": Ibid., 6.

179   "point for development": Ibid., 7.

181   obstacles and setbacks: "Emotional and Social Intelligence
       Leadership Competencies: An Overview," Key Step Media, https://www
       .keystepmedia.com/emotional-social-intelligence-leadership
       -competencies/, accessed March 28, 2023.

183   "integrated and healthy": Barbara L. Fredrickson, "The
       Broaden-and-Build Theory of Positive Emotions," *Philosophical
       Transactions of the Royal Society of London. Series B: Biological Sciences*
       359, no. 1449 (2004): 1367–77, https://doi.org/10.1098/rstb.2004.1512.

183   possible solutions: B. L. Fredrickson, C. Branigan,
       "Positive Emotions Broaden the Scope of Attention and Thought-Action
       Repertoires," *Cognition and Emotion* 19, no. 3 (May 2005): 313–32,
       doi:10.1080/02699930441000238.

183   overall well-being: B. L. Fredrickson and R. W. Levenson,
       "Positive Emotions Speed Recovery from the Cardiovascular Sequelae
       of Negative Emotions," *Cognition and Emotion* 12, no. 2 (March 1998):
       191–220, doi:10.1080/026999398379718.

183   "healthy longevity": Fredrickson, "The Broaden-and-Build
       Theory of Positive Emotions."

183   "person-centered care": J. Perlo, B. Balik, S. Swensen, A.
       Kabcenell, J. Landsman, and D. Feeley, "IHI Framework for Improving Joy
       in Work," white paper, Institute for Healthcare Improvement, 2017.

184   each Saturday morning: "Joy in Work Results-Oriented
       Learning Network Case Study: Mayo Clinic," Institute for Healthcare
       Improvement, 2021, https://www.ihi.org/Engage/collaboratives/joy
       -results/Documents/IHI_Joy-in-Work-ROLN_Case-Study_Mayo-Clinic
       .pdf, accessed April 13, 2023.

184   throughout the team: Amar Shah, "Defying the Odds
       to Create Workforce Joy and Well-Being," Institute for Healthcare

Improvement, January 5, 2023, https://www.ihi.org/communities/blogs
/defying-the-odds-to-create-workforce-joy-and-well-being, accessed April
13, 2023.

184   "cultivate joy": "Joy in Work Results-Oriented Learning
Network Case Study: Mayo Clinic," Institute for Healthcare Improvement,
2021, https://www.ihi.org/Engage/collaboratives/joy-results/Documents
/IHI_Joy-in-Work-ROLN_Case-Study_Mayo-Clinic.pdf.

187   goals when necessary: Lewina O. Lee, Peter James, Emily
S. Zevon, Eric S. Kim, Claudia Trudel-Fitzgerald, Avron Spiro, Francine
Grodstein, and Laura D. Kubzansky, "Optimism Is Associated with
Exceptional Longevity in 2 Epidemiologic Cohorts of Men and Women,"
Proceedings of the National Academy of Sciences 116, no. 37 (2019): 18357
–62, https://doi.org/10.1073/pnas.1900712116.

187   "direction of their lives": Karen Reivich and Andrew Shatté,
*The Resilience Factor: 7 Essential Skills for Overcoming Life's Inevitable
Obstacles* (New York: Three Rivers Press, 2003), 40.

187   "improve your situation": Ibid., 41.

187   "with self-efficacy": Ibid.

190   rumination, and avoidance: C. R. Snyder, Kevin Rand, and
David Sigmund, "Hope Theory," in *The Oxford Handbook of Hope*, ed.
Shane J. Lopez and Matthew Gallagher (New York: Oxford University
Press, 2018), 257–76.

190   components of burnout: M. Pompili, M. Innamorati, V.
Narciso et al., "Burnout, Hopelessness and Suicide Risk in Medical
Doctors," *La Clinica Terapeutica* 161, no. 6 (November–December 2010):
511–14, PMID:21181078.

190   anti-burnout effect: Angela B. Pharris, Ricky T. Munoz, and
Chan M. Hellman, "Hope and Resilience as Protective Factors Linked
to Lower Burnout Among Child Welfare Workers," *Children and Youth
Services Review* 136(C) (2022).

190   health and well-being: H. Gustafsson, P. Hassmén, and
L. Podlog, "Exploring the Relationship Between Hope and Burnout in
Competitive Sport," *Journal of Sports Science* 28, no. 14 (December 2010):
1495–504, doi:10.1080/02640414.2010.521943.

190   our own destiny: Annie McKee, *How to Be Happy at Work:
The Power of Purpose, Hope, and Friendship* (Cambridge, MA: Harvard
Business School Press, 2018), 92.

190   reach our potential: Ibid., 5.

191   "just as likely": Barbara Fredrickson, *Positivity: Embrace the
Hidden Strength of Positive Emotions, Overcome Negativity, and Thrive*
(New York: Crown, 2009).

194   very little stress: A. Keller et al., "Does the Perception That
Stress Affects Health Matter? The Association with Health and Mortality,"
Health Psychology 31, no. 5 (September 2012): 677–84, doi:10.1037
/a0026740.

195   among the men: Kelly McGonigal, *The Upside of Stress: Why
Stress Is Good for You, and How to Get Good at It* (New York: Avery, 2016),
69.

195   affect their health: Octavia H. Zahrt and Alia J. Crum,
"Perceived Physical Activity and Mortality: Evidence from Three
Nationally Representative U.S. Samples," *Health Psychology* 36, no. 11
(2017): 1017–25, https://doi.org/10.1037/hea0000531.

195   spot of stress: Ibid.

196   opportunity to grow: McGonigal, *The Upside of Stress*, 17.
197   engagement, and collaboration: Alia Crum, "Evaluating a
Mindset Training Program to Unleash the Enhancing Nature of Stress,"
Academy of Management Proceedings 2011, no. 1 (November 30, 2017):
1–6, https://doi.org/10.5465/ambpp.2011.65870502.
198   "your stress instincts": McGonigal, *The Upside of Stress*, 60.
198   "This matters": Ibid., 120.
201   organizational levels: Nathan Eva, Mulyadi Robin,
Sen Sendjaya, Dirk van Dierendonck, and Robert C. Liden, "Servant
Leadership: A Systematic Review and Call for Future Research,"
Leadership Quarterly 30, no. 1 (2019): 111–32, https://doi.org/10.1016/j
.leaqua.2018.07.004.
202   of their organization: Larry Spears, "Character and Servant
Leadership: Ten Characteristics of Effective, Caring Leaders," Regent
University, July 7, 2022, https://www.regent.edu/journal/journal-of
-virtues-leadership/character-and-servant-leadership-ten-characteristics
-of-effective-caring-leaders/, accessed April 5, 2023.
203   an entire organization: Jerry L. Chi and Grace C. Chi, "The
Impact of Servant Leadership on Job Burnout Among Employees of a
Christian Hospital," *International Journal of Management and Human
Resources* 1, no. 1 (2013): 86+, https://link.gale.com/apps/doc/A401381747
/AONE?u=anon~186b0ca7&sid=googleScholar&xid=eeba2bb7, accessed
April 6, 2023.
203   "hindrance stressors": Kevin W. Westbrook, Duncan Nicol,
Julie K. Nicol, and Denise Thornton Orr, "Effects of Servant Leadership
Style on Hindrance Stressors, Burnout, Job Satisfaction, Turnover
Intentions, and Individual Performance in a Nursing Unit," *Journal of
Health Management* 24, no. 4 (2022): 670–84, https://doi
.org/10.1177/09720634221128100.
204   risk of burnout: Zhenyao Cai, Yimin Mao, Ting Gong,
Ying Xin, and Jiayun Lou, "The Effect of Servant Leadership on Work
Resilience: Evidence from the Hospitality Industry During the COVID-19
Period," *International Journal of Environmental Research and Public
Health* 20, no. 2 (2023): 1322, https://doi.org/10.3390/ijerph20021322.
204   other people's trauma: C. M. Grunhaus, T. J. Ward, V. E.
Tuazon, and K. James, "The Impact of Supervisor Servant Leadership on
Counselor Supervisee Burnout and Secondary Traumatic Stress," *Teaching
and Supervision in Counseling* 5, no. 1 (2023): 1–12, https://doi
.org/10.7290/tsc05csj9.
204   better job outcomes: Guangya Zhou, Rani Gul, and
Muhammad Tufail, "Does Servant Leadership Stimulate Work
Engagement? The Moderating Role of Trust in the Leader," *Frontiers in
Psychology* 13 (July 5, 2022), https://doi.org/10.3389
/fpsyg.2022.925732.
211   protects against burnout: Z. Hashem and P. Zeinoun, "Self-
Compassion Explains Less Burnout Among Healthcare Professionals,"
Mindfulness 11 (2020): 2542–51, https://doi.org/10.1007/s12671-020
-01469-5.
211   higher job satisfaction: Elise S. Vaillancourt and Louise
Wasylkiw, "The Intermediary Role of Burnout in the Relationship Between
Self-Compassion and Job Satisfaction Among Nurses," *Canadian Journal
of Nursing Research* 52, no. 4 (2019): 246–54, https://doi
.org/10.1177/0844562119846274.

Chapter 7: 3Rx

214   "hard to recover": Christina Maslach and Michael P. Leiter,
        *The Truth About Burnout: How Organizations Cause Personal Stress and
        What to Do About It* (San Francisco: Jossey-Bass, 1997), 17.

217   "continue to grow": Stacy Weiner, "Thousands of Medical
        Residents Are Unionizing. Here's What That Means for Doctors, Hospitals,
        and the Patients They Serve," Association of American Medical Colleges,
        June 7, 2022, https://www.aamc.org/news/thousands-medical-residents
        -are-unionizing-here-s-what-means-doctors-hospitals-and-patients-they.

218   "acceptable trade-off": "The U.S. Surgeon General's
        Framework for Workplace Mental Health & Well-Being," Office of the U.S.
        Surgeon General, 2022, https://www.hhs.gov/sites/default/files/workplace
        -mental-health-well-being.pdf, 4.

220   decreased patient safety: T. Bell, M. Sprajcer, T. Flenady, and
        A. Sahay, "Fatigue in Nurses and Medication Administration Errors: A
        Scoping Review," *Journal of Clinical Nursing* 32, no. 17–18 (January 2023):
        5445–60, https://doi.org/10.1111/jocn.16620.

221   error by 22 percent: F. McCormick, J. Kadzielski, C. P.
        Landrigan, B. Evans, J. H. Herndon, and H. E. Rubash, "Surgeon Fatigue:
        A Prospective Analysis of the Incidence, Risk, and Intervals of Predicted
        Fatigue-Related Impairment in Residents," *Archives of Surgery* 147, no. 5
        (2012): 430–35, doi:10.1001/archsurg.2012.84.

221   family complaints: C. L. Garcia et al., "Influence of Burnout
        on Patient Safety: Systematic Review and Meta-Analysis," *Medicina*
        (Kaunas, Lithuania) 55, no. 9 (August 30, 2019): 553, doi:10.3390
        /medicina55090553.

221   could have been prevented: J. P. Cimiotti, L. H. Aiken, D.
        M. Sloane, and E. S. Wu, "Nurse Staffing, Burnout, and Health Care–
        Associated Infection," *American Journal of Infection Control* 40, no.
        6 (August 2012): 486–90, doi:10.1016/j.ajic.2012.02.029; erratum in
        American Journal of Infection Control 40, no. 7 (September 2012): 680.

225   binge-watching Netflix: Catherine Price, "Why We All Need
        to Have More Fun," *New York Times*, December 23, 2021, https://www
        .nytimes.com/2021/12/23/well/mind/having-fun-suceeding-coronavirus
        -pandemic.html.

225   for work recovery: Alyson Meister, Bonnie Hayden Cheng,
        Nele Dale, and Franciska Krings, "How to Recover from Work Stress,
        According to Science," *Harvard Business Review*, July 7, 2022, https://hbr
        .org/2022/07/how-to-recover-from-work-stress-according-to
        -science?utm_medium=email&utm_source=newsletter_daily&utm
        _campaign=mtod_notactsubs, accessed May 17, 2023.

226   body's inflammatory response: U. Naidoo, "Eat to Beat
        Stress," *American Journal of Lifestyle Medicine* 15, no. 1 (December 2020):
        39–42, doi:10.1177/1559827620973936.

226   factors for burnout: M. Söderström, K. Jeding, M. Ekstedt,
        A. Perski, and T. Åkerstedt, "Insufficient Sleep Predicts Clinical Burnout,"
        Journal of Occupational Health Psychology 17, no. 2 (2012): 175–83,
        https://doi.org/10.1037/a0027518.

226   well-being benefits: Caroline Colvin, "Mental Health Benefits
        Untapped by Many Workers, Study Finds," HR Dive, March 23, 2023,
        https://www.hrdive.com/news/unused-mental-health
        -benefits-2023/645829/.

227   taking time off: Juliana Menasce Horowitz and Kim Parker,

"How Americans View Their Jobs," Pew Research Center, Social & Demographic Trends Project, March 30, 2023, https://www.pewresearch .org/social-trends/2023/03/30/how-americans-view-their-jobs/.

228 burning them out: Kira Schabram, Matt Bloom, and DJ DiJonna, "Research: The Transformative Power of Sabbaticals," *Harvard Business Review*, February 23, 2023, https://hbr.org/2023/02/research -the-transformative-power-of-sabbaticals?utm_medium=email&utm _source=newsletter_daily&utm_campaign=dailyalert_notactsubs &deliveryName=DM255601.

229 emotional regulation: A. A. Green and E. V. Kinchen, "The Effects of Mindfulness Meditation on Stress and Burnout in Nurses," *Journal of Holistic Nursing* 39. no. 4 (December 2021): 356–68, doi:10.1177/08980101211015818; erratum in *Journal of Holistic Nursing* 40, no. 3 (September 2022): NP1–NP5.

231 oneself by withdrawing: Tani Singer and Olga M. Klimecki, "Empathy and Compassion," *Current Biology*, September 22, 2014, https:// www.sciencedirect.com/science/article/pii/S0960982214007702.

232 Two Reactions to the Suffering of Others: Ibid.

232 "without experiencing distress": T. Dowling, "Compassion Does Not Fatigue!" *Canadian Veterinary Journal* 59, no. 7 (July 2018): 749–50.

235 fell by 10.1 percent: Marc Mosset al., "The Effect of Creative Arts Therapy on Psychological Distress in Health Care Professionals," *American Journal of Medicine* 135, no. 10 (October 2022): 1255–62.E5, https://doi.org/10.1016/j.amjmed.2022.04.016.

235 stronger resiliency: Kristen A. Torres et al., "Creative Arts Intervention to Reduce Burnout and Decrease Psychological Distress in Healthcare Professionals: A Qualitative Analysis," *Arts in Psychotherapy* 83 (April 2023), https://doi.org/10.1016/j.aip.2023.102021.

236 creative practice: Kevin Beaty, "An Unlikely Union Between a Hospital and a Writers' Workshop Is Helping Medical Workers with Trauma," Denverite, March 21, 2023, https://denverite.com/2023/03/20 /an-unlikely-union-between-a-hospital-and-a-writers-workshop-is -helping-medical-workers-with-trauma/.

238 of the study: C. P. West, L. N. Dyrbye, D. V. Satele, and T. D. Shanafelt, "Colleagues Meeting to Promote and Sustain Satisfaction (COMPASS) Groups for Physician Well-Being: A Randomized Clinical Trial," *Mayo Clinic Proceedings* 96, no. 10 (October 2021): 2606–14, doi:10.1016/j.mayocp.2021.02.028.

238 camaraderie of connection: Mayo Clinic Program on Physician Well-Being, "Research Translated into Strategies in Practice," Mayo Clinic, https://www.mayo.edu/research/centers-programs/program -physician-well-being/platforms-excellence/research-translated-into -strategies-practice.

247 "people I care about": Emine Saner, "Forget Regret! How to Have a Happy Life—According to the World's Leading Expert," *Guardian*, February 6, 2023, https://www.theguardian.com/lifeandstyle/2023 /feb/06/how-to-have-a-happy-life-according-to-the-worlds-leading -expert.

Index

Note: Page numbers in *italics* indicate figures.

About the Author

KANDI WIENS, EdD, MSEd, MBA, is a senior fellow at the University of Pennsylvania, the director of the Penn Master's in Medical Education Program and the Penn Health Professions Education Certificate Program, and the academic director of the PennCLO Master's Program. She often teaches in various graduate-level programs across the University of Pennsylvania. Kandi holds a master's as well as a doctoral degree from the PennCLO Executive Doctoral Program at the University of Pennsylvania, an MBA from the University of Oregon, and a BS in business administration from Montana State University. She is a researcher, a national speaker, and an executive coach whose work focuses on helping leaders hone and use their emotional and social intelligence to amplify their positive impact and protect themselves from burnout. To learn more about Kandi's work, visit www.kandiwiens.com.